Using the Force: Creativity, Community and *Star Wars* Fans

ALSO AVAILABLE FROM CONTINUUM:

Brooker:

Batman Unmasked

Jones and Jolliffe:

The Guerilla Film Makers Handbook, 2nd Edition

Levy:

Oscar® Fever

McMahan:

Alice Guy Blaché: Lost Visionary of the Cinema

Rayner:

The Films of Peter Weir

Vincendeau:

Stars and Stardom in French Cinema

USING THE FORCE

Creativity, Community and *Star Wars* Fans

Will Brooker

2002

The Continuum International Publishing Group Inc
370 Lexington Avenue, New York, NY 10017

The Continuum International Publishing Group Ltd
The Tower Building, 11 York Road, London SE1 7NX

www.continuumbooks.com

Printed in the United States of America

Library of Congress Cataloging-in-Publication Data

Brooker, Will, 1970-
Using the force : creativity, community and Star Wars fans / Will Brooker
p. cm.
Includes bibliographical references and index.
ISBN 0-8264-5287-6 (hc) ISBN 0-8264-1466-4 (pbk)
1. Star Wars films—History and criticism. I. Title.
PN1995.9.S695 B76 2002
791.43'72—dc21 2002002079

Contents

Acknowledgements

Thanks to:

The one hundred fans whose responses to my original request form the backbone of this research.

All the authors, artists, and directors who permitted me to reproduce their work here, and apologies to those I was unable to contact.

Tim Meader, Becky Mackle, and Frazer Bowdery for meeting me to discuss their love of *Star Wars* and for providing the key interviews in three of the chapters.

Andrea Alworth for her research assistance, often under an alias.

David Barker at Continuum for taking it on and seeing it through.

Corrie Schoenberg at Continuum for her excellent organisation of promotions and publicity.

Fiona Graham for the index, the transcripts, the bibliography, and for being my most loyal fan during the writing of this book.

Liz and Pete Brooker for taking me, finally, in 1978.

Joe Brooker, even if he always preferred the Empire to the Rebels.

George Lucas, still, for the memories.

Illustrations

Preface

1977: I HATED *STAR WARS*

Confession: In 1977, I hated *Star Wars*. Americans were forming lines around the block to watch the movie for the fourth time running, but in Woolwich, southeast London, me and all the other seven-year-old kids were still being made to go to Silver Jubilee parties and wear cardboard hats in red, white, and blue. *Star Wars* didn't reach the Odeon in Woolwich until 1978. And even in 1978, I hated *Star Wars*. Everyone was talking about it, so it must be rubbish. It was some boring rubbish about a see-through robot—how babyish—and everyone else loved it, so I wouldn't.

Kids were bringing the bubblegum cards into school to swap, and someone must have given me one out of pity, because I sat at home one evening copying the drawing from the back of a card: the muscle man in the yellow trousers and white shirt, the lady in the rude dress next to him. I didn't even know what I was drawing, but I knew what it symbolized. It was *Star Wars*, whatever that was: it was everywhere, it was the thing people were talking about. My mum and dad went to see it—reinforcing my sense that it was something grown-up and alien, like the BBC news—and came back late at night to report that while I might like the bit at the end where people fought with light swords, my little brother would probably be scared of the beginning. Light swords. I imagined a duel scene, the two men holding swords with lightbulb hilts. Well, maybe I'd like that bit, then. Maybe the movie was worth seeing just to find out if I'd like that bit, and I could say the rest was rubbish. I might even tell my parents they'd made a big mistake thinking I'd like the light swords. . .

I ran out of the Odeon cinema in Woolwich. I was a TIE fighter. I was an X-Wing. I ran until I collapsed. I was crazy for *Star Wars*; it was my fuel. It was love and drugs for the first time and in the same night. For the next six years, I lived *Star Wars*. I wrote sequel stories and drew comics predicting the third episode in which Ben Kenobi would return from the dead and distract Vader so Luke could strike him down. I sat with my best mate, painting medals and bracelets on our mini action figures with gold enamel and melting the floor of the Creature Cantina playset so it would look authentically blaster-damaged. I played endless games with my brother, moving the figures around on the floor and speaking in bad American accents. He always took the role of the Empire—every birthday and Christmas he'd ask for another white-armored trooper, identical to the last—while I elevated the trilogy's minor alien characters to a mercenary group called Hammerhead's Gang. I joined the official fan club and studied the tiny illustrations on the newsletter, searching for clues in the preproduction art for what was then *Revenge of the Jedi* (wasn't that man on the skiff wearing Han Solo's shirt and waistcoat?). I scribbled notes in felt-tipped pen during a rescreening of the first film, trying to get down as much of the dialogue as I could. When it was finally shown on television, I held a cassette recorder up to the screen and taped the entire sound track; later I transcribed Greedo's alien dialogue phonetically. I can still reproduce his conversation with Han Solo, off the top of my head.

That's my story, or part of it. You might have a similar one of your own. There are many such stories, inflected by national culture, age, and gender, and that's what this book is about: the different ways in which people engage with *Star Wars*, the role it has in their lives, and their relationship to it. *Star Wars*, as my brief account shows, is not just a film or a trilogy, or a trilogy and two prequels. For many people, including me, it is the single most important cultural text of our lives; it has meshed with memories of our childhoods, with our homemade tributes—from the amateurish childhood comics to the professional product of an adult fan—with our choices of career or education, and with our everyday experiences. Even in 1977, *Star Wars* was a phenomenon. For many people now, it is a culture: a sprawling, detailed mythos they can pick through with their eyes closed; a group of characters who may have been more important role models than friends and family; and a set of codes—quotes, in-jokes, obscure references—that provide instant common ground for fellow fans meeting for the first time and that bind established communities together.

My story illustrates how *Star Wars* can permeate someone's life, at least from the ages of seven to thirteen. I admit I also feel the need to show my credentials. I carried out this research partly out of sheer love and loyalty for the saga and the culture, and the fans I interviewed by e-mail or in person trusted me with personal information because they believed I was a fan. Several of them were wary that I would portray them and other fans as comedy misfits with a ridiculous fixation on a kiddy film. I couldn't do that without ridiculing myself. I am inside the *Star Wars* culture, and I consider that a benefit rather than a hindrance to academic research.

On one level, this is a work of cultural studies. It engages with, and sometimes challenges, previous research into science fiction fandom; it explores issues of interpretation and cultural power. However, I think this book would have failed if it alienated the very people it discusses. If a study of fans by a fan cannot be read and enjoyed by those fans, something is wrong. So I am walking a thin line here, trusting that it is possible to be serious and accessible at the same time, most of the time.

At around five o'clock in the evening on Saturday, June 24, 2000, I e-mailed a webmaster of TheForce.net, one of the most established *Star Wars* fan sites. I explained that I was researching a book on *Star Wars* audiences and asked that anyone interested mail me their age, occupation, location, and a paragraph about why the films were important to them. The announcement went up on the news board at six. A minute later, I received my first message. When I finished reading it and returned to my in-box, I had three more. By half past six I was feeling like Mickey Mouse in *The Sorcerer's Apprentice*; after reading one mail, I'd go back to discover another five. The pages of my account were filling up and expanding. At seven o'clock I mailed the webmaster again and asked him to take the notice down. I kept the first hundred replies.

I wrote back individually to around sixty of my respondents. With most of them, I exchanged between two and five messages, building up some degree of personal relationship; with a few, I exchanged closer to twenty. Some sent me scanned pictures, some directed me to their websites or digital films. One invited me to his house to watch him and his mates watching *Empire*; another travelled to London to let me interview her about her role in the *Star Wars* Chicks website. Those one hundred people constitute the main body of my primary research; without them there would be no book, and so this is partly for them, with thanks.

It is already clear that much of my research was based on internet communication: e-mail conversations, analysis of websites, downloading digital films, and trawling online libraries of short stories. While the book contains three substantial face-to-face interviews, I have never met most of my correspondents and know them only through text. I see this research method as entirely appropriate rather than as a drawback: most of my correspondents have never met the other fans they communicate with regularly and know them only through text. Becky Mackle, the webmistress interviewed in chapter 9, talks to three hundred women on her mailing list but has only met five of them. The fanfic authors in chapter 7 have made friends with a shared interest from all over the world, swapping their stories by e-mail; the contributors to TheForce.net discussion boards argue fiercely over points of canon, as demonstrated in chapter 5, but may never know what their antagonists look like, where they live, or even their age and gender.

Star Wars fandom was flourishing before the advent of the World Wide Web in the mid-1990s. In 1996, when I wrote a chapter on the uses of and references to *Star Wars* between the end of the original trilogy and the launch of the Special Editions,[1] internet sites only warranted a footnote; I gave more attention to print fanzines like *Luminous Beings Are We* and *Force Sensitive*. *Star Wars* fan fiction, as noted in chapter 7, has been circulating in print form—lithographed or photocopied and mailed the old way, in envelopes—since the release of *A New Hope* in 1977, and conventions have not only been enabling fans to gather for decades but also continue to run in 2001 despite the availability of e-mail and online networks. However, the internet transformed the nature of *Star Wars* fandom as it did many other communities: communication across the world became instantaneous and cheap; whole fan novels could be sent to another nation in seconds; a global network of fans could argue in real time on a discussion board; and by the late 1990s, amateur filmmakers could launch their productions on a web platform and screen it to a potentially vast audience.

Perhaps most important, fans could easily and quickly find other fans and become part of a community. As we see in chapter 9, Becky Mackle

---

[1]Will Brooker, "New Hope: The Postmodern Project of *Star Wars*," in Peter Brooker and Will Brooker (Eds.), *Postmodern After-Images,* London: Arnold (1997).

was unable to admit her passion for *Star Wars* as a girl, when her peers were more interested in Care Bears. At eighteen, she joined a small, all-male science fiction group and became the token female, meeting the boys' expectations by taking an interest in Leia's hairstyles and fashion. In 1999 she discovered the Star Wars Chicks site and, after twenty-five years as the only female *Star Wars* fan she knew, discovered hundreds of like-minded women at one stroke. "It adds validation," she explains. "I'm not alone, I'm not a freak." The internet enabled many fans to take their first step into a larger world, and it is fitting that online communication forms the heart of my research, as it links and unites so many of the various fan communities I discuss.

I am writing about *Star Wars* partly because it constitutes one of the most potent cultural myths of my life, and I am writing about fans partly because I am one myself. But the phenomenon of *Star Wars* fandom is important way beyond my own personal investment. The saga is one of the key cultural benchmarks of the last thirty years—someone who had never seen any of the films would surely recognize Vader's helmet, the sound of a lightsaber, and the slogan "May the Force be with you"—yet while the films' appeal is broad, it also runs deep. The creative energy that the fans discussed in this book channel into their appreciation of *Star Wars*—spending every weekend running a website or mailing list, writing novel-length fiction, posting throughout the day on discussion boards, devoting an entire summer to the production of a short digital film—rivals any other fandom of my experience. The commitment and ability of fans of, say, *Beauty and the Beast, Alien Nation, Blake's Seven* or *Blade Runner* may in some cases equal that of *Star Wars* devotees, but the communities formed around George Lucas's saga are nevertheless outstandingly dedicated and skilled even in this context.

The difference is that *Star Wars* generates this level of full-on fan commitment at the same time as it continues to operate as a multi-million-dollar global franchise, a commercial enterprise run by an increasingly stubborn and reclusive creative mastermind. *Star Wars* inspires the devotion of a cult, yet is far too big, too successful, too current, to fit that term's usual definition. The fans who are discussed below feel an intense possessiveness, insistent that *Star Wars* belongs to them because of their lifelong immersion in the saga; but *Star Wars* still belongs to Lucas, whose vision of the continuing narrative is diverging more and more from that of the average thirty-something fan.

PREFACE

Star Wars is not a dead franchise, kept alive in cultural memory by the fan minority, but an industry, delivering product to a worldwide audience. The prequel trilogy is not aimed at the diehards who run websites, but at the cinemagoer who took his kids to see *The Phantom Menace* as a fun blockbuster and will never write a fan story about Obi-Wan Kenobi. To Lucasfilm, Ltd., *Star Wars* is not a cult text or a folk myth but an ongoing business, a series of trademarks and properties that need to be protected; their main relationship is not with the type of dedicated fan discussed here—who could all boycott the saga with very little effect on box office receipts—but with mainstream moviegoers and their children.

The fans of *Twin Peaks, The Prisoner, Doctor Who* or *Starsky and Hutch* are custodians of their chosen text, rehabilitating and sustaining the characters through their own creations. *Star Wars* fans feel that they should be the custodians, but are faced with a situation where someone else still owns the story, is pitching it to a far wider audience than their dedicated group, cares not at all for their interpretation of the saga, and will attempt to shut down their sites forcibly if they contradict his version of the characters and plot. The result is an unhappy conflict, with many fans trying to balance their gratitude and admiration for the Lucas who created the first trilogy with their distaste and lack of respect for the director who, in their eyes, is now despoiling the myth they grew up with. So although *Star Wars* fandom in many ways echoes the structures and practices of other fan communities—as detailed in several academic studies of *Star Trek*, for instance—it also presents an unusual case; while this book confirms earlier theories of media fandom, it also explores new territory.

Each of the ten chapters explores a different aspect of *Star Wars* fandom, presenting a different angle on the same core issues of community and interpretation. How is the saga important to these people in terms of social identity and group bonding? What meanings do they draw from the *Star Wars* texts? How do they back up their theories by drawing on secondary material such as novels, comic books, computer games or reference texts? To what extent do the meanings they take from the films clash with other interpretations, particularly those of Lucasfilm?

Although each case study returns to these common themes, chapters 1 and 2 deal with the ways in which *Star Wars* shapes its fans' personal identities and binds them into groups with a shared expertise, while chapters 3, 4, 5, and 6 explore ways of engaging with the films, through close analysis, critical examination, debate around canon, and speculation based on existing evidence. Chapters 7 and 8 discuss two approaches to creative expression through *Star Wars*—fiction and film, respectively—and the final two chapters ask whether gender and age affect a fan's interpretation of the saga.

More specifically, the first chapter surveys the range of e-mail responses I received to my initial request, and discusses the major influence *Star Wars* has had in many people's lives, from shaping their choices of career and education to influencing their outlook on spiritual faith. Chapter 2 examines the dynamic of a group watching a *Star Wars* film, using the case study of a young man from Essex, England, and his mates to suggest how the saga works as a springboard for in-jokes, banter and lighthearted quizzes, providing a shared focus and playing an important role in bringing friends together. Chapter 3 looks at another way of viewing the films: the solitary, close analysis of the dedicated fan who pores over the texts line by line, dedicated as a detective, to compare the special edition with the original.

Chapter 4 begins with an e-mail interview with Simon Pegg, the writer and actor whose sitcom, *Spaced,* included a criticism of *The Phantom Menace* in virtually every episode. Pegg is representative of a trend among fans in their late twenties and early thirties who grew up with *Star Wars* and feel they now have a better grasp of and more of a claim on the mythos than George Lucas himself. To this group, *The Phantom Menace* was a slap in the face, a betrayal of their fan loyalty, and provoked an internal struggle whereby they cling to their nostalgia for the original trilogy but have little faith in Lucas's current ability to continue the saga.

The fifth and sixth chapters explore the debate on the internet bulletin boards of TheForce.net around the issues of canon—where a *Star Wars* text ranks on the hierarchy of "official" to "unofficial"—and speculation, the guessing games that, at the time of writing, centered around the unfolding plot of *Episode II*. These chapters return to the questions of how fans back up their interpretations with expert reference to the smallest details of *Star Wars* texts, and the ways in which various contradictory readings of the films are proved or disputed.

Chapter 7 concentrates on the twin communities of "slash" and "genfic," fan-authored stories that explore, respectively, gay and straight relationships among *Star Wars* characters; I argue here that, despite the fact that slash exists under constant fear of censorship by Lucasfilm, it has a great deal in common with the mainstream genfic and indeed with the "official" *Star Wars* novels. The next chapter presents a contrast through the fan-film community. Like fiction authors, these writers and directors are taking the familiar tropes of the *Star Wars* mythos and developing them in original directions, in this case through digital cinema: live action, animation, music video and parody, ranging from one-minute effects tests to CGI extravaganzas and narratives up to twenty minutes long.

This textual strategy—to retain a core of recognizable elements but take them on a tangent—is the basis of both genfic and slash, but Lucasfilm's reaction to this form of creativity is very different. Slash writers operate covertly, knowing that Lucas disapproves and would love to close the practice down completely, whereas *Star Wars* filmmakers promote their work openly, aware that Lucasfilm has recruited fan directors to work on official comics or even *Episode II*. Together, these chapters raise the specter of Lucasfilm as a tyrannical Empire, stamping out rogue interpretations where it fails to assimilate them, and by extension constructing the fan creators as a rebel alliance.

The penultimate chapter demonstrates that although *Star Wars* seems to have little to offer girls and women, it nevertheless enjoys a significant female fandom across several distinct communities, from the teen sites built around adoration for Luke Skywalker to an explicitly feminist project of reevaluation based on the argument that Boba Fett is female. Finally, I turn to a younger generation and ask whether fans under eleven years of age share any of the attributes we have seen in their older counterparts; whether the distaste for *The Phantom Menace* is lost on them; whether they, experiencing the saga in the right order, take a different perspective on the overarching *Star Wars* narrative; and whether they display any of the creativity and imagination of the fans who first saw *Star Wars* in 1977.

1

STAR WARS AND EVERYDAY LIFE

Ross:	Okay, umm. Did you ever see, um, Return of the Jedi?
Rachel:	Yeah.
Ross:	Do you remember the scene with, um, Jabba the Hutt? Well, Jabba had, as his prisoner, um, Princess Leia.
Rachel:	Oooh!
Ross:	Princess Leia was wearing this, um, gold bikini thing. It was pretty cool.
Phoebe:	Yeah, oh, Princess Leia and the gold bikini, every guy our age loved that.

—"The One With the Princess Leia Fantasy," *Friends*

Star Wars is hard to avoid. On a Friday night in England, sitting in and flipping around the television channels, you could go from the *Simpsons* episode guest starring Chewbacca[2] to the sitcom *Spaced,* where the protagonist, Tim, is dealing with his hatred for *The Phantom Menace,* to the BBC news with an update on George W. Bush's "son of Star Wars" defense initiative, to *Car Wars,* a show about vehicle crime, to *The Adam and Joe Show* with its stop-motion animation of Luke and Jabba

[2]"The Springfield Files," *Simpsons*.

mini action figures. Even *Buffy The Vampire Slayer*, screened as the late show at one in the morning, plays out with a tune by Nerf Herder, named after one of Leia's insults to Han Solo. *Star Wars* references are so deeply embedded in our popular consciousness that we encounter them every day without even trying.

For many of my respondents, though, the *Star Wars* saga was a defining influence on their lives and continues to play a major role in their day-to-day relationships. It inspired them to become involved in technology or art, in psychology or the military; it informs their belief framework and their personal ethics. They incorporate the films into their workplaces, their homes, and their relationships through quotations, toys, posters, costumes, even permanent tattoos. The addresses on the e-mails they sent me were almost without exception badges of their loyalty—Sith_inc, Vader's Castle, JediMistress, UbobaFett—and many signed off not even with "May the Force be with you," but with the code MTFBWY. *Star Wars* is hard for anyone to avoid: these fans have embraced it.

"I Am A *Star Wars* Geek"

I promised earlier that I would not portray *Star Wars* fans as freaks or obsessives. Sometimes, however, they choose the label for themselves. Scott Beetley, a twenty-one-year-old college student from Texas, headed his mail with "I Am A *Star Wars* Geek" and took me on a tour of his day "so you know how goofy I am about these movies. . . . "

> In the morning, I wake up in a room covered with *Star Wars* posters. No lie, I have 11 posters and a few photos of my girlfriend. From my ceiling are 9 vehicles, podracers, TIE fighters, an X-Wing, and so on. In the corner is a bookshelf with over 100 action figures grouped by film and relation to the "Expanded Universe." In my bathroom is a "Naboo Space Battle" shower curtain, with matching waste basket, soap tray, cup and toothbrush holder. I get on my computer where I have a Battle Droid for my wallpaper, and a glowing lightsaber mouse cursor. I have a C3PO mouse and Boba Fett mouse pad. Then I go online, where I chat and hang out with friends I have made on various *Star Wars* message boards. It's actually quite pathetic. Usually, I go to work later, and tell friends any interesting rumors I've heard on the internet, and see my girlfriend, but then it's back home to get onto the computer to talk to my friends later in the evening. I am a complete junkie. If

> there was a support group, I'd be a prime candidate. I am not a total hermit, nor am I what most would stereotype as a computer nerd. I am a working musician, and have been dating my girlfriend for over four years, so there is nothing wrong with me that I have to stay inside all day and dream *Star Wars*, I just do.[3]

There is an interesting conflict at the heart of Scott's account. As he presents himself to a stranger, he proudly, albeit lightheartedly, admits to being a junkie with an obsession that is "actually quite pathetic." On the other hand—no doubt aware of the popular conception of fan as geeky loser[4]—he is quick to dodge the stereotypes of "hermit" and "computer nerd." Scott is happy to be a bit of a joke, but only on his own terms; he revels in the details of his childish passion, but stresses that he has a social life off the computer, a respectably cool job, and a girlfriend of four years.

This last point is perhaps the most important, as Scott uses it to confirm his normalcy: "There's nothing wrong with me." Some categories of weird fan ("junkie") are fine; others—hermit, geek, and surely by implication gay geek—are not so fine. The same distinction is made by another respondent, David Stagl, a twenty-five-year-old audio engineer from Chicago: "I live a pretty normal life, have a girlfriend I'll be marrying soon, go to the movies all the time . . . but I am a huge fan that checks the web everyday for news."[5]

These definitions of normality—obsessive fandom is acceptable as long as it avoids the unacceptable social types of perpetually single misfit and homosexual—are interesting with regard to the later chapter "Slash and Other Stories," which discusses gay readings and writings of *Phantom Menace* characters, and the general ambivalence, verging on distaste, that is displayed by many fans for this homoerotic interpretation of the films.

Scott is by no means alone in transforming his bedroom into a shrine to the saga. Erin Womack, a high-school student from Virginia, tells the story of her "second generation" fandom—the term is hers and will come up again in the final chapter of this book. "I was no more than eleven

---

[3]Scott Beetley, personal e-mail (June 24, 2000).

[4]The "I Grok Spock" image immortalized on *Saturday Night Live* with William Shatner; see Henry Jenkins, *Textual Poachers,* London: Routledge (1992), p. 9.

[5]David Stagl, personal e-mail (June 24, 2000).

when I really started to study the films . . . my collection grew and grew until there was an entire room in my family's house reserved for it."[6] Robert Oliver, a professor from Georgia, happily boasts, "I have a pantry full of toys."[7] Scott, nineteen, from Michigan, admits "You can't look anywhere in my room and not see something related to *Star Wars*."[8] Mike Hall, twenty-one, from Virginia, has "a bedroom dedicated to nothing but *Star Wars* stuff, and I can barely move around in the room anymore."[9]

What this small group of fans have in common—the reason I have grouped them separately—is a hard-core passion for the film in itself, not as it relates to any specific area of their lives such as career choice or hobby, but almost as a transcendental presence. In some ways they can be compared to the next respondents who cite *Star Wars* as a parallel to and illustration of their spiritual beliefs, although in these cases *Star Wars* itself is the object of faith.

Colin F. writes a one-sentence message: "*Star Wars* is my life."[10] Robert Oliver reports that "I spent $1500 to see Episode 1 three days early, and it was the most beautiful experience of my life . . . I know the perfect love that is *Star Wars*."[11] Mike Hall claims, "*Star Wars* rules my imagination and fascination."[12] Scott from Michigan offers, "I've completely memorized every line, every sound and every movement in each film. If you want to see any of the movies but can't find the video, just ask me and I'll act it out for you."[13] Months after Erin saw her first *Star Wars* film, "the characters represented everything for me . . . I fell madly in love."[14] Scott Beetley concludes his account with, "I love it. It consumes me."[15] Dev, a fifteen-year-old farm worker from Okeene, Oklahoma, writes

> All I know is that I LOVE *Star Wars*. *Star Wars* is always in my mind, I'm always thinking about what's going to happen or what's already happened in the *Star Wars* Galaxy. Without it I would probably be lost.[16]

---

[6]Erin Womack, personal e-mail (June 24, 2000).
[7]Robert Oliver, personal e-mail (June 24, 2000).
[8]Scott, personal e-mail (June 24, 2000).
[9]Mike Hall, personal e-mail (June 24, 2000).
[10]Colin F. personal e-mail (June 24, 2000).
[11]Oliver, ibid.
[12]Hall, ibid.
[13]Scott, ibid.
[14]Womack, ibid.
[15]Beetley, ibid.

"Love of the Light Side"

Although Dev's dependence on the fictional creations of George Lucas may seem extreme, he is not so far removed from those respondents who have drawn on *Star Wars* as guidance for their own ethical or spiritual beliefs. Intriguingly, in some of these cases the *Star Wars* saga is cited not just as a supplement that illustrates and parallels existing religion, but as a workable, persuasive ethical system that traditional religion has failed to provide. This investment in *Star Wars* as a moral primer is very different in tone from the chain of forwarded e-mails that tried to persuade fans to register their faith as "Jedi" on the Australian and British censuses of 2001: it is personal and entirely sincere. Not for nothing is *Star Wars* known by many fans as the Holy Saga, or the Holy Trilogy.

John Scott, a high-school student from South Carolina, states that "most of the people I have met who don't like *Star Wars* or haven't seen it watch it and undergo a change, almost a religious conversion. So now when I'm speaking about *Star Wars* I am referred to as The Missionary."[17] At its purest, this spiritual inspiration is expressed as a basic sense of right and wrong related to the twin aspects of the Force. Philip Guillet, a twenty-one-year-old psychologist from New York, writes that

> Its message is so positive and optimistic, making us all feel special . . . like we belong to something much bigger than ourselves. For many, including myself, what occurs in those movies is a personification of what we are all struggling through: forces of good and evil tugging at our mind. The seduction of the Dark Side gives us incentive to turn to evil, however, the devotion and love of the Light Side is what may keep us on the side of good.

Philip's account of human spiritual conflict relates so closely to Lucas's concepts that it could almost be a speech by Obi-Wan Kenobi. Other respondents gave a more general sense of the ways in which the films had affected their ethical perspective, echoing Philip's opinion that the saga offers an optimistic, positive message as well as a clear-cut moral structure. A twenty-eight-year-old computer student from Oklahoma wrote, "It gave

[16]Dev, personal e-mail (June 24, 2000).

[17]John Scott, personal e-mail (June 24, 2000).

me an optimistic outlook and gave me a view of good and evil."[18] "If I had to say I learned one thing from *Star Wars* . . . Aim High . . . and reach for the stars . . . and your dreams can come true as well,"[19] added a marine biologist.

Some replies made more specific reference to the Jedi Knights, extrapolating a code of behavior and belief from the evidence of Yoda, Obi-Wan, Qui-Gon Jinn, and Luke Skywalker. "One thing I love the most is the teachings of the Jedi, especially Yoda," says Tiffany Pessotti, a high-school senior from Cape Cod. "Yoda's teachings can easily be spread into your everyday life."[20] Kes Massey, twenty-seven, from the United Kingdom, paraphrases Yoda's counsel—"Judge me by my size, do you?"—and the Jedi philosophy that anger, hatred, and prejudice pave the road to the Dark Side.

> I think I learnt much about morality from *Star Wars*, about not giving in to majority opinion, about respect for others whatever opinion you have of them, about having a calm attitude to life, and how the "inner" person matters more than the "outer" appearance.[21]

Philip Guillet, cited earlier, incorporates Yoda even more directly into his life, using the instrumental theme associated with the Jedi Master to soothe himself and prepare for his own role as a psychologist.

> *Star Wars* represents my own personal beliefs of religion and spirituality . . . Yoda's theme song calms me from a day and gives me strength to continue helping others in a warm and caring way. He, Obi-Wan, Qui-Gon and Luke are such respectable figures that some of us can't help but aspire to be like them. Sure, we may not be able to lift droids, rocks or X-Wings, but we could "use the Force" in other ways such as helping, loving, caring and supporting, and be our own personal Jedi.[22]

Intriguingly, there do exist a handful of Christian websites that use the notion of becoming a "real Jedi" as a way into organized faith rather than

---

[18]Captain Riggs, personal e-mail (June 24, 2000).
[19]Robert Davis, personal e-mail (June 24, 2000).
[20]Tiffany Pessotti, personal e-mail (June 24, 2000).
[21]Kes Massey, personal e-mail (June 24, 2000).
[22]Guillet, Ibid.

as an expression of a secular and personal ethical code as in Philip's account. While these sites accept the appeal of *Star Wars* as a powerful fantasy, and actively draw comparisons between its mythical aspects and the teachings of the Bible, they encourage their visitors to see the films as a diluted version of the "real" conflict between good and evil. The tone of address and rhetoric play a very clever game, mapping the familiar elements of the *Star Wars* narrative onto the key concepts of Christian faith, never criticizing or mocking the reader's love for the movies but always promising something even better. You like *Star Wars*? You'll love Jesus. This is from "God's Jedi," part of a South Carolina Baptist Church home page:

> In its truest, purest form our faith is a story of love, forgiveness, passion, power, suffering, defeat, hope and victory that should make *Star Wars* look like a nursery rhyme. The question isn't "what does *Star Wars* have that Christianity doesn't," but "why is the Christian epic more wondrous and relevant than even *Star Wars*?" Christianity has the Force, but it is called God . . . There is an evil empire, a dark side, with which Christians must contend. It is made up of sinful man, propelled forward by his own weakness and desire. Its emperor, Satan, is far more terrifying than any black clad personification of darkness rendered on the big screen.[23]

By extension, of course, the common fan dream of becoming a real Jedi can come true through Jesus—in a manner of speaking.

> And as Christians we are meant to be the Jedi of this life, servants always, emissaries of good, lovers of light, defenders of the weak and helpless. . . . Equipped with scripture, not lightsabers, believers are called to face down the forces of evil every minute of every day and to live by the example of the Master, Jesus. We do not have magic powers that manipulate the Force, but we can seek the power of God in prayer.[24]

Another site, "How To Become A Real Jedi," takes much the same tack. Essentially a promotion for Frank Allnutt, author of *The True Force,* it

---

[23]Dr. Ed Leap, "God's Jedi," http://www.collegestreetbaptist.org/people/leap.html (accessed June 2001).
[24]Ibid.

stresses that while "the Force in *Star Wars* is a make-believe supernatural power that created all things," "the Bible tells us there is a True Force, who is God."[25] Satan, of course, represents "evil or paraforce." Becoming a Jedi is entirely possible, because apparently Jedi stands for "JEsus DIsciples." Once you have your head around that, all manner of glories follow: "He will come for His Jedi." "Jesus will give new bodies to all His Jedi." "May the True Force Be With You!"[26]

Given that the mix-and-match mythology of *Star Wars* can persuasively be mapped onto Christianity, it is perhaps surprising that none of my one hundred respondents mentioned Christianity when describing their relationship with the films. However, I did receive messages from one young man, Neal Bailey, whose own internal conflicts offer a fascinating parallel with the sites discussed. Neal, aged twenty, from Washington, D.C., described himself as an atheist. However, part of him longed to embrace God, and he envied the Jedi for their ability to feel and sense the object of their faith as a tangible Force.

> I really wish I could believe in God. More than anyone I know. I pray nightly, and get no response. It's rather dismal, really. So imagine the way *Star Wars* affects that tugging in my heart. If I could see the power of God by being able to enhance my ability to do good, if I could use my power to take evil and destroy it while doing minimal harm . . . I'd be a priest, and a theist. . . . The Force is a physical manifestation of religion. As an atheist, I don't believe in God because I can't see him, feel him, touch him. Were I a Jedi, this crisis of faith would be solved, and I would be a far better person.[27]

Note that Neal's confession, its self-deprecation echoing Scott Beetley's comment that "it's actually quite pathetic," approaches the relationship between the films and the faith from the opposite direction to the websites cited above. Frank Allnutt promises that by becoming Christian, you become a Jedi; Neal Bailey imagines that were he a Jedi, he could become a Christian.

---

[25]Frank Allnutt, "How To Become A Real Jedi," http://www.frankallnutt.com (accessed June 2001).
[26]Ibid.
[27]Neal Bailey, personal e-mails (June 24, 2000; June 30, 2000).

Daniel Patascher, a twenty-one-year-old university student from Pennsylvania, also incorporates the "Jedi code," as he derives it from the *Star Wars* films, into his own belief system. Daniel, however, has a specific perspective: he is part of the Straight Edge youth movement, which rejects drink, drugs, and promiscuity.[28] While Frank Allnutt draws a direct parallel between the Jedi Knights and the soldiers of Jesus, Daniel considers their purity, celibacy, and commitment to a cause akin to the Straight Edge lifestyle.

> Jedi take nothing that may harm them, and they try to do what is best for a given situation. A Jedi is set in his/her beliefs for life, as am I. Their strict adherence to the Force is similar in a way to my strict adherence to stay "clean" and "pure." . . . I constantly refer to SW collecting as my natural HIGH.[29]

His beliefs lead Daniel to an intriguing reading of scenes from the original trilogy. While other correspondents respected Yoda's wise teachings and in one case even turned to his theme tune as therapy, Daniel examines the gimer root that Yoda habitually sucks upon and suspects "he may have some illegal substance in his stick."[30] Turning to the Jabba's palace scene from *Return of the Jedi,* Daniel views the assorted revelers and criminals with a contempt that is clearly related to his own distaste for drug use and loose morals. Applying his experience to the fictional text, Daniel questions the scene's realism on one level, and on another the implied ethical backgrounds of the "heroic" protagonists.

> Jabba's palace is a despot for the slum of the SW universe [*sic*]. Just like our world, there is always a place for somebody. What gets me is that it was pretty easy to penetrate . . . Lando and Leia both get in unharmed. In the real world, infiltrating a gang's areas is pretty hard unless you were involved in gangs your whole life. Lando obviously was part of that "scene" but Leia moves in right under Jabba's nose, and she grew up in wealth and fame.[31]

---

[28]See www.straight-edge.com

[29]Daniel Patascher, personal e-mails (June 24, 2000, July 2, 2000).

[30]Ibid.

[31]Ibid.

Han Solo, on the other hand, is admirable for his journey from spice-dealing to Rebel general: "His part is much like a drug dealer who goes to jail, rehabilitates and then teaches children the error of their ways."[32] This moral progression is clearly an important part of the narrative to Daniel for its correspondence with his own views, although he admits that he is bringing to the foreground an element that the actual text pushes to the background—"the process by which Han becomes a leader in the rebellion is understated in the movie."[33]

Han's rehabilitation is echoed by the story of Kevin Shank, a twenty-five-year-old respondent from Toledo, Ohio. The ellipses here appear in the original.

> I was 3 when it came out, from my earliest memories I remember *Star Wars*, the toys more than anything, I used to lose myself with adventures . . . after *Return of the Jedi* I was going through my teen years, and *Star Wars* was uncool, so off the toys went to another kid far far away. It wasn't until I got out of the army, I saw a *Star Wars* figure and realized there was something missing out of my life . . . *STAR WARS* . . . I then replaced drugs, with collecting *Star Wars* stuff, now I have a sleeve of *Star Wars* tats on my left arm . . . I got Booush [sic], IG-88, and young Anakin, the relation between them is this mystical force of romance . . . people ask me why I get *Star Wars* stuff tattooed on me, and I have to sit down and explain soul searching . . .

Like Daniel Patascher, Kevin finds a "high" in *Star Wars* to replace drug use—"I went to a comic convention and felt like a little giggly girl," he adds—but while Daniel relates the films to his belief system, drawing out elements that serve the Straight Edge philosophy and criticizing the "good guys" for their possible involvement with drugs or gangs, Kevin elevates *Star Wars* to the same level as his other, vaguely expressed religious beliefs. Although "not a Christian, but more Buddhist in nature," he explains, "I do have a sort of *Star Wars* religion, I feel there is [*sic*] reasons on why I'm here or what I'm doing . . . I've had lots of weird things happen to me."[34]

---

[32]Ibid.

[33]Ibid.

[34]Kevin Shank, personal e-mail (June 24, 2000).

One final point worth noting in Kevin's account is the original reason he became involved with *Star Wars*: "I would have to say I related to Luke Skywalker. Why? I didn't have a father in my life until I was 8, so I had this mystery on who my father was."[35] Like many kids, Kevin found escapism in both the films and the games he would invent around them—"I used to lose myself with adventures"—but Luke's journey, from the murder of his uncle to the death of Obi-Wan and the unbearable revelation offered by Darth Vader, must have been especially poignant for this young boy.

Only one other respondent shared a similar memory of the films' importance as therapy. Barbara Gardner, twenty-nine, from New Jersey, made no mention of any religious belief, but her use of the films for her own emotional well-being and support was as significant as any of the examples discussed.

> I was seven when *Star Wars* came out, and so grew up with the trilogy, and it probably saved my life. As a teen, my mother died young and unexpectedly of cancer, and my stepfather was abusive, and being an only child, *Star Wars* was my distraction, my escape, my addiction and my dreams, all wrapped up in one. As an adult, I have continued to be a fan, and it holds both the same appeal for me that it did when I was young, and an added meaning for all that it represents of the life I escaped when I immersed myself in that universe, reading and writing and playing in it.[36]

Again, we can only imagine what it meant to Barbara when Princess Leia discovered that her father was the Dark Lord who had imprisoned and tortured her. In cases like these, the fan use of *Star Wars* as inspirational escapism and as a source of emotional guidance and comfort is anything but trivial.

"Dressed as a Jedi"

My immersion in *Star Wars* as a seven-year-old was not unusual. Many kids spent the months after their first viewing writing stories, playing

---

[35]Ibid.

[36]Barbara Gardner, personal e-mail (June 30, 2000).

action-figure games, dressing up in makeshift costumes and drawing pictures of their favorite scenes.[37] What is more unusual is the continuation of this *Star Wars*–related creativity into adulthood. In some cases, the childhood passion was channeled into an adult career choice, as detailed below; in others, it inspired a college major.

Greg Howe, eighteen, from Boulder, Colorado, and a "Student of the Arts," writes, "I actually think my love of art can be traced back to *Star Wars*."[38] Sevaan Franks, a nineteen-year-old from Ontario who studies film at York University, cites *Star Wars* as "the first movie I can ever remember seeing . . . since then it has embedded itself in my day-to-day life and has become a big influence for my future in film."[39] Steve D'Alimonte shares a similar experience of viewing *Star Wars* at a very early age—he was eighteen when he wrote to me—and having it affect his entire field of study. "It has had a huge impact on my life. I loved it as a child for the cool ships and lightsabers, and now I can appreciate on so many more thematic levels (but the ships and lightsabers are still awesome) . . . let's just say it is why I am studying film at university."[40] Cindy Eickhoff, nineteen, an art major from Montana, is of the same generation, and her first viewing of the film had a similarly long-term effect. "I found my love for the visual arts through George Lucas' masterpiece. Now I am an award-winning artist that looks forward to making my own movies someday."[41]

Finally, Thomas Hodges from Philadelphia offers a tale of epiphanic conversion that in some ways overlaps with the *Star Wars*-as-religion mentality. As well as shaping his jobs and choice of degree, George Lucas's creation gave Thomas the philosophy that he could realize anything he put his mind to. Unique among my respondents, Thomas actually dreams of completing the circle and putting his skills to work on a future episode of the saga. His story is vividly told; we discover him aged five on a rainy Memorial Day in 1977, crowded into an old-fashioned cinema with his folks.

---

[37]The illustrated screenplay for *A New Hope* has a charming appendix featuring the felt-pen sketches young fans sent to Lucasfilm during the late 1970s. London: Titan Books (1997).

[38]Greg Howe, personal e-mail (June 24, 2000).

[39]Sevaan Franks, personal e-mail (June 24, 2000).

[40]Steve D'Alimonte, personal e-mail (June 24, 2000).

[41]Cindy Eickhoff, personal e-mail (June 24, 2000).

> Then the opening crawl; being 5, I knew only a few of the words so Mom read them to me. I remember watching in awe as the Blockade Runner came into view, then the Star Destroyer seemed to go on forever . . . it was breathtaking. . . . My imagination exploded. I began to think that anything was possible, anything I could dream, could be made real. When the film was over, I was changed forever. When we walked into the theatre, it was raining cats and dogs . . . as we walked out . . . a beautiful sunset. I felt like Luke Skywalker at that moment as he looked onto the Twin Suns. It was when we arrived home, it began. Since that Memorial Day weekend, I've been drawing. Creating images that stem from my imagination. Since High School I've worked as a freelance comic artist for a few years then returned to school. I'm in my last year at the Art Institute of Philadelphia. My Major, computer animation. When I graduate, I plan on reaching my ultimate goal . . . working on a *Star Wars* film.[42]

While some young fans were able to direct their creative enthusiasm into a field of academic study directly related to the films, others retain their passion as a hobby on the sidelines of work or college. Despite the fact that it may gain them no credit in academia or the workplace, their childhood creativity has evolved and matured into a considerable talent. The various genres of *Star Wars* fan fiction and fan film represent such a large and complex body of online work that they merit their own chapters below. The webmasters and webmistresses of *Star Wars* fan sites, who devote their time and skills voluntarily to communities like Star Wars Chicks, are discussed at various points throughout the remainder of the book. For reasons of space, other facets of fan art, such as computer-generated images, are only touched upon, while "old media" artifacts like printed fanzines and acrylic paintings have had to be omitted.[43]

A significant number of my respondents were engaged in another type of creative tribute to the saga, that of literally becoming the characters. Two of them, a sixteen-year-old from Salt Lake City named Brian Barker[44] and Lisa "Ping" Hilton, had gone to the premiere of *The Phantom Menace* in costume dressed as a Jedi (or Sith, in Brian's case). Germain Breton,

---

[42]Thomas Hodges, personal e-mail (June 24, 2000).

[43]These latter forms of fan creativity are covered quite fully in earlier academic discussions on fandom such as Jenkins' *Textual Poachers* and Bacon-Smith's *Enterprising Women,* Philadelphia: University of Pennsylvania Press (1992).

[44]Brian Barker, personal e-mail (June 24, 2000).

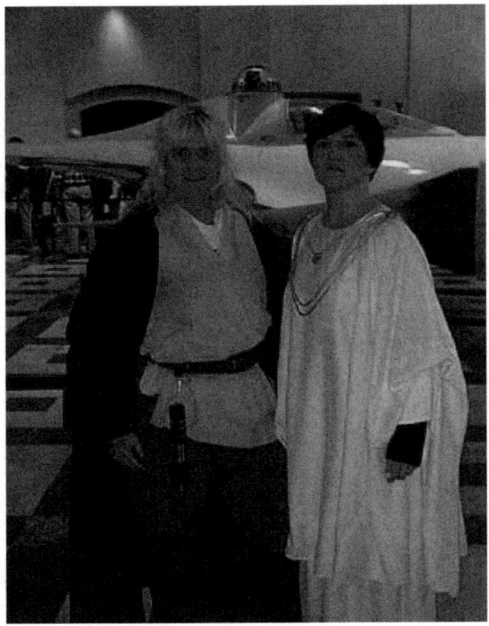

Pamela (left) with another fan as Mon Mothma

twenty-six, from Montreal, had spent the last eighteen years of his life building replica props and costumes from the *Star Wars* saga and sent me a photograph of himself dressed in Mandalorian battle armor like Boba Fett's. Pamela Kinley, a forty-five-year-old actress from Virginia, explained that following her first viewing of *Star Wars* in 1977, "I made costumes of many of the characters (as did my husband) which includes Princess Leia, giving range to my imagination and scope."[45]

Pamela implies that she takes on different *Star Wars* roles to exercise her talent as an actress and costume designer, and her website shows her in various outfits, including a Sith and a Jedi.[46] Princess Leia is arguably one of the less interesting choices for a woman, compared to the *Star Wars* characters who are implicitly coded as male. Like Lisa Hilton's

[45]Pamela Kinley, personal e-mail (June 24, 2000).

[46]Pamela Kinley, http://fantasticdreams.50megs.com/index.html

decision to attend the premiere as a Jedi, Pamela's donning an Obi-Wan–style robe, tunic and pants inevitably, if unintentionally, draws attention to the fact that while the Jedi Council in *The Phantom Menace* includes two female members, the first four films in the *Star Wars* saga offer us four male Jedi Knights and no female.[47]

We can compare Pamela and Lisa's examples with TheForce.net Valentine's Day feature, which asked readers to send a snap of themselves and their significant other in costume. Of the seven (uniformly heterosexual) couples who were posted as the best, four of the women are Jedi or Sith. While it would be misguided to automatically read a feminist intention into these costume choices—it is interesting that two of the remaining women chose Leia at her most girlish and virginal, in the white gown with "Danish pastry" hairdo—we might identify a note of challenge in the caption one of the female fans gives herself, "Obi Wannabe." There is a curious discrepancy between the number of female Jedi in fan photographs and the number in the official *Star Wars* texts.

The last of the seven couples is most interesting. Jeff poses as an Imperial Guard, Lisa as "Lady" Fett, entirely androgynous under her mask in the first photograph and only revealed as a woman in the second, where she submits to Jeff's kiss on the lips. The question of Boba Fett's gender will come up again in the chapter "Star Wars Chicks," which discusses the online Campaign for a Female Boba Fett. As the webmistress of that site points out, Fett is assumed to be male although there is no supporting textual evidence in the first four movies. Germain Breton presumably spent days creating a Mandalorian battle costume because he assumed the character was male; he does not send me a picture of himself as Queen Amidala.

Jeff and Lisa's two photographs, then, disrupt the generally accepted view of the character by allowing him to appear in his conventional guise as a fearsome mercenary, then showing "him" in a romantic clinch with an Imperial guard. However, just as the concept of female Jedi Knights, even if we never see any, is validated by the appearance of two female Jedi Masters in *The Phantom Menace,* so the notion that a male bounty

---

[47]Compare with Stephanie A. Hall's photograph of a female "Corellian," that is, Han Solo, in Bacon-Smith's *Enterprising Women*, op. cit., p. 21; this "masquerade" seems to have a similar project of infiltrating the more challenging and powerful male roles.

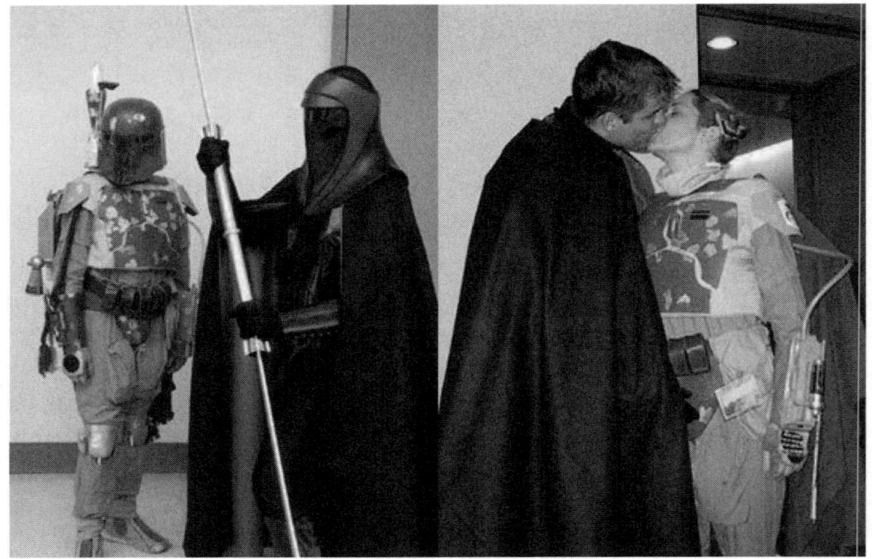

Jeff and Lisa as Imperial Guard and Lady Fett

hunter may not be all he seems is present in the original trilogy. The narrative of revelation in Jeff and Lisa's pictures borrows directly from the primary text of *Return of the Jedi,* where the apparently male bounty hunter Boushh unmasks himself as Princess Leia and draws Han Solo into a kiss.[48] These women's costumes pick up on ideas that are either suggested or not ruled out by the primary text, and make them visible; there may be no critical intention behind them, but they nevertheless encourage a reappraisal of the films' assumptions about gender, and their effect is occasionally quite radical.

"Fett looked like an Intergalactic Police Officer"

The fans in the previous section had either chosen a college major based on their passion for *Star Wars* or were pursuing creative projects based on

---

[48]Pamela Kinley's site includes a picture of a woman as Vader, tacitly reminding us that until *Return of the Jedi,* nothing tells us for certain that the Dark Lord is not a Dark Lady.

the film in their spare time. The spheres of work and fandom were either deliberately kept separate—you don't go to the office dressed as Darth Vader—or had not yet merged. Other respondents were fortunate enough to have combined the two, many of them acknowledging that their current field of employment could be traced directly back to their childhood viewing of the saga.

Brian Stewart, a twenty-nine-year-old computer network analyst from West Virginia, attributes his interest in computers and technology to his first experience of *Star Wars* in 1977.[49] Randall Johnson, twenty-three, from Oregon, announces "when I first saw *Star Wars*, my passion for film began"; he currently works in video production.[50] More generally, A.J. Confessore, thirty-one, from New Jersey, was inspired to become an entertainer by his first viewing of *Star Wars* at age eight: "I have performed *Star Wars* stand-up comedy at conventions. I'd write more now but I'm too busy being ambitious."[51]

Rudy Grasha, an Indiana police officer with the e-mail address A3gangcop, provided a vivid account of the inspiration behind his career. Note how Rudy, like Daniel Patascher, negotiates the generally accepted associations about characters' ethical standpoints in order to have them fit more comfortably with his own outlook:

> At the age of 9 I had my first glance of Boba Fett and to me Fett looked like an Intergalactic Police Officer. Yes, at times Fett is employed by shady individuals, but it is only to collect a bounty. If there is a bounty on one's head, I would think that she/he/it has done some wrong. Fett is simply collecting a paycheck, not breaking the law. In some states, Bounty Hunters are actually recognized and even considered Enforcement Officers (although sadly, here in Indiana they are not). But to get technical, some of the good guys weren't so "good," like in the case of Han Solo. Han Solo was a drug (spice) trafficker and smuggler. Although Han was set up, causing Jabba the Hutt to place a bounty on his head, he still did wrong and I would be forced to arrest him like I do anyone else.[52]

---

[49]Brian Stewart, personal e-mail (June 24, 2000).

[50]Randall Johnson, personal e-mail (June 24, 2000).

[51]A. J. Confessore, personal e-mail (June 24, 2000).

[52]Rudy Grasha, personal e-mail (July 4, 2000).

Prevented by Indiana's legal system from precisely emulating Fett's role as a bounty hunter, Rudy has to do the next best thing: join the police force and reconstruct Fett as a borderline cop, justifying the character's role in breaking up the Han-Leia romance by taking a real-world hard line on Han's past as a smuggler. Once the bounty hunter has been satisfactorily reappraised, Rudy can indulge what he wryly calls his "FETTish."

> At the house, Fett ranges from small figures, signed Fett helmet, to statues, to signed movie posters, to even my home-made Fett costume. At work, he is proudly displayed on and around my desk. In my take home police car, Fett is displayed there along with his "Bantha Skull" insignia that I have drawn onto the inside overhead light. The skull is always talked about when transporting subjects to the station. In 1997 I had the skull insignia tattooed on my arm. It couldn't have been a better idea.[53]

We should note the gulf between this no-nonsense, masculine use of Boba Fett—the businesslike rehabilitation of the character, the stamping of his skull brand on the cop car, the work desk, even the body—with the image of Lisa as Fett kissing her boyfriend. It seems that the character's mask and relative lack of dialogue leaves him open to a variety of contradictory readings.

Other respondents were able to incorporate their enthusiasm for the saga into a range of different jobs. Shawn Farrell, a twenty-six-year-old librarian and systems analyst from New York, writes that "there are numerous ways I've been able to involve what I do professionally with what I like personally—through library programming and events related to *Star Wars* and reviewing any of the new titles for library collections."[54] Bill Karp, who is thirty-five and an industrial designer, "recently designed and manufactured displays for both the Special Edition and *Episode I* promotions with Pepsi-Cola (my most recognized design is the R2-D2 can cooler for convenience stores)."[55] John Tenuto, a thirty-one-year-old from Illinois, offered a fascinating story about the ways in which he and

[53]Ibid.

[54]Shawn Farrell, personal e-mail (June 24, 2000).

[55]Bill Karp, personal e-mail (June 28, 2000).

his wife, as sociology professors, used elements of the saga to put across theoretical concepts.

> We both use *Star Wars* in our classrooms as examples of sociological theory. For instance, Queen Amidala's make-up is a wonderful example of Erving Goffman's notions of dramaturgy and covering a stigma. Also, Han, Leia, and Luke are used by my wife as examples of Freud's thinking. We are also both long-time fans of the series of films, attend conventions, and use that information in class while discussing subcultures.[56]

On that note, look at where my first shot of *Star Wars* in 1978 has got me. This entire book is an example of childhood passion channeled into an academic career.

Armed Forces

Seven of the one hundred responses were from Americans in the military: three in the Air Force, two in the Army, and two at military academies. This was the largest single group with a common career or interest—they were scattered across the United States, and none knew each other—and their uses and readings of the *Star Wars* films also had a great deal in common.

We would expect some overlap between the U.S. military and the adventures of Luke Skywalker: type the words "star wars" into a search engine and half the results will concern the Strategic Defense Initiative. Moreover, if some kids are inspired to get into computers, filmmaking, or the police force by early exposure to the saga, surely others' imaginations would be sparked by the heroic dogfights of *New Hope,* the Hoth ground battle of *Empire,* and the grand clash of the Imperial Navy with the Rebel fleet in *Jedi,* and would have pursued their dreams until they became pilots or soldiers.

Yet in fact, there was little evidence of such a connection in the replies I received. None of the seven even picked up on the ironic double meaning of "star wars" in relation to their careers. None offered a direct link between their current position and their childhood experience of the

---

[56]John Tenuto, personal e-mail (June 24, 2000).

movies, although almost all had seen and adored the saga at an early age. Three even stated explicitly that the films had little bearing on their choice of career. Norman Fuss, a thirty-three-year-old army officer studying at Yale, explained: "Unfortunately, I can't claim that *Star Wars* motivated me to join the service."[57] Twenty-year-old Virginia Military Institute student Magnus Nordenman wrote, "Personally, I am not sure I can say that SW has had a big impact on my choice of school or, hopefully, my future in the armed forces."[58] Their comments were echoed by twenty-three-year-old Floridian ex-airwoman Monica Reinhart: "I didn't join the Air Force because I was influenced by SW to do so."[59]

These respondents did indicate that *Star Wars* was incorporated regularly into their working lives, partly through their own collections of merchandise and toys that they loyally took with them on deployment despite luggage weight restrictions, and often by the use of quotations. Jeff Godemann, an Air Force meteorologist, issues regular forecasts to air crews during war and in peacetime. "I do end flight weather briefings with a good-natured, 'May the Force be with you,' from time to time . . . I recall flights of F-16's in Korea using the call-sign 'Jedi.' "[60] Magnus Nordenman recalls an occasion when his fan knowledge became a currency within the school's harsh rite-of-passage system known as the "Rat Line."

> When I was a rat I was caught by two older cadets, and I prepared myself for a tough quiz on the meals served today. The question I got instead was: "in the *Star Wars* galaxy, what was the emperor's former title and last name?" I answered the questions correctly (Senator and Palpatine). After this I was hammered with questions about *Star Wars*. That day I didn't have to do any push-ups![61]

Norman Fuss offers a view from the Army, which he claims is "full of *Star Wars* references."

> The command and control building at the Army's National Training Center at Fort Irwin, California is known as the "*Star Wars* building."

---

[57]Norman Fuss, personal e-mail (July 3, 2000).

[58]Magnus Nordenman, personal e-mail (June 24, 2000).

[59]Monica Reinhart, personal e-mail (June 28, 2000).

[60]Jeff Godemann, personal e-mail (June 29, 2000).

[61]Nordenman, op. cit.

> It is where the movements of every vehicle and unit are tracked during the year-round war games fought there. The helicopters used by especially-feared commanders are referred to as "Death Stars" because they bring terror and destruction from the sky.[62]

Jacob Neher, deployed to South Korea at the time of writing, elaborates on his similar experience.

> Around work you can always see *Star Wars* playing a part in life. In my unit we put little personal quotes on our vehicles, mine has "Use the Force". . . . Once during a SCUD drill my crew was performing, our generator went out, in the darkness all you could hear was my voice saying "Do you want me to get out and push?" And the darkness was broken by laughter.[63]

Quoting in these circumstances may have a special resonance—Jacob misquotes Leia's complaint about the Millennium Falcon hyperdrive, Jeff repeats the blessing given to the Rebel soldiers before a mission—because of the close parallel between the real-world situation and the film's milieu. Regularly dealing with state-of-the-art military hardware and making combat decisions is likely to give fans a closer identification with *Star Wars* characters in the same position. Norman Fuss gives an example of "using the Force" that in some ways echoes those respondents who drew on the Jedi code for their own ethical guidance, but adds an edge of greater urgency.

> I think that the most relevant part of *Star Wars* to me in the field is the lessons ascribed to mastering the light side of the Force. Being calm, at peace and not giving in to anger, fear, aggression or excitement during periods of stress is key. I distinctly remember a night training exercise when I was a young lieutenant. I was put in charge of a night armor attack that quickly ran into contact. As the shouted incoherent reports of my subordinate units came over the radio, I remember a feeling of calm almost to the point of detachment came over me. I told them to calm down and just report what they saw. They mastered their excitement, we completed the attack successfully and I learned an important lesson straight out of the movies: giving in to anger and fear might be the easy path, but it is not the stronger one.[64]

---

[62]Fuss, op. cit.

[63]Jacob Neher, personal e-mail (July 2, 2000).

[64]Fuss, op. cit.

What also emerged strongly from these responses was an eagerness to map elements of the fictional texts, specifically the *Star Wars* governments and armies, onto their own experience of the real world and to read off a political meaning from the saga. We have seen this approach in the Christian websites, in the Straight Edge interpretation, and in Rudy Grasha's take on Boba Fett; some of the military fan readings were even more involved.

The narrative of the original trilogy, with its rebellion against a totalitarian Empire, is open to any number of political interpretations. *New Hope's* scenes of roadblocks and troops on every corner in Mos Eisley, for instance, would fit an allegory of British soldiers in Northern Ireland. However, Jacob Neher did not hesitate in relating the politics of *Star Wars* to his own role in the military.

> As a *Star Wars* fan I have always been partial to the Hoth battle scene in Empire . . . I always imagined taking part in something like that, given my chance to fight against a tyrannical government and system. I think part of my decision to join the US Army, rather than the Navy, is part of those ideals.[65]

Magnus Nordenman, while making a distinction between his choice of a career in the armed forces and his libertarian beliefs, saw connections between his political stance and the narrative of *Star Wars*—"for example, the rebels fighting against an evil empire with an all-encompassing state and no tolerance for other lifestyles!"[66] But just as Jacob's comparing the U.S. Army to a progressive, guerrilla force battling to overthrow a totalitarian Empire would seem questionable to some, so Magnus's reading of the Imperial ideology is also open to debate. Norman Fuss went into exceptional detail on this matter, conscientiously applying his own real-world knowledge of military conventions and political history to the fictional armies of *Star Wars*. Following Magnus's response, I asked Norman whether he subscribed to the view that the Empire was culturally intolerant, even fascist.

> The politics of the Empire seem more in line with Imperialism or Colonialism rather than the abject subjugation of the Nazi era. The

[65]Neher, op. cit.

[66]Nordenman, op. cit.

> Rebellion only started once recourse to redress through the representative bodies was exhausted. Perhaps it is analogous to the American revolution in a sense, but an absolute comparison breaks down because the *Star Wars* rebels are fighting to regain rights they once had (representation and sovereign rule) where the Americans claimed these rights but were not permitted them. Is the Galactic Empire racist? Was the British Empire? All we see is their non-tolerance of non-humans in their officer ranks, but who knows what the stormtroopers look like under their masks? Perhaps they are humanoid (although not human). Perhaps the Galactic Empire is a mix of Nazism with unchecked Imperialism. There is no reference to any Holocaust-type of action directed at any minority in the films (Alderaan was a planet of Humans).[67]

Norman's responses display a keenness to have the *Star Wars* saga make sense in real-world terms, applying different models from his own experience in order to rationalize the sometimes inconsistent evidence from the films. Note that despite his misgivings about the Empire's political leanings, he retains a fascination for the Imperial troops—who are, after all, far more like a recognizable army than the ragtag bunch of heroes who make up the Rebel Alliance—and because of his own experience sometimes identifies with Vader's men "regardless of their allegiance"[68] and, indeed, their repeated incompetence.

> The Imperial Army has to be a conscript army. There are just too many soldiers needed to man all their ships (I forget the exact numbers, but some material on the manning numbers for the Death Stars run into the millions) and the tactics they use suggest a lack of concern for the individual soldier (frontal assaults through one forced point of entry in the rebel blockade runner and through the elevator at the detention block). The lack of training at the individual level also suggests a hurriedly trained conscript force (despite Ben Kenobi's assertion of "only Imperial stormtroopers are so precise" when referring to the blast points on the Jawa Sandcrawler, most stormtroopers can't hit the broad side of a barn with a blaster).[69]

This meticulous application of technical knowledge to the fictional text is unusual, but not unique. David West Reynolds' official *Visual Dictionaries*

---

[67]Norman Fuss, personal e-mail (July 5, 2000).

[68]Ibid.

[69]Ibid.

are based around an archaeological project to treat "the world of *Star Wars* like ancient Rome or Egypt";[70] the *Technical Companions* by the same author have a similar attention to "realist" detail. West Reynolds' approach is also taken up and continued by the fan site *Star Wars Technical Commentaries,* run by Dr. Curtis Saxton.

> These pages examine particular technical aspects of *Star Wars*. The motivation of this project is to synthesise and explore a self-consistent reality for that universe . . . note that these pages have no relation to real physics work; the project intends to rationalise a fantasy. This hobby simply uses the methods and language of science to consider the question: "If the *Star Wars* universe was real, how would its phenomena be understood?" All contents are subject to revision and correction without notice: the primary objective for these pages is accuracy and rational consistency.[71]

Like Norman's correspondence, *Technical Commentaries* takes pains to relate established military structures to the evidence of *Star Wars*, although Saxton makes his own task more difficult by engaging with the "expanded universe" of the novels, computer games, and comics as well as the primary texts of the four films. Saxton's approach is far more consistent and rational than the collected works of the various authors and artists who construct the *Star Wars* canon and Expanded Universe, and he consistently has to stretch a point to try to pull in some careless anomaly from the secondary texts.

> High General & High Admiral: Ranks explicitly introduced in *The Imperial Sourcebook;* they are inserted into the general convention because *Star Wars* naval and military forces are larger in scope than Earthly equivalents, thus requiring more levels of higher officers. By an ideal symmetry they look as if they ought to be at the same level (and on another level a Surface Marshal should equal a Fleet Admiral), but the *Imperial Sourcebook* swaps them.[72]

Saxton's site covers such issues as the military advantages of Imperial Walkers, the potential fallout of the Death Star debris over Endor, and

---

[70] David West Reynolds, author bio, *Star Wars: The Visual Dictionary,* London: Dorling Kindersley (1998).

[71] Curtis Saxton, *Star Wars Technical Commentaries,* http://www.theforce.net/swtc/

[72] "Imperial Nomenclature," ibid.

the extent of Darth Vader's combat injuries. A very similar approach is taken to other specialist topics, again from a military perspective, at the online fanzine *Echo Station.* George Hill, author of the site's "Required Gun" articles, has in common with Norman Fuss an Army background and a desire to explain the *Star Wars* armies in terms of his own knowledge. Like Norman, Hill is most concerned with the Imperial weaponry and strategies, which he discusses with snappy enthusiasm and constant reference to his military experience.

> Today we have what are called Cavalry Scouts. These guys are very special folks—and I was lucky enough to work with some of these guys, nut cases each one, God bless'm. They use M-3 Bradleys, Armored HumVees, motorcycles, Kiowa Helicopters, dune buggies and sometimes whatever they can, to get in and out and find the OPFOR. The Empire uses three items. First are the Probe Droids . . . then they have the Speeder Bike scouts . . . then for the heavies: the AT-ST scout walkers who run in and find the hot spots and locate the heavier concentrations of enemy forces—looking for weaknesses and causing general havoc.[73]

Like Norman Fuss, Hill concludes his account with a snipe at the stormtroopers' lack of accuracy. "One of the worst insults I have heard on the firing ranges is 'You're shooting Like A Stormtrooper!' I laugh at Ben's line 'Only Imperial Stormtroopers are so precise.' This makes me believe a firearms instructor would make a great living there on Tatooine. That, and Imperial trainers need a good butt kicking."[74]

If this approach seems to lead in Hill's case to slight bravado and a celebration of deadly weaponry for its own sake ("the SAW is 1/3 lighter than the '60, and can fire at 1100 RPM, which is why soldiers would fight for the right to carry it—it rocked"[75]) the same method of rational, "real-world" analysis has also been applied to more peaceable aspects of *Star Wars*. At *Echo Station*, government employee Jody Reeves considers the way the Republic and Senate would operate,[76] aeronautics PhD Scott

[73]George Hill, "The Required Gun" pt. 2, http://www.echostation.com/features/guns2.htm (April 5, 1999).

[74]Hill, "The Required Gun" pt. 1, http://www.echostation.com/features/guns.htm (March 19, 1999).

[75]Hill, "The Required Gun" pt. 2, op. cit.

[76]Jody Reeves, "A Capitol Idea," http://www.echostation.com/features/politics.htm (January 30, 1997).

Schimmels explains possible theories behind the TIE and X-Wing propulsion,[77] and martial arts expert Nick Jamilla discusses the master/apprentice relationship with relation to his own kendo training.[78]

Finally, Jacob Neher demonstrates another aspect of *Star Wars* fandom that may not be confined to the military but certainly results from the Army lifestyle of regular overseas deployment and having to adapt to very different cultural situations. Although Jacob was one of those who firmly identified a correlation between the heroic Rebel uprising and his own role as an American soldier fighting "against a tyrannical government and system,"[79] this story shows that his fandom also served as a bridge in intercultural communications.

> Because of my job, I am taken to places where I cannot pursue my hobby, but on the other side of that, I do get to see how *Star Wars* is seen in other cultures . . . I have had great experiences. Here in South Korea, the US Army has a program that lets Korean soldiers join the ranks of the US Army and be a part of our team, we call them KATUSAs (Korea Augmentation to the United States Army). I was walking down the street with one the other day and passed a *Phantom Menace* poster. As we passed it the KATUSA pointed it out and told me I should go and see the movie because it was great. As his English was not too good, I started to explain to him that I was a huge *Star Wars* fan and have already seen it numerous times, he was surprised because he was a great *Star Wars* fan also, we ended up trading several different collectibles and have been good friends ever since. I have also come across *Star Wars* items in other countries and when you go to look at them and there is another person in another country looking at them it is a great ice breaker to get to know that person better.[80]

The KATUSA remains a KATUSA, unnamed despite the friendship; but this story from a twenty-one-year-old soldier, told with endearing boyishness—the common bond was sealed with an exchange of toys—is a sweet reminder that despite its backbone of military conflict, despite

---

[77]Scott Schimmels, "Flying Star Wars Style," http://www.echostation.com/features/propulsion.htm (May 5, 1999).

[78]Nick Jamilla, "On Becoming a Jedi," http://www.echostation.com/features/apprentice.htm (May 21, 1999).

[79]Neher, op. cit.

[80]Ibid.

its fetish for weaponry and its allegorical associations of a valiant America resisting evil foreign Empires, *Star Wars* can also work as a common culture that binds people together. Rituals of quotation, memories of playground space battles, friendly trivia contests, attempts to imitate the sound of a lightsaber or Vader's labored breathing: this is the stuff of many a male friendship. The next chapter takes us into a group of young men who love *Star Wars*. It examines the role the films played in bringing them together and providing them with a shared bank of references, a fictional mythos inflected with their own in-jokes; a world both Lucasfilm's and their own.

2

WATCHING *STAR WARS* TOGETHER

> George, your kids are keeping it real back there, watching *The Phantom Menace* DVD . . . he and I agree: Liam Neeson ain't no Harrison Ford. And Sarah Smile agrees with me that Ewan McGregor is much, much hotter than Luke—what's his name? The kid, you know, who smashed his face up.
>
> —Kurt Andersen, *Turn of The Century*
> London: Headline (1999), p. 96

This chapter and the next are about two different ways in which fans watch their favored text: the group viewing, as a participatory community commenting on and interacting with the film: and the close analysis, which is more likely to be carried out alone. My discussion of the latter is based on e-mail interviews, while for the group viewing I visited the home of one of the few British fans who had read TheForce.net notice and contacted me.

The group gathered at Mark Williams' rented house in Chatham, a small town in Kent, southeast England. My contact, Tim Meader—twenty-five years old, and hugely tall, over six feet six—had invited a bunch of fellow fans with various work or social connections. Phil Espline and Mark Williams had been working with Tim at a solicitor's office for the last seven years. A few years ago, Phil had introduced the guys to his childhood friend Duncan Wilson, who now works as a financial adviser. Duncan, in turn, brought his fiancée, Emma Mepstead, into the group of friends. We took a vote and decided to watch *The Empire Strikes Back* together.

Group viewing is, of course, not unique to *Star Wars*. My recent research on *Dawson's Creek* audiences[81] suggested that many of the show's female fans gather to watch it in gangs of four or more, and the subsequent discussion of the episode's romantic entanglements is as pleasurable as the program itself. Constance Penley and Camille Bacon-Smith have discussed the importance of the group to female *Star Trek* fans; Bacon-Smith observes that watching videotapes of Kirk and Spock helped the community she joined mourn the death of a member and come to terms with their own emotional response.[82] Henry Jenkins also comments on the weekly viewing of *Star Trek* as a group activity; in one of his examples, the viewing is followed by discussion and then creativity as the viewers spin their own stories about the episode and become amateur producers.[83]

Recent history provides many other examples. In the late 1960s, students would assemble religiously in dorm rooms on Wednesdays and Thursdays to watch the campy TV show *Batman,* while socialites in New York enjoyed the show together in the TV lounge of the "21" club.[84] John Fiske noted in 1987 that gay Americans were gathering for "D&D (dinner and *Dynasty*)" parties,[85] a trend echoed in 1990 by the *Twin Peaks* parties with their servings of coffee and cherry pie during the weekly installment.[86] Elihu Katz and Tamar Liebes faithfully transcribe the commentary of families from various ethnic backgrounds as they watch *Dallas,* commenting on the ways in which the group relates the glitzy American lifestyles back to their own.[87] Writing in the early 1990s, Marie Gillespie discusses the viewing and discussion of the soap *Neighbours* among young British Asians as a "socially shared act and experience . . . young people can draw upon it collectively to make sense of their own lives."[88]

---

[81]"Living on Dawson's Creek: Teen Viewers, Cultural Convergence and Television Overflow," *International Journal of Cultural Studies*, Vol. 4, No. 4 (Dec. 2001).

[82]Camille Bacon-Smith, *Enterprising Women,* Philadelphia: University of Pennsylvania Press (1992), p. 267.

[83]Jenkins, *Textual Poachers*, p. 52.

[84]Will Brooker, *Batman Unmasked*, London: Continuum (2000), p. 214.

[85]John Fiske, *Television Culture*, London: Routledge (1987), p. 71.

[86]See David Lavery (Ed.), *Full of Secrets: Critical Approaches to Twin Peaks*, Detroit: Wayne State University Press (1994).

[87]Tamar Liebes and Elihu Katz, *The Export of Meaning: Cross-Cultural Readings of Dallas,* Oxford: Oxford University Press (1990).

The group dynamic I witnessed around *Star Wars* is by no means unique, then, but it has the distinction that these fans are far more immersed in their chosen text than most of the groups mentioned above. The diners at "21" were laughing at the double entendres of *Batman,* but in all likelihood had no interest in the comic book source; in a year, if that, there would be another amusing distraction. The Morrocan Jews whose family viewings are transcribed by Liebes and Katz enjoy *Dallas*, but not to the point where they read spin-off novels or even recognize the actors from other shows. The *Twin Peaks* fans may have been dedicated to working out the show's central mystery at the time it was screened, but they hadn't lived with it since they were children and played Laura Palmer games in the schoolyard.

With the exception of the *Trek* fans, this group experience is different from other communal viewings in that *Star Wars* has played an important role in these viewers' lives for well over a decade. As the transcript shows, they know much of it by heart and have an expertise that goes beyond the primary text itself into the secondary realm of novels, computer games and comic books. Tim and his friends are doing far more than passing time with a trashy text as ironic entertainment like the *Batman* and *Dynasty* audience, far more even than the *Dallas* and *Neighbours* viewers who use the shows as a means of exploring issues in their own everyday lives; they are touching base with something familiar and precious to them, and by doing it together they are cementing their own friendships. Every time someone delivers half a line of dialogue and another person finishes it, these young men are performing an unacknowledged ritual, celebrating a film they all love and reminding themselves of what they all have in common.

"I Do The Gonk Droid"

Star Wars had been important to Tim and his friends since they were young. They all experienced the saga first through either *Empire* or *Return of the Jedi*; Duncan and Phil used to play with the action figures at school,

---

[88]Marie Gillespie, *Television, Ethnicity and Cultural Change,* London: Routledge (1995), p. 149.

and remember enacting scenes from the movies in a large playground group. During the long drought between official *Star Wars* films, Duncan sustained himself with the spin-off novels and bought them for Phil at Christmas, drawing him into the culture of the Expanded Universe. In 1999 Mark and Tim went to New York together and came back buzzing about the *Phantom Menace* trailer; on the film's release in the U.K., the guys made an event of it and went to the cinema in a large group. Emma, by contrast, had never seen a *Star Wars* film until 1999. Duncan half joked that he had forced her to watch the trilogy in one go, "as a clause for engagement."

Of course, there is no such thing as a typical group of fans, and Tim's friends can only serve as one example. While they could all be said to belong to the broad community around *Star Wars*, they also belong to several other social communities based on class, gender, ethnicity and religion. Although there was no mention of it during the discussion of the films, everyone but Tim was part of a Church of England youth group. All of them were white, British, and educated to sixth form level, the equivalent of high school in the States. Most of them, of course, were male. A group of teenagers or Asian-Americans or graduates or women, or a combination of those factors, would very probably have reacted differently to the film. However, I suggest that their affiliation to the wider *Star Wars* fan community would mean that all these group responses had a great deal in common. Tim's friends are not rare in their participation and playful involvement with the film during screening, and the fact that *Star Wars* has, in one way or another, played an important part in their shared histories is not unusual.

Before carrying out this participant observation at Mark's house, I surveyed my other e-mail contacts, asking them what role watching the saga played in their friendships and how they might customarily view the film with a group. Daniel Patascher, the Straight Edge teen, told me that

> 3 years ago I met a good friend, Rob, who was just as big into *Star Wars* as me. We have watched it together and we try to get other people who have never seen it to watch it. . . . We do quote A LOT!! We talk back to the screen especially in parts where we don't see eye to eye with good old George . . . [89]

[89]Daniel Patascher, personal e-mail (July 8, 2000).

Matt Stein, a seventeen-year-old student from New York, went to see *The Phantom Menace* in a group, "three times in one day." When watching the trilogy at home with friends, he says

> We do talk to the screen at times, always yelling at Luke for doing something stupid, 'cause he is a little dumb . . . there are a few lines which we tend to quote during the movie such as "Use the Force Luke," or "I am your father." We just tend to goof around because we all pretty much know the movie by heart. I also have a Jedi robe which I made myself, and it has become a ritual to wear that during any *Star Wars* showing. A number of the people I've watched *Star Wars* with have felt compelled at one time or another to do a Yoda impression, though I don't like that 'cause only Frank Oz can do that voice.[90]

Jeff, thirty-three and a grocery store manager, from Ohio, disagrees about the sanctity of the original voice talents; for him, performing the more distinctive character parts is integral to the viewing experience.

> Usually I do it before the dialog is spoken . . . Yoda, Jabba and the Emperor. All of the Yoda lines, they're all great and unique. I like to do the sound that Jabba makes when he's being choked and his final "exhale" as he's choked to death. And his laugh. My older brother likes the Emperor and some of the Stormtroopers' lines ("Look sir, droids!" from *Star Wars*). And I do the lightsaber sound effects too! I jus' remembered that I do the Gonk droid. It makes a "gonk" sound. It's hilarious. I act out scenes when Vader has his hand stretched out to Luke asking him to join him and then he pulls back his hand and makes a fist . . . other scenes would have to be when the Jawa replied back to Uncle Owen, throwin' both arms up in the air.[91]

Scott Beetley, the "*Star Wars* geek" from chapter 1, boasts that when watching the trilogy with his friends "I can do all the movies, line for line."[92] "JkthRipper" and his buddies turn the mastery into a contest: "By this point, we can quote pretty much the entire movies, so often we will try to keep up with the film and see who fouls up a line first."[93] Steve

[90]Matt Stein, personal e-mail (July 6, 2000).
[91]Jeff, personal e-mail (July 5, 2000).
[92]Scott Beetley, personal e-mail (July 5, 2000).
[93]JkthRipper, personal e-mail (July 5, 2000).

Ash, thirty-three and a computer programmer, is more selective and only repeats key dialogue from the Jedi characters—"Now, that's a name I haven't heard in a loooong time"—and adds, "It's very important to do an impression whenever these lines are quoted."[94] In addition to echoing the characters, Steve adds his own commentary: "I mutter 'oh God, here we go' as soon as Wicket appears, and cheer at each Ewok death."[95]

Robert Davis, a twenty-four-year-old from Ohio, told me that on one occasion he "got a copy of the *Star Wars* drinking game . . . picked up some beers . . . and took my Special Edition collection over for a party with some friends from college . . . we had a blast."[96] The drinking game[97] instructs players to take a sip of their beverage every time Luke whines, Yoda uses bad grammar, or something goes wrong on the *Millennium Falcon*. Not surprisingly, Robert reports that "there are sections of that night that are rather fuzzy to me at the moment."[98]

The most elaborate response, against my expectations, came from a sixteen-year-old girl living in Massachusetts. Keara Martin and her best girlfriend, Tina, "talk for at least ten minutes a day about *Star Wars* during the school year," and their viewing rituals around *Star Wars* films frequently involve themed hairstyles, costumes, and catering as well as the more usual quoting and commentary.

> I have *A New Hope, The Phantom Menace* and most of the others memorized. I'm not kidding when I say that I can recite the entire movie if given a cue. My buds and I also yell, "Luke, you idiot!" "Quit whining," "Luke, I am your father . . . ew, and he kissed Leia" and other things. Also, we are pretty weird in that we whistle at young Obi-Wan Kenobi (we're teens, he's cute, that's all there is to it), make fun of Anakin being a shrimp, and I scream out lines from my fanfic. I also wear a Darth Maul t-shirt, and generally have my lightsaber and an action figure on hand. Also, there's a *Star Wars Encyclopaedia* handy for notes, and I generally have my hair done to match the females in the movie. I also enjoy pulling out my Mara Jade, Leia and Amidala costumes on special occasions. On days like the anniversary of release or a new book, I wear Amidala

---

[94]Steve Ash, personal e-mail (July 5, 2000).

[95]Ibid.

[96]Robert Davis, personal e-mail (July 5, 2000).

[97]www.infinityrealm.com/swdrink.htm

[98]Robert Davis, op. cit.

> lipstick, have on an Anakin watch, two snap bracelets, a braid in my hair, and a pez dispenser. I act out fight scenes if I'm really hyper, rewind the end of *Return of the Jedi,* whimper a bit when Qui-Gon dies (actually, that would be Tina) and always play *Star Wars* music when we can afterward. We name our cookies "Wookiee cookies" and drink Sprite, called "Yoda Soda."[99]

While these patterns of group viewing do exhibit some variation, then—Keara's drawing on her own fan fiction is unique among my respondents—the similarities are more striking. Watching the favored text, especially with friends, involves an often sarcastic commentary, a practice of quoting lines that sometimes edges into competition, occasional rituals of dressing up or drinking, and some more involved participation like acting out scenes. JkthRipper compared the group viewings to *Mystery Science Theater 3000,* the TV show where three characters marooned in space comment acerbically on old movies; there is surely also a parallel with *Beavis and Butt-Head*'s guffawing at MTV videos.

While the previous sample is small, it does provide some context to the viewing with Tim's friends and indicates that their group response to the *Star Wars* text is far from exceptional.

My observation of the group was carried out in the informal setting of Mark's front room; beers were shared around, and I joined in the discussion rather than leading it or, on the other hand, deliberately keeping quiet. I used a cassette recorder for brief interviews before the film, asking the men and Emma about their experience of *Star Wars* and their relationships with each other, then tape-recorded the conversation during the screening of *The Empire Strikes Back*—the original version—which the group chose as their favorite. I also took notes during both the interviews and the film, in order to be sure of who was speaking at any one time and to clarify points of the recording. After transcribing the results at home, I invited the group to look over my version of the evening's conversation and correct any mistakes; their amendments were minor but I have incorporated them faithfully.

I have chosen to present the transcription first, as a straight account of the conversation and commentary that took place during the screening,

[99]Keara Martin, personal e-mail (July 6, 2000).

and to analyze it afterwards.[100] Note that because I have included all my more embarrassing mistakes and "innits"—the London contraction of 'isn't it'—alongside the other remarks, this will be in some small part a self-analysis as well and an examination of how a complete newcomer fits into the established fan-group through a shared knowledge and enthusiasm. It will also be apparent that the comments frequently connect *Star Wars* with popular British TV shows of the 1970s and 1980s. American readers may need some briefing on *Grange Hill* (a long-running kids' soap set in a London school), John Inman, the effeminate star of *Are You Being Served?* and Victor Meldrew, the grumpy old protagonist of another sitcom, *One Foot in the Grave*.

"Isn't that the bloke out of *Cheers*?"

[*"A long time ago, in a galaxy far, far away . . . "*]
Phil: Every single time you watch the crawl, you always read it.
[*Star Destroyer looms on-screen*]
Tim: Is that the *Avenger,* is it?
[*Luke rides tauntaun across Hoth landscape*]
Mark: What does he [the tauntaun] say?
Tim: Muppet, muppet! Is that before he [Mark Hamill] has his accident?
[*Tauntaun falls*]
Duncan: These films are quite violent, aren't they?
Will: *Phantom Menace* isn't though.
Duncan: It is when he [Obi-Wan] cuts him [Darth Maul] in half.
Emma: You don't see any blood.
Duncan: No, you do, when he cuts him in half, like that, and blood spurts, only little bits—

[100]Tamara Liebes and Elihu Katz present an alternative method in their excellent study of *Dallas* audiences, *The Export of Meaning,* but I found that positioning annotations alongside the transcription would in this case be too clumsy. David Morley's *The "Nationwide" Audience,* London: BFI (1980), is the classic study of discussion during television viewing and indirectly influences my own approach.

Tim: [to Emma] I bet you fancy Han Solo, don't you. Ahhh, [mockingly] every woman fancies him.

Mark: They tried to make Jar Jar like between R2 and Chewbacca. But you could never understand what Jar Jar Binks was saying.

Duncan: I think he [Lucas] was trying to be too clever, wasn't he?

Emma: But it [Jar Jar] was for the kids, that character was for the kids.

Duncan: Think of [a young relative] Rhiannon, she loves Jar Jar Binks.

Emma: But she talks like that. [laughter]

Mark: [noticing Leia on-screen] That's the other thing about watching *Return of the Jedi*—you get to see what's-her-face in a bikini! Come on, boys! [laughter]

Emma: It's like out of *Friends,* isn't it?

Mark: That was everyone's first crush, wasn't it?

Will: I hate to be a real geek but they got it wrong in *Friends*. She had the *New Hope* hairstyle and the *Jedi* bikini.

Duncan: Yeah, she did.

[*Leia: I'd just as soon kiss a Wookiee.*]

Tim: [exactly with Han's line, in accent] I can arrange that.

[mild laughter and cheers]

Tim: Isn't that the bloke out of, er, of *Cheers*?

Will: Yeah. It's Cliff, isn't it?

Tim: I was always him, in the playground.

Will: What, you were that minor character?

Tim: Yeah, well, do you know the figure, the Rebel Commander—

Will: That wasn't him, though, was it?

Tim: Well, no, he was just offscreen there.

Will: Do you know Mr. Bronson out of *Grange Hill* is in this?

Mark: Yes, he is!

Will: Does he die? Most of the Imperials die.
Phil: He makes a mistake, doesn't he? [as Vader] Apology accepted—
Tim: No, that's Captain Needa. He's Admiral Ozzel, the guy out of *Grange Hill*.
Duncan: I'm sure he said apology accepted—
Tim: Apology accepted, Captain Needa. He's [as Vader] as clumsy as he is stupid, [as himself] Admiral Ozzel.

[appreciative laughter]

[*Luke frees himself from the Wampa cave*]

Duncan: The funniest thing is, when I first saw it I didn't understand what this was about. 'Cause obviously you hadn't seen the first one.
Will: How did you make any sense of it?
Duncan: You knew in the playground—
Tim: You had all the figures, even if you hadn't seen the film.

[*Luke stumbles through the snow*]

Tim: [as Obi-Wan] You will go to the Dagobah system.

[extensive appreciative laughter]

Tim: [noting See-Threepio] He looks like John Inman. He walks like John Inman.
Will: He does come across as quite camp, doesn't it. [Threepio] Oh my!

[laughter]

Duncan: That's quite normal for Mark.
Mark: He's my hero!

[laughter]

[*Han on-screen in Hoth outfit of coat with furred hood*]

Mark: Parkas in *Star Wars*—how cool is that.
Will: That's right, that's what you wear at school, innit.

[*Obi-Wan: You will go to the Dagobah system . . .*]

[some laughter]

[*Obi-Wan: Yoda, the Jedi Master who instructed me.*]

Tim: Ah, but did he?

Will: [as Han]: And I thought they smelled bad . . . on the outside!

[laughter]

Mark: That's such a great line. He's a cheeky chappie, isn't he, Han Solo. Do you like Harrison Ford, generally?

Will: I used to, I don't anymore.

Phil: Samuel L. Jackson, he oozes cool, whatever he does. No matter what. From *Pulp Fiction* even to Mace Windu. He's incredible.

[general agreement]

[*Han cuts open the tauntaun's body with Luke's saber*]

Will: That's the only time in the trilogy you see a non-Jedi using a lightsaber.

[agreement]

Tim: In the books it seems to indicate you have to be Force-sensitive to turn one on. Obviously not.

Duncan: That's part of your training, isn't it, to build your own?

[*Snowspeeders fly over Hoth looking for Han and Luke*]

Phil: I had one of them.

[general "So did I."]

Duncan: And they had the electric thing—lights.

[general: "Yeah."]

Tim: [as Han] Good morning.

Will: [as Han] Nice of you guys to drop by.

[*Han: Good morning. Nice of you guys to drop by.*]

[*Leia visits Luke in medical center*]

Tim: This is weird, 'cause this is the brother and sister kissing each other, isn't it?

Mark: And Chewbacca laughs. [as Han] Laugh it up, fuzzball!

[extensive appreciative laughter]

Tim: [about Chewbacca] That makes me quite sad now that he's dead.

[*Leia: Why, you stuck up . . . half-witted . . . scruffy-looking . . . nerf-herder!*]

Phil: [quoting Han, but not with accent] Who's scruffy looking?

[*Shot of Star Destroyer*]

Tim: That's the Executor—I named my car after that.

[laughter]

Mark: That was the second one [car].

Tim: Yeah, it was the Iron Fist before that.

Duncan: What was the Iron Fist?

Mark: That was the one with the stuck-on—[distracted by appearance of actor on-screen] Mr. Bronson.

Will: Yeah, Mr. Bronson.

[*Darth Vader addresses officers Piett and Ozzel*]

Mark: James Earl Jones, what a great voice.

[*Han and Chewbacca prepare the Millennium Falcon for takeoff*]

Mark: What's that bit where he says to C-3PO, do this and do that, and ask him this and ask him that . . . and hurry up!

Tim: That's *Return of the Jedi*.

[*Vader: He is as clumsy as he is stupid.*]

[some laughter]

Tim: It says somewhere that the Emperor was in control of all the armed forces, from his base on Coruscant.

Will: The Emperor . . . was he? In control?

Tim: Yeah, using his mind—

Will: That sounds a bit, sort of, hokey.

Tim: Which is why when he died, all his forces—

Will: I don't really go for that.

[*Vader chokes Admiral Ozzel*]

Emma: Wasn't the guy who was actually in the suit, Darth Vader, he said all his lines, and he thought he was actually gonna be in it?

Will: Yeah, what's his name, I've forgotten his name, Dave Prowse.

Mark: Dave Prowse, yeah.

Will: He's got a Birmingham accent, is he Brummie?

Tim: West Country, innit?

Phil: I thought it was West Country.

Will: I think you're right, I don't know what I'm saying, but he's still always slagging James Earl Jones, and saying his own voice would have been better.

[moment later]

Tim: [Vader as West Country] Oi foind yer laack of faith disturbin'.

[outburst of laughter]

Will: Oi am your father.

Mark: Oi be your faather.

[laughter]

Emma: Come to the dark soide.

Tim: I be your father, and I, I'm yer brother too!

[extensive laughter]

Duncan: Oi think your mother was a goat.

[fading laughter]

[*Imperial walkers attack Rebel base*]

Phil: I always wonder, how did they get these down onto Hoth?

Tim: It's in the computer game, *Force Commander*. It's like a landing barge.

Will: [skeptically] A landing barge, what's that like then? But in the film, how did they get them down?

Phil: You never see them land, do you? They're just there.

Tim: I don't know how they do it, but in the game—

Will: Well, how do they do it, a landing barge?

Tim: Yeah, it's like a big prisonlike thing, they all come down like that, and it drops them off, and it lifts up—

Phil: That's like, computer game license.

Will: Yeah, right.

Duncan: Did you notice, in *Phantom Menace,* that one of the people they nominated for Chancellor, is, uh, Bail Antilles?

Will: Yeah.
Tim: Of Alderaan.
Duncan: And the interesting thing about that is, Princess Leia's dad is Bail Organa.
Will: There is debate around that—
Duncan: And I thought perhaps it was a mistake in the film, as if they should have said Bail Organa.
Tim: I dunno, cause Bail Antilles is Wedge's dad, innit?
Will: Well, no, it's complicated, cause C-3PO's old master was Captain Antilles, in *New Hope,* so, like, don't you know more than one person with the same name? Couldn't there be more than one person called Bail?
Tim: Did you have the AT-AT? [toy Imperial Walker]
Duncan: With the AT-ST you had the button at the back, didn't you, to make its legs move. The new toys don't look a patch on the old toys.
Mark: The French ones are more muscles.
[laughter]
Duncan: The other good thing about the old ones is they had the lightsaber come out.
Will: Yeah, that wasn't really very good though, was it?
[laughter]
[*Luke leaps from underside of a walker*]
Tim: That would have broken Luke's legs there.
Duncan: He used the Force.
Mark: They are timeless, aren't they? Any other film from the 70s, you know it's from the 70s, but with this . . . the effects are so good, and the imagery.
[general agreement]
[*Han and Leia aboard the Falcon, preparing to escape Hoth*]

Mark: In *Return of the Jedi* you see Han touch her tit, touch Leia's tit. He does!

Will: Are you sure?

[Emma laughs]

Mark: He does get down there, he goes "here you are," and he touches her tit.

Will: I've never seen that.

Mark: Well, look out for that. [distracted by Han on-screen] That was the Harrison Ford point. [i.e., lifted index finger] He does that in every film.

Duncan: No, only in the serious ones.

Mark: In *Patriot Games,* he did it in that.

Duncan: And in *Clear and Present Danger.* I think he also did it in *Air Force One.* Things like *Six Days, Seven Nights,* and *Sabrina,* things like that, he didn't do it in that cause he's a romantic character.

[*Luke takes X-Wing on course for Dagobah*]

Mark: [as Luke] That's right, Artoo.

[laughter]

[*Luke: There's nothing wrong, Artoo.*]

Tim: Ahhhh! [mocking]

Duncan: That's later, when they escape.

Mark: Oh yeah, that's right, yeah.

[*Millennium Falcon enters asteroid field*]

Duncan: Did you see this on the Spectrum [1980s home computer]? This bit of music was exactly the same.

Will: On the Spectrum, they couldn't do music like this. Was it any good?

Duncan: Yeah, it was like wireframe. But they did *Return of the Jedi,* and that wasn't vector graphics.

Will: No, it was raster graphics.

Duncan: It was like a forced 3-D angle.

[*Falcon flies into asteroid "cave," actually creature's mouth*]

Phil: You never see how they get into that worm. You don't actually see it, all it does is you see them coming out, you don't see them getting in.

Emma: They don't realize they're in it, do they?

Will: Yeah, they must fly down right into his mouth.

[*Luke arrives on Dagobah*]

Duncan: [as Yoda] Away put your weapon!

Tim: [testing him] What's the first line?

Duncan: That's it, isn't it?

Tim: No, it's "Feels like what." [as Yoda] Feels like what? [as Luke] Like we're being watched.

Phil: Right. [as Yoda] Away put your weapon, I mean you no harm!

Tim: [as Yoda] Help you I will, yes! Good food!

[laughter]

Duncan: Do you think R2 is where they got the inspiration for Dusty Bin?

[*Emma turns away in disgust when Artoo spits out mud*]

Mark: [suddenly] Oh, I know when it is! [that Han touches Leia's bust]

Tim: He's been thinking about it all this time . . . breast part of brain.

[laughter]

Mark: You know when, um, with the Ewoks, on what's the planet called?

Tim: Endor.

Mark: The forest of Endor, and they're in the bunker, and she gets shot and he goes down like, "are you alright," and that's when it is. Check it out.

[*Yoda: Away put your weapon! I mean you no harm!*]

Tim: Round of applause! [as Yoda] Why are you here? [as himself] I know all this conversation, I better shut up. [as Yoda]

Found someone, you have, I would say, hm? [as himself] That is [mutual friend] Dave Basset, you cannot deny that. [laughter] [as Yoda] Mudhole? Slimy? My home this is!

[laughter]

Phil: George Lucas always said that the way Mark Hamill was here is totally brilliant, because he can't hear anything that Yoda was saying, he was just talking to a puppet.

Mark: Yeah, but sometimes they have someone say it, like in *Roger Rabbit* with the cartoon, someone speaks it, just so the actor can—

Phil: Apparently it wasn't, he was just acting as if the character was there, but it doesn't look like that, it looks as though they're having a conversation.

[*Vader enters meditation booth to address the Emperor*]

[*Vader: Yes, my master.*]

Tim: I've got that on my PC. That's what it says to me, and when I log on it says "What is thy bidding?"

[laughter]

[*Vader: He will join us or die, my master.*]

Tim: I don't understand that bit, because there are only meant to be two Sith at one time.

Will: That's a fair point. Palpatine should know that there can only be two, the Master and the Apprentice.

Mark: Then again, in *Return of the Jedi,* he tells him to kill Darth Vader and take his place.

Will: But the Emperor told Vader to convert Skywalker to the Dark Side, so there could be three of them.

[*Luke on Dagobah with Yoda*]

Tim: [as Yoda] . . . when nine hundred years you reach—

[*Yoda: For eight hundred years have I trained Jedi . . .*]

[general reaction to Tim's mistake with Yoda dialogue]

Will: Nine hundred years is *Jedi,* isn't it, when nine hundred years you reach, look as good you will not.

Tim: Yeah.

[*Han and Leia inside asteroid*]

[*Han: There's an awful lot of moisture in here.*]

Tim: That's one of the ten most perverted lines, isn't it?

[*Han and Leia stumble back to the Falcon*]

Mark: That's bad acting.

Tim: That's *Star Trek* acting, isn't it?

Will: *Doctor Who.*

[*Dagobah: Luke prepares to enter the tree*]

Tim: That's where a Dark Jedi died.

Will: Apparently.

Tim: Why does he see Vader in there?

Will: It's because he takes his weapons, surely.

Duncan: It's because he uses his lightsaber first.

Will: It's anger, then, isn't it?

Mark: That's 'cause of his insecurity, isn't it, that he takes the weapons.

Duncan: Yeah, but he didn't have to light his saber first, and he attacks first.

Mark: Oh, I see, right.

Will: He wins, doesn't he, but he loses 'cause he's using the Dark Side to win.

Duncan: See, he did it first.

Will: And he's using it for attack rather than defense.

Duncan: And he's got it up.

Will: No, that's a parry, isn't it?

Mark: No, he's got to, you've got to finish him off, otherwise what are you supposed to do, keep batting him away? You've got to finish him off, so where do you cross over?

Will: Yeah, that's a good point. You're saying if a Jedi kills someone, is that supposed to be turning to the Dark Side?

Mark: Exactly.

Tim: I always thought they used the Dark Side when they used that mind trick, altering someone's will.

Mark: That's just like a white lie, it's just something they do, isn't it?

[*Bounty hunters on board the Star Destroyer*]

Will: Dengar's ex-Imperial Navy. I read it yesterday in the *Star Wars Visual Dictionary*.

Tim: He got beaten by Han Solo in a swoop race.

Will: Ah, well, you're referring to *Tales of the Bounty Hunters* there.

Tim: And the *Star Wars Encyclopaedia*.

Will: But that's not canon though . . . it's in the *Star Wars Encyclopaedia*?

Tim: Yeah.

Will: Well, *Tales of the Bounty Hunters,* that's not really an official text. But the *Encyclopaedia* is.

Tim: I've got all the books, and I read the *Encyclopaedia*.

Will: But the books aren't official really, are they?

Tim: But he [Lucas] passes them all, doesn't he?

Will: Yeah, he does, but some bits in the books are contradicted by the films.

Duncan: I read [spin-off novel] *The Crystal Star* or something—

Will: Vonda MacIntyre.

Duncan: —it didn't really seem to go anywhere.

Will: I don't like the idea of Han and Leia being married, having kids, it's like soap opera.

Duncan: I didn't mind it in the first three. But *The Courtship of Princess Leia,* I didn't like that very much at all.

Will: Kids running around in the books, that's annoying.

Tim: They're all grown up now, they're sixteen, seventeen, they're Jedi Knights themselves. There are about a hundred Jedi Knights now. Chewbacca's nephew's one—

Mark: Chewbacca's nephew?
Tim: Yeah, Lowbacca.
Mark: Lowbacca?
Will: Oh, that's just bizarre, that's silly. What books are these?
Tim: There's the *Young Jedi Knights* series, and then the *New Jedi Order*. It carries it on.
Duncan: He's a . . . Salvatori, he's a fantasy writer.
Tim: And there's the *Jedi Academy*.
Duncan: Yeah, Kevin Anderson, I didn't really like them. They had the Sun Crushers in them, didn't they? I didn't really like them.
[*Imperials in Star Destroyer*]
Emma: Those soldiers remind me of *Spaceballs*.
Duncan: Dark Helmet.
[laughter]
Emma: Yeah, I liked that.
Will: So you'd seen *Spaceballs,* and you hadn't seen *Star Wars*.
Mark: So you saw *Star Wars*, and thought it's taking the piss out of *Spaceballs*!
Duncan: Use the Schwartz!
[laughter]
[*Slave 1 follows the Falcon*]
Tim: IG-88 was there as well, wasn't he?
Will: You and your books. Those aren't official! *Battle of the Bounty Hunters*. [laughter] Well, where was he then?
Tim: I can't remember now, but somewhere offscreen.
Will: [skeptically] Offscreen.
Tim: It adds to the film, so you know why everyone's there.
Mark: Even if he has no part in it.
[laughter]
Tim: He does, though, cause in *Jedi* he transfers his body into the second Death Star, doesn't he?

Will: That's pretty silly, though, innit?

[*Yoda: Always in motion is the future.*]

Duncan: Is it "always in motion" or "always emotion"?

Phil: I've always thought it was "always emotion."

Mark: It's so clever, the clothes, the way they don't look futuristic, it's just normal clothes, just casual.

Will: What Luke's wearing is like combat trousers, like clothes fashionable in the late 90s.

Mark: Yeah, but with pockets at the front rather than the side.

Will: Well, Lando's clothes don't.

[*Bespin: Threepio is hit by a laser*]

Tim: What I don't understand is, Threepio gets shot there, but when he's reactivated, he says "stormtroopers."

Will: Maybe that was what he was thinking, before he got shot.

Emma: He's probably short-circuited.

Duncan: It was the last thing on his mind.

[*Chewbacca brings in Threepio's dismantled body*]

Tim: He's like Lassie. Or the kangaroo, Skippy.

[*Lando: You look absolutely beautiful. You truly belong here with us among the clouds.*]

Duncan: Have you ever used that one yourself, there, Tim?

Mark: You know that film with Eddie Murphy, *Coming To America,* the one who uses the Soul-Blow on his hair.

Duncan: That's Eric LaSalle out of *ER*.

[*Han is about to be carbon-frozen*]

[*Leia: I love you.*]

[*Han: I know.*]

Emma: [complains] He doesn't say "I love you" back.

[*Vader and Fett in carbon-freeze: Vader is contemptuous*]

Will: He hates him, doesn't he? The Empire hates bounty hunters.

Tim: Boba Fett saves Vader's life, though.

[laughter]

Mark: [sarcastic] Oh, what book is that?

Tim: It's a comic, called *Boba Fett: Enemy of the Empire*. It's set just before the film. They're fighting on this volcanic ledge, and Vader does this Force push-off—and, oh, I can't remember now.

Will: I think this is confusing the films.

Phil: How does that [Solo in carbonite] float there?

Will: It's the same as a landspeeder. I think that's technically called a repulsor-lift—ah, it's all made up.

[*Vader and Luke duel*]

Duncan: He does it again, same as in the cave, and he attacks first again.

[*Threepio: Ouch! Oh, ah, that hurt! Bend down, you thoughtless—ow!*]

Mark: He's like Victor Meldrew, innit?

Will: Vader creates a wind to lift him back up, doesn't he? No, it's when Luke's falling down. I might be forgetting this. And Vader produces a wind to lift him back up.

Tim: No, that's where he says join with me, and—

Will: No, I'm sure he tries to lift him back up—

Tim: No.

[laughter]

Will: Maybe I'm imagining it.

Tim: [triumphantly] You read it in a book!

Duncan: Yeah, you and your books.

[laughter]

[*Vader gazes down exhaust chute after Luke*]

Mark: How does Darth Vader shower?

[*Final shot, pulling back from main characters onboard Rebel ship*]

Tim: [about freighter]: That's a Nebulan B Frigate. [laughter] I like my ships. I love the names of the ships.

[End credits]

"Mr. Bronson out of *Grange Hill* is in this"

There is a great deal of rich and fascinating material here, and I shall try to pick through it systematically.

First, we should examine the different levels of intertextuality at work in the discussion. Tim and his friends appeal to several distinct frames of reference, often when trying to prove a point in friendly argument. I would categorize them as follows:

1. *Intratextual:* a reference to the *diegesis*, or internal story space, of *Empire Strikes Back*. This would be a remark about character or plot that relies on information from the film itself, rather than any knowledge of actors, writers, or novelizations. For instance, Tim's remark, "That would have broken Luke's legs there," is a gentle complaint about realism: Luke has leapt from the underbelly of a gigantic Imperial walker and lands without injury. Duncan could have responded with a mocking explanation that it was probably a stuntman falling from a height of two meters, that is, referring to the context of the film's production; or he could have asked how long Tim thought the film would have lasted if Luke had broken his legs in the first battle, breaking out of the story world to appeal to conventions of narrative, or he might have brought in secondary texts by mentioning a *Star Wars* novel where Luke jumps from a similar height.

Instead, he replies simply, "He used the Force." This answer stays entirely within the framework of *Empire Strikes Back* and explains the apparent lapse in realism in terms of what we have already been shown in the film. Luke is honing his Force abilities in the Wampa cave, so we can imagine that he has enough control over the mysterious power to cushion his landing. Other examples of this approach would include the extended discussion about why Luke discovers a specter of Vader inside the hollow tree on Dagobah. The argument I have with Duncan and Mark about whether Luke is showing unnecessary insecurity or aggression is based entirely on visual evidence from the scene—"See, he did it first . . . and he's got it up"—rather than any external knowledge.

2. *Intertextual:* This category itself must be divided into several levels. First, there are remarks that cross-reference the other two films in the original trilogy—most obviously, the ironic awareness that the twins, Luke and Leia, enjoy a passionate kiss in this episode—and, at another remove, the extended saga of prequels. Tim's point about the Emperor's plan to

recruit Luke alongside Vader—"I don't understand that bit, because there are only meant to be two Sith at one time"—draws on the knowledge that viewers now have from *The Phantom Menace* and points out an apparent inconsistency between the two. Similarly, when Tim questions Obi-Wan's claim that Yoda taught him as a young Jedi—"Ah, but did he?"—he is referring to the fact that, in Episode One, Obi-Wan's master is Qui-Gon Jinn.

Second, we see frequent attempts to explain contradictions or provide a context through reference to the wider canon of *Star Wars* lore, texts that are still "official" within the hierarchy, but that lie outside the films themselves and so would probably only be familiar to fan readers. While debates about this are taken up during the screening, and will be revisited extensively in chapter 5, "Canon," this category would include evidence from the *Star Wars Encyclopaedia,* such as Tim's contentious remark that the bounty hunter Dengar, a minor character in *Empire Strikes Back,* "got beaten by Han Solo in a swoop race."[101]

While the *Encyclopaedia* is accepted as canonical in this specific instance, this is not always the case; the group still makes a distinction between "official" texts on one hand, and on the other, novels, computer games or comics that, despite their Lucasfilm branding, have less credibility. The line between the two is hazy. The theory that building one's own lightsaber is a test of Jedi training goes unchallenged, perhaps because this rite of passage is supported not just by the *Encyclopaedia*[102] but also by incidental evidence in the primary film texts and directly by a semi-canonical source: Luke performs the task in the novel *Shadows of the Empire,*[103] and Vader admires the finished weapon in *Return of the Jedi*.

However, the more far-fetched theories, which Tim presents as gospel—that the Emperor was controlling the Imperial forces with his mind, that a Dark Jedi died in the tree on Dagobah, that Boba Fett saved Vader's life, that Chewbacca's nephew is now a Jedi Knight, and that IG-88 transfers his consciousness into the Death Star—are treated with friendly contempt, even though they are drawn from secondary texts and faithfully

---

[101]Stephen J. Sansweet, *Star Wars Encyclopaedia*, London: Virgin (1998), p. 72.
[102]Ibid. p. 178.
[103]The novel's events take place between *Empire* and *Jedi* and were adapted into a Lucasfilm game and sound track album; of all the spin-off *Star Wars* books, this comes the closest to canon.

documented in the *Encyclopaedia.*[104] It will be clear enough from the transcription where my own instinct draws the line between canon and non-canon, and Tim's boundaries are clearly different. As I'll discuss later, our debates on this subject seem to play a key role in the evolving relationship between the established group and myself as newcomer.

Third, there are intertextual references to material with an incidental or even tenuous relationship to *Star Wars*. These include actors' careers or life stories, such as Mark and Duncan's discussion of Harrison Ford's other films, Tim's early question about Mark Hamill's car crash, and the extended riff about Dave Prowse's belief that he would be playing Darth Vader with a West Country accent. There are some references to *Empire*'s place in film history, such as Mark's comment that the saga seems timeless and undated compared to other movies made in the 1970s; and an ongoing game during the first half of the film to spot Cliff and Mr. Bronson, from *Cheers* and *Grange Hill* respectively, among the opposing galactic armies. The appreciative nods to Mel Brooks's spoof *Spaceballs* and to the "Princess Leia Fantasy" in *Friends* would also fall into this category.

The group sometimes makes a cross-reference to a text entirely unrelated to the saga, for humorous effect: R2D2 looks like Dusty Bin, the cheap mascot from the 1970s game show *3-2-1*; C-3PO resembles the camp *Are You Being Served?* actor John Inman and the old grouch Victor Meldrew from *One Foot in the Grave*; and Chewbacca reminds Tim of either Lassie or Skippy the Bush Kangaroo. In terms of *Star Wars* canon, of course, these texts are not even in the ballpark.

3. *Extratextual:* I use this final category to account for references to entirely personal experience that has no obvious relationship to the primary text. Emma's comment that Jar Jar Binks talks like Duncan's brother's girlfriend's daughter Rhiannon had to be explained to me afterwards, and I never discovered the identity of Dave Bassett, who apparently has the misfortune to look like Yoda. These references are obviously entirely dependent on this specific group of friends, and I have little doubt that other groups would share similar obscure in-jokes based on acquaintances and personal history. We saw in chapter 1 that many fans incorporate

[104]The *Encyclopaedia*, faced with this problem of distinguishing between canon and quasi-canon, opts for a middle ground whereby events like the Dark Jedi's presence in the Dagobah tree are treated as potentially true rather than absolute fact. Sansweet, ibid. p. 64.

Star Wars into their jobs, hobbies, and spiritual outlook. Tim's comment that he named his car after an Imperial Star Destroyer is an improvisation along the same lines.

"He doesn't say 'I love you' back"

Much of the research into television audiences over the past twenty years has focused on the ways in which gender, ethnic background, national culture, and class shape a viewer's interpretation of a mainstream text.[105] As white, lower-middle class, English males, Tim and his friends are members of a "dominant" group whose responses are often treated as the norm. In this section I suggest that there is a degree of performance and irony in the "masculine" response to the film, and furthermore that Englishness and the frequently overlooked factor of age play a key role in defining the group's bank of shared cross-references. I also consider the idea that the group's ethnicity means that they ignore aspects of the film text that a Black British audience might single out. Initially, though, we should consider Emma's position as the sole woman present.

Driving from the station, Mark and Tim had warned me that "a girl" would be present in the group and that her responses would be naïve and inappropriate. Emma is not a fan of the saga in the same way as Duncan and his friends, and her comments are accordingly of a different nature. The important point, I think, is not that Emma is a woman, but that she is a woman and non-fan. Aficionadas of *Star Wars* have, as my later chapter suggests, developed various ways of engaging with the saga that are distinct from those of their male counterparts, but Emma's response is different again. As someone on the borders of the community, encountering the saga and the group as "Duncan's girlfriend," it seems that she plays up her own stereotypically "feminine" response to the films, probably aware

---

[105]For further examples of the way national culture, class, gender, or ethnicity can shape interpretation, see Morley, op. cit.; Liebes and Katz, op. cit.; Gillespie, op. cit.; Jacqueline Bobo, "The Color Purple: Black Women as Cultural Readers," in Deirdre Pribham (Ed.), *Female Spectators*, London: Verso (1992); and my article "Readings of Racism: Interpretation, Stereotyping and *The Phantom Menace*," *Continuum* vol. 15 no. 1 (April 2001).

that anything she says will be regarded as ignorant by the male experts alongside her. Tim's mocking question, "I bet you fancy Han Solo, don't you?" establishes the preconception early during the screening, and instead of resisting it, Emma chooses to accommodate their expectations.

Rather than even attempt to compete with their insider knowledge—the question about David Prowse's accent is the one exception—she only makes comments from a "girly" perspective, such as her exaggerated expression of disgust when Artoo spews out mud from the Dagobah swamp. Her remark that Han didn't tell Leia he loved her is the prime example; it is a criticism based on standards of emotional behavior and gender roles in relationships, with no reliance on specialized knowledge about the characters or story. Duncan might have pointed out that Solo goes into carbon freezing with his hands manacled and emerges somehow with them freed; Emma creates her own perspective by suggesting that Leia wanted reassurance, not a snappy comeback.

Mark, on the other hand, seems to adopt a stereotypically "laddish" role in the group, playing up the opposite position as a lusty wide-boy or man-about-town. His attempt to remember the point where Han brushes Leia's breast becomes a running gag—"He's been thinking about it all this time," Tim remarks in wonder—and is consolidated by his corner-of-the-mouth advice to "check it out," "look out for that," which constructs him as a dealer of "dirty" moments in mainstream films. The recommendation of *Jedi* as the film where you get to see "what's-her-face in a bikini" is, of course, along the same lines.

It seems quite possible that this act is laid on for Emma's benefit, almost as a complementary role to her "naïve," stereotypically female response. Although Mark's "Come on, boys!" seems to deliberately exclude her, she is the one who immediately responds with the *Friends* reference, and she laughs indulgently at his mucky-mouthed reference to "Leia's tit." It is interesting to note that, while keeping up this banter, Mark also accepts and continues a joke about himself as camp: When Duncan suggests that C-3PO's slightly effeminate mannerisms are "quite normal for Mark," the latter exclaims, "He's my hero!" Having established his own sexual tastes through a lightly ironic performance of laddishness, Mark can deal with gags at his own expense.

We should remember that these young men were meeting me for the first time and were aware that they were not just presenting themselves to a stranger, but also that their remarks were for publication; on one level, then, they were probably quite careful about the way they came across. Before the screening I had mentioned the critic Robin Wood's theory that C-3PO had a form of "pedophile relationship" with R2-D2[106]; the group met this suggestion with slight unease and a lack of enthusiasm. When I brought up the topic of slash fiction, Tim stressed that he had no knowledge of the genre or any wish to know about gay readings of the Jedi relationships. Perhaps not surprisingly, Tim and Mark in particular seem to have felt the need to establish their heterosexuality before there could be any gags about idolizing campy robots.

Tim and his friends, unlike most of my e-mail respondents, are English. As such, the way they read the film and link it to their own cultural context would be different from that of, say, Americans Robert Davis and Scott Beetley. In fact, this group's reading is grounded not just in British culture but in the experience of British culture from a specific generational perspective; while Emma was the youngest, at twenty, Duncan, Phil, Tim, and Mark were all between twenty-five and twenty-seven years old. Most of their humorous cross-references and comparisons are to British popular culture from the 1980s, when they were growing up—*Are You Being Served?, 3-2-1,* Mr. Bronson in *Grange Hill,* ZX Spectrum games, parkas, *Doctor Who*. It is quite probable that these jokes or links would simply not be understood by American viewers, who would no doubt make entirely different connections.

Moreover, a younger fan like Keara Martin, who was born in 1983, might even find that the references to American culture like *Cheers, Spaceballs,* and *Lassie* were over her head, or certainly that they lacked the same cultural weight. There is a sense of nostalgia to this group's enjoyment of *Empire,* based partly on shared memories of what it meant to be a *Star Wars* fan in 1980: the first wave of toys compared to the more recent models, the limited scope of home computer games, the discussions in the playground when everyone else had seen the film and you only had the figures. My final chapter, "*Star Wars* Generations," discusses more fully the way that interpretive communities can be shaped by age as well as by more obvious factors like gender and ethnicity.

Finally, the group is Caucasian. While there may seem sparse examples in the transcription of a specifically "white" reading, we should not fail

[106]Robin Wood, *Hollywood from Vietnam to Reagan*, New York: Columbia University Press (1986), p. 173.

to examine the role that ethnicity might play in this interpretation; we would surely look for it in a group of non-white fans. One interesting point is the discussion that begins with a joke about Lando Calrissian's smooth chat-up lines to Leia: Mark immediately jumps to a mention of an Eddie Murphy film, based on the fact that it features a comically "pimpish" Black character, and the group enjoys the comparison. It would surely be wrong to label this reading as racist in its laughter at a Black stereotype, but it is perhaps dependent on the group's being entirely white; it seems likely that a group of Black viewers might respond to *Empire* in a different way, perhaps criticizing the portrayal or pointing out the general underrepresentation of Black characters in Lucas's otherwise culturally diverse universe.

"I know all this conversation, I better shut up"

Much of the group's engagement with *Empire* consists of quoting lines of dialogue before they are delivered on-screen, usually in an imitation of the character's voice. Quoting in this way displays individual knowledge of the text, memory skills and imitative ability and is rewarded by the group's appreciative laughter. It also plays an important part in bonding the group, as members help and support each other in addition to competing and mocking, and the process is a key factor in my "initiation" into the little community.

The rules to this game of quotation are unspoken, yet made clear through the group's reaction or lack of it. First, a quotation preferably should be delivered in imitation of the actor's voice and just prior to or at the precise moment of the character's delivery of the actual line.

> [*Leia: I'd just as soon kiss a Wookiee.*]
> Tim: [exactly with Han's line and accent] I can arrange that.
> [mild laughter and cheers]

Here Tim is applauded for his multiple skills of timing (on cue), memory (the exact words), and imitation (the Han Solo voice). He achieves the same standard with "You will go to the Dagobah system," as Obi-Wan is about to speak the dialogue, and Tim demonstrates his ability to imitate a different character by adopting Alec Guinness's solemnly theatrical tones rather than Harrison Ford's drawl. By contrast, when Phil says, "Who's scruffy looking?" the dialogue is correct and the timing is right, but there is no effort whatsoever to imitate the character, and his delivery of Solo's line in a half-hearted Kent accent earns him an embarrassed silence.

If a quotation were delivered too far in advance, it would lose its relevance; delivered after the actual line, there is clearly very little skill involved. However, there are several examples in the group discussion where a member illustrates a point by giving the line of dialogue in character rather than "straight," and effectively gains bonus points. For instance, Tim's "as clumsy as he is stupid" involves his slipping into Darth Vader's voice in midsentence, then going back to his own accent in conclusion. Phil does the same during this exchange, indicating that he is quoting Vader by performing the voice, rather than taking the easier route of prefacing the line with "Vader says to him." Mark, in a later conversation, recalls the scene where "Chewbacca laughs," then immediately drops into Han's role to give the reaction line, "Laugh it up, fuzzball!" The laughter that greets these performances serves as recognition of a vivid, confident impersonation, the opposite of Phil's "Who's scruffy-looking?"

If a quotation is delivered incorrectly or at the wrong point, the participant will be affectionately mocked for misremembering the line. The group jeers Mark's attempt to preempt Luke's dialogue—"That's right, Artoo"—but note that the atmosphere is supportive in terms of helping a participant to remember the line and its timing. Duncan offers, "That's later, when they escape," and Mark takes the advice: "Oh yeah, that's right, yeah." A similar process occurs a little later, when Tim, who establishes himself as the expert at Yoda's dialogue, tests Duncan's memory and coaches him.

> Duncan: [as Yoda] Away put your weapon!
> Tim: What's the first line?
> Duncan: That's it, isn't it?
> Tim: No, it's "Feels like what." [as Yoda] Feels like what? [as Luke] Like we're being watched.

Tim is effectively leading a masterclass here, showing a knowledge not just of Yoda's first line but also of Luke's reaction, and easily performing both roles in a reenactment of the exchange. Phil joins in with an impression of Yoda—"Away put your weapon, I mean you no harm!" but Tim holds his position as the expert on the character's dialogue, going into an extended, word-perfect performance which, significantly, he deliberately cuts short. "I know all this conversation, I better shut up." He knows he can carry off all the Yoda dialogue, but censors himself for fear of boring the group and becoming overbearing; however, he offers one more line as a postscript, just to make the point that he really could go on for longer. A moment later he accepts correction when he slightly misquotes a line; the mistake is important in terms of showing that his knowledge is not absurdly, geekily encyclopedic.

The game depends on all the players being on a level as good amateurs; a newcomer who could recite every single word from the screenplay, and did so, would be regarded like a professional soccer player steaming onto a kids' pitch and racking up twenty goals in the first five minutes. There is a delicate balance between displaying skills of imitation and textual knowledge, and showing off. A participant will therefore tend to hold back after having successfully delivered a quotation, so as not to dominate the shared game. To quote continuously, however accurately, would seem boorish and arrogant.

Although there is some sense of competition, then, this is more often a group experience. Sometimes a quotation is split between two people—"Good morning," "Nice of you guys to drop by," is a two-man delivery of a single Harrison Ford line—and sometimes it develops into a longer-running joke. The Darth Vader skit is the best example, and even Emma joins this one, drawing on a well-known line and adapting it to the broad West Country accent of Dave Prowse. The gag develops as a group creation, started off by Duncan. My contribution—"Oi am your father"—is improved by Mark's "Oi be your faather," with its more accurate dialect and drawn-out vowels. Tim's addition, suggesting that this "Darth Farmer" character was involved in all manner of incestuous confusion, represents the peak of the joke, and Duncan's contribution comes as the laughter is fading.

Once a participant has quoted a line from the film, the actual line itself—when it comes—also earns appreciative laughter, as it recalls the successful imitation. Obi-Wan's "You will go to the Dagobah system" gets a response when it occurs a few minutes after Tim's quotation; it becomes a payoff line, the second half of a running gag. Hearing the actual dialogue enables the group to judge whether Tim had the script down pat and how well he re-created the accent, and there is pleasure in hearing Alec Guinness precisely echoing Tim's rendition. Similarly, "He is as clumsy as he is stupid" becomes a comedy line because it had raised a laugh previously in the discussion, and after the challenge to remember Yoda's dialogue, the words "Away put your weapon! I mean you no harm!" have acquired a resonance that prompts Tim to ask for a "round of applause" when they are finally delivered in the film by Frank Oz.

"You and your books"

For the newcomer to the group, learning these rules and successfully playing the game is an important, though again completely tacit, process of initiation. I entered the friendly competition once it had been established that quoting dialogue was part of the group's interaction with the film; although the process was subconscious, there is probably something in the fact that I waited a decent period before chiming in with a brief "Oh my!" as Threepio. No doubt I would have clammed up if nobody had laughed at my Han Solo line, "I thought they smelled bad . . . on the outside," a few minutes later; but having got the desired response, I shared the "good morning" dialogue with Tim in a following scene and became drawn into the collective activity.

Just as Tim establishes himself as the Yoda expert—and as someone who can reel off the names and categories of spaceships—so the other members have their own fields of specialized knowledge, which is subtly made clear by their contributions. Mark's specific area of interest emerges through his comments about the actors' careers and his attempts to place *Empire* within a historical context by comparing the effects and costumes to other films of the time. Duncan, in turn, makes detailed remarks about Harrison Ford's characteristic performance in various films and identifies an actor in *Coming to America* as Eric LaSalle. Tim and Mark join in by identifying Cliff from *Cheers* and Mr. Bronson from *Grange Hill,* but this knowledge is arguably less specialized. Duncan at one point shows a technical knowledge or detailed memory of 1980s computer games based on *Star Wars*; Tim, on the other hand, is established as the group's expert on more recent PC *Star Wars* games.

Most notably, a running joke is established around Tim's investment in non-canon texts such as books, comics, and computer games. Duncan is also a fan of the books and draws on that intertextual knowledge to explain plot points; but Mark exhibits a mocking skepticism about these details that happen "just offscreen." It is this debate around canon and non-canon that really works to integrate me, as an outsider, into the group, at least for the duration of the film. My slightly cutting remarks about the "landing barge," which Tim argues lowers the walkers onto Hoth, are backed up by Phil: "That's, like, computer game license." Mark then takes my side when Tim once again draws on secondary, quasi-canonical materials with his discussion of Lowbacca, and comments sarcastically, "Oh, what book is that?" when Tim brings up the theory that Boba Fett saves Vader's life.

Near the end of the transcript, my argument with Tim has become familiar enough to work as the basis for an ironic reversal. I repeatedly claim, erroneously, that I remember seeing Vader creating a "force wind" to lift Luke out of the exhaust chute, despite Tim's mockery.

Tim: No, that's where he says join with me, and—
Will: No, I'm sure he tries to lift him back up—
Tim: No.
[laughter]
Will: Maybe I'm imagining it.

Tim's gleeful "You read it in a book" is a fitting punch line to this twist in our established relationship—for once I am trying to prove an event with no basis in the primary text, while he remains skeptical—and Duncan joins in, affectionately scolding, "You and your books." Tim and I, despite having met just two hours earlier, have reached a point where our opposed stances towards the canon are known to the group and to each other and can be parodied. Our enjoyment in the exchange stems from a recognition of this fast friendship; at the start of the evening I was a stranger, and already it has become acceptable to have a joke at my expense.

This rapid initiation and bonding is surely similar to that which united Jacob Neher and his KATUSA. When I joined Tim's group we went through a stage of mutual testing, feeling for alliances and exploring common ground; once it was established that I had a similar—although, crucially, not identical—level of expertise and enthusiasm for the saga, we immediately had a vast bank of shared references to draw upon. Some of these references were, as I've suggested, dependent on the fact that I am more or less of Tim's generation and grew up as a young man in the same national culture, but for the most part it was our fandom that gave us a common vocabulary.

I knew about the rule of two Sith, the debatable history of Dengar and Solo, and who plays the Rebel Commander; and my immersion in this arcane, trivial mythos was enough to grant me membership, for a few hours at least, of a community that had been established over many years. Of course, I only engaged with the group on one level. *Star Wars* is not all that binds these people together, and I only encountered one aspect of their lives. A mutual knowledge of the saga had enabled me to achieve almost instant familiarity with a group of strangers, but I still know very little about them as people and our contact faded within a month.

Similarly, it would be wrong to pretend that I was ever genuinely on an equal footing with Tim and his friends. All the time we were sitting with beers and talking at the screen, I was the only one with a tape recorder next to me on the sofa and a notebook in hand. They were aware, just as I was, that I would be able to go home and write what I wanted about them under their real names; and although I have aimed for a fair, objective analysis, there is still something uncomfortable in the fact that, having been invited into Mark's house, I now blithely comment that perhaps he deliberately adopted a laddish performance to avoid being thought of as gay. Repaying a subject's trust while retaining a critical distance is a difficult balance to achieve, and a great deal of power ultimately lies in my hands as researcher and writer.

However, I think it is remarkable that for one hundred and twenty minutes, the hierarchies were so fully dissolved and replaced with new ones, or rather old ones—the hierarchies of the playground, where the kid with the most trivia or the best Yoda impression can hold court. For a while, I think we were all back at school in 1980, with our parkas and action figures, cussing each other and doing the voices.

3

WATCHING *STAR WARS* ALONE

The Emperor wants to control outer space, Yoda wants to explore inner space. That's the fundamental difference between the good and the bad sides of the force.

—Moff, *Human Traffic* (directed by Justin Kerrigan)

The special edition of *Star Wars: A New Hope,* which was released for the film's twentieth anniversary in 1997, is listed on Paul Ens' fan site as having sixty-nine differences from the original.[107] The *Empire Strikes Back Special Edition* has fifty-five, and the revamped *Jedi* thirty-eight. According to another count at Jay Pennington's Special Edition FAQs, Paul's total is conservative: Jay's study of *A New Hope: Special Edition* consists of fifteen pages with thirteen entries each, most of them illustrated.[108]

George Lucas has stated that his main purpose in reworking the original trilogy was maintenance and preservation.

> The most obvious thing that's happened is we've gone back to the original negative, cleaned it up considerably, redone a lot of the optical effects, the wipes, the dissolves and improved the quality of the film, because it was deteriorating. One of the things I wanted to do was

---

[107]Paul Ens, *Special Edition Annotations*, www.theforce.net/swse/

[108]Jay Pennington, *Treadwell's Star Wars Special Edition FAQs*, www.jax-inter.net/users/datalore/starwars/sepage.htm

> preserve the film so that it could still be a viable piece of entertainment in the twenty-first century. Films do deteriorate, and they disappear. This one had deteriorated a lot more than anybody expected in twenty years. So that was the primary concern. The audience will get a brand new print that's very clean and actually better than the original release in terms of technical quality. It's less grainy, it's less dirty, and it's just a better print.[109]

Many of the changes, according to his account, were purely for technical purposes, and the rejigged effects shots such as improved space dogfights in *A New Hope* also fall into this category, although he makes a distinction between these and the altered scenes that affect character and narrative. "I've also added the Jabba the Hutt scene with Han Solo, which was a scene that had been cut out due to time and money constraints. When I finished the third film, I really wanted to go back and put that scene back in because it was relevant to what happens to Han Solo at the end of the movie"[110]

Lucas' comments tend to play down significantly the number and extent of the changes between the *SE,* or *Special Edition,* and the films that fans quickly redubbed the "original trilogy." While his account makes the reworking sound primarily like a matter of cleaning up the print and soundtrack, for fan sites like those of Paul Ens and Jay Pennington, the *SE* was a cause for painstaking comparisons that involved poring over the different versions moment-by-moment, freeze-framing, contrasting, and in most cases providing an analysis of the implications, drawing on an intimate familiarity with the saga and its universe. This mode of watching *Star Wars* is a solitary, intensive examination, a process of constructing personal theories and interpretations, and is far removed from the group viewing we discussed in the last chapter, despite their common ground in an extended knowledge of the chosen text. Watching *Empire* with a group of friends was an experience something like going to a ball game: analyzing it alone is more like the traditional practice of scholarship, the reclusive study of a dense primary text.

This chapter looks at the way fans perform a close analysis of the *Star Wars* films, with a specific focus on comparisons between the *SE* and the

---

[109]Interview with George Lucas, starwars.com (January 15, 1997).
[110]Ibid.

original trilogy. It is based on four websites and two lengthy e-mail reports. The first group comprises Paul Ens' and Jay Pennington's online studies, along with two extended reviews on the home pages of Chris Foxwell[111] and two teenage girls named Samantha and Heather.[112] The two original reports were carried out at my request by Keara Martin—the girl with the Pez dispenser and Yoda Soda—and Scott, the nineteen-year-old from Michigan who cropped up early in chapter 1 with his claim that he could act out the entire trilogy from memory. I asked my two correspondents to list what they considered the key changes from original trilogy to *SE,* and to discuss the reasons for their choices. My intention was to see which aspects of the reworking were important to these fans and how they would place them in the context of the wider saga or the expanded universe of secondary, quasi-canonical *Star Wars* texts. Combined with the website studies—which, although I have corresponded with the authors, were constructed independently of my research—they present a suggestive account of the detailed attention that fans will devote to their favored text.

For the record, all these contributors are American. Jay Pennington, a video editor from Florida, and Paul Ens, a web designer from the San Francisco Bay area, were the oldest at thirty and twenty-six, respectively, when they created their sites. Keara was sixteen at the time of writing; Chris Foxwell is a twenty-two-year-old anthropology/astronomy major from Boston.

From the five commentaries, I have categorized the areas of fan attention into the distinct groups that I found most interesting: technical improvements, questions of "realism," implications for canon, and changes to character. Although some went into far more detail than others—Jay Pennington's is an all-inclusive analysis, whereas Chris Foxwell and Heather's sites only claim to offer personal reviews—a consistent list of key changes cropped up in every account. The expansion of Mos Eisley, the computer-generated Jabba, the reinstated Biggs scene,[113] the Wampa ice creature, the redecoration of Cloud City,[114] the addition of Jabba's "Jedi

[111]Chris Foxwell, "Thoughts on the New Ending to *Return of the Jedi,*" wso.williams.edu/~rfoxwell/starwars/Starwars.htm

[112]Samantha and Heather, *Star Wars Special Edition Reviews,* www.geocities.com/Hollywood/Lot/3143/starwars/swreview.html

[113]All from *A New Hope: Special Edition.*

[114]Both from *Empire Strikes Back: Special Edition.*

Rocks" band, and the extended Endor celebrations[115] were common to all these reports, which suggests a ground level of agreement on which alterations were most significant, even though there was a great deal of variation beyond this baseline.

"An extra Chewie growl"

Jay Pennington's site shows a remarkable, almost frightening attention to technical details. His notes begin with the 20th Century Fox logo, pointing out that "the fanfare is the old Alfred Newman with Cinemascope extension, as always, not the newly recorded performance (conducted by Bruce Broughton) Fox has used recently."[116] A typical description, in this case a comparison of old and new shots of the Falcon in the Death Star hangar halfway through *A New Hope,* comments that the original matte painting "had originally been farmed out to Disney in 1976" and praises the skill with which

> The Millennium Falcon has been replaced, the floor extended, the far wall filled in, the walls of the "pit" enhanced, matte edges in the upper and lower left corners blended, and the starfield even moves from right to left as they should, due to the Death Star's rotation! The Falcon has the *ESB* paint scheme, but what the hell.[117]

Jay's analysis reckons up the precise length of the added footage—"The first dive of the X-Wings toward the Death Star . . . is about one second longer than the one it replaced; 33 video frames longer, but that doesn't precisely translate to the number of frames of film"[118]—and traces the sources of the sound track that was used to cover the extended scenes. "The music during Boba Fett's departure now utilizes portions of the score that had been previously been cut: the cue is now left intact, and instead of ending with Chewie's first shot at Slave I, it continues to the end of

---

[115]Both from *Return of the Jedi: Special Edition.*
[116]Pennington, op. cit.
[117]Ibid.
[118]Ibid.

the scene."[119] Jay spots every flub that Industrial Light and Magic (ILM) has failed to correct—"the first two frames of the shot where Vader opens fire on Luke are missing the TIE on the left-hand side!"[120]—and every change to the sound track, however minor—"An extra Chewie growl as Lando enters to invite everyone for dinner."[121]

Few of the other commentaries even approach this level of detail and technical expertise, although it is significant that the other fans do note the subtle cleanup operation even when they lack the precise vocabulary to explain it. Keara explains that

> Even as a little girl I noticed the slightly gray boxes around the TIE fighters and X-Wings. I loved the scene, don't get me wrong, but the obvious signs of special effects nagged at me like a mosquito by my ear. When I first viewed *ANH* of the *SE,* I was amazed. I kept walking up to the screen and attempting to find the touch-up lines, but there were none . . . The same proved true for Hoth, it was refreshing not to see any lines on ships or have to see through the dashboard.[122]

Paul Ens also engages in a high level of detailed analysis, but even he stops short of Jay Pennington's standard, and his remarks are generally reserved for changes which seem to have more potential significance. He observes that Wedge's snowspeeder tow rope in the Hoth battle is far more noticeable in the *SE,* but only draws it to our attention because it could be a "deliberate change" rather than "just a side-effect of the general clean up."[123] The distinction is very subtle, but it implies a perceived difference between the straight improvement of faulty effects shots and an authorial decision to draw more attention to a specific element: an artistic choice, rather than a necessity.

For the most part, the other accounts only comment on changes when they have implications beyond the purely technical. Heather notes the alteration to one of Luke's lines in *Empire*—"instead of saying 'You're lucky you don't taste very good' Luke says 'You're lucky you got out of

---

[119]Ibid.

[120]Ibid.

[121]Ibid.

[122]Keara Martin, personal e-mail (July 6, 2000).

[123]Ens, op. cit.

that' or something like that"—but the observation is casual, reflecting her opinion that this was "an utterly pointless change."[124] The new matte painting of the Death Star hangar may be admirable for its blended edges, but it does not change the pace of the scene, introduce elements that were previously not in canon, or make us view Han Solo in a different light. Some of the additions, while no greater as technical achievements, have far more important effects in terms of our understanding of the story.

"Scientifically sloppy"

The internal realism of the *Star Wars* mythos—the sense that we are glimpsing characters, technology, and cultures that have a complex history outside the film—is a major part of the saga's appeal, and flaws of this nature were clearly jarring to some of the fans in my study. Keara Martin saw the gray boxes around the X-Wing fighters as a constant nagging reminder that this was just an effects sequence, and accordingly she was far more immersed in the polished dogfights of the *Special Edition*: "For the first time I was able to fully become caught up in the movie. I literally found myself screaming at the pilots . . . there weren't any special effects as far as I was concerned, just pure storyline."[125] Similarly, Jay Pennington treats the correction of a scene involving the Millennium Falcon's top hatch—one shot showed it with an air lock, one without—as a cause for celebration. "Now there's no confusion. Just after the hatch above Lando opens, another one above the bright light opens in turn! A guy in my row [at the cinema] made a 'YES!!' gesture when we saw this, and I must agree!"[126]

Keara has serious issues with some of the changes to the *Special Editions,* and only approves some of them. The Ewok song at the end of the original *Return of the Jedi* meets with her disdain on grounds of realism—"Please, the Ewoks, with their raspy little voices, sound that clear?"[127]—and the new version is praised for its more authentically primitive sound. Chris

[124]Heather, op. cit.
[125]Martin, op. cit.
[126]Pennington, op. cit.
[127]Martin, op. cit.

Foxwell takes a similar line, arguing that the new composition "is performed by 'woodland' instruments and 'primitive' percussion suitable to a race as technologically advanced as the Ewoks."[128] On the other hand, Keara lambasts the Death Star explosion in the *SE* of *A New Hope* for its scientific inaccuracy:

> First of all, chances are you've seen *Star Trek* movies or shows. No big deal—except that George Lucas used their shockwave. That's right, and why did that shockwave only go in one direction? It was scientifically sloppy, even though the minor implosion and then smaller fire was an attribute. Also, the new explosion didn't show enough fire. Something that big, with that much oxygen, could be burning, theoretically, for up to an hour.[129]

Most of the other fans in this sample also note the revamped explosions of Alderaan and the Death Star, sourcing the effect, as Keara does, to the rival science-fiction mythos of *Star Trek*. Their view of it, however, is largely neutral or positive. Paul Ens comments on "a similar effect to that used in *Star Trek 6* when the Klingon moon Praxis explodes";[130] Jay Pennington calls it "A 'Praxis Moon' ring of fire," judging that "the destruction of Alderaan is much improved,"[131] while Heather simply remarks that "they finally fixed those terrible seventies explosions. Alderaan was really bad in the original."[132] We should note, then, that while I identify a common agreement in terms of the most significant changes, there is not necessarily any consensus among fans about whether these changes are successful.

"100% canonical"

In the twenty years that passed between the release of *A New Hope* and its remaking as *A New Hope: Special Edition,* the *Star Wars* mythos was

---

[128]Foxwell, op. cit.

[129]Ibid.

[130]Ens, op. cit.

[131]Pennington, op. cit.

[132]Heather, op. cit.

padded out by a host of secondary, semi-canonical texts, most of them dating from the 1990s and following on from the success of Timothy Zahn's trilogy of novels (1991–1993). Zahn's narrative continued from the end of *Return of the Jedi* and introduced a new secondary cast including the Imperial Grand Admiral Thrawn and the Emperor's aide Mara Jade; Steve Perry's *Shadows of the Empire* (1996) slotted in between Episodes V and VI of the existing saga and brought in a rival for Vader named Prince Xizor and a Han Solo substitute, the Corellian Dash Rendar. While some novels traced the future of the Rebel heroes, expanding the narrative to include Han and Leia's Force-sensitive children and Luke's attempts to rebuild a Jedi academy,[133] books of short stories were establishing histories for the minor characters in the existing trilogy, focusing on creatures from the background of Jabba's palace and the Mos Eisley Cantina.[134]

By the time *A New Hope* was remade and rereleased, the *Star Wars* universe was far bigger than it had been twenty years earlier. In the long drought between official primary texts, fans had taken what they could get, and characters like Mara Jade and Xizor had become favorites; they appeared in comic books, on trading cards, and as mini action figures. However, they still stood outside the canonical text, which at its purest level consisted solely of the *Star Wars* film trilogy.

The *Special Edition* had the power to change all that, and in some ways it did. According to Stephen Sansweet, in the introduction to his authorized *Encyclopaedia,* the canon in 1998 was not based around the original trilogy, but on "The *Star Wars Trilogy Special Edition*."[135] That is, anything left out of the *SE* was now untrue, and anything in it was gospel. The Millennium Falcon, then, always had two hatches; Chewbacca had always growled when Lando invited his friends for refreshment; Alderaan had never suffered a 1970s-style explosion. This may make little difference on one level—whether or not Luke's line to Artoo is altered has no real relevance

---

[133]See Kevin J. Anderson, *Jedi Academy Trilogy,* London: Bantam Books (1994); Barbara Hambly, *Children of the Jedi,* London: Bantam Books (1995); Nancy Richardson, *Junior Jedi Knights* series, London: Berkley Books (1995); Kevin J. Anderson and Rebecca Moesta, *Young Jedi Knights* series, London: Berkley Books (1995–1996).

[134]See Kevin J. Anderson (Ed.), *Tales from the Mos Eisley Cantina,* London: Bantam Books (1995); Kevin J. Anderson (Ed.), *Tales of the Bounty Hunters,* London: Bantam Books (1996); Kevin J. Anderson (Ed.), *Tales from Jabba's Palace,* London: Bantam Books (1996).

[135]Stephen J. Sansweet, *Star Wars Encyclopaedia*, London: Virgin (1998), p. xi.

to the scene—but as we shall see, the changes had some weighty implications for Han Solo's character in particular. They also have consequences for the status of the canon and its relationship to the Expanded Universe of novels.

As Paul Ens notes, most of these changes occur during the souped-up Mos Eisley scenes of *A New Hope*.

> To the left, some Asp droids (originally featured in *Shadows of the Empire*) are loading cargo into a transport . . . Luke's landspeeder enters the scene, the shot moves to the right and more of the new Mos Eisley can be seen. In the sky, a few ships (Imperial Landing Crafts) land and take off, including Dash Rendar's Outrider (again, from *Shadows of the Empire*) . . . Luke's speeder heads down the street away from the camera. The landspeeder passes behind a large ronto carrying two Jawas. A swoop (yet another *Shadows of the Empire* creation) nearly hits the front of the ronto, which rears up like a horse . . . As the landspeeder crosses the frame, two more rontos can be seen below what could be the crashed ship spoken of in *Tales from the Mos Eisley Cantina*.[136]

Although Jay Pennington cautions that what looks like the Outrider could well be "a ship of the same design," and even though Paul's account has an air of pragmatic doubt about it, these changes mark a dramatic shift in the hierarchy between canon and quasi-canon. Steve Perry's fictional creations are now drawn into the primary text, where they have the status of anything dreamed up by George Lucas. The Asp droid is now as "official" as C-3PO, whereas the Sith Service droid T-12, like scores of other whimsical minor characters, is still confined to the semi-canonical narrative of the comic book *Dark Lords of the Sith*.[137] If that's really the Outrider over Mos Eisley, then Dash Rendar immediately has far more currency as a canonical figure; if swoops are official vehicles, then the story about Han Solo beating Dengar in a race on the lightweight speeder bikes also carries more weight. With one shot, what was rumor becomes true.

It is in this context that Jay Pennington expresses regret that Vader's Star Destroyer was never referred to by the explicit designation fans prefer—"Too bad he didn't say Super Star Destroyer, or even make its name, *Executor*, 100% canonical by mentioning it in a movie." Similarly,

---

[136]Ens, op. cit.

[137]By Tom Veitch and Kevin J. Anderson, Dark Horse Comics (1994–1995).

Keara Martin was incensed to find that her own heroine wasn't even allowed a cameo; while Dash Rendar was invited in, Mara Jade was left out in the cold. "Why wasn't she in Jabba's Palace? Zahn had told her story in a book, we'd known that she was there since 1991! So why on earth didn't we just see a redhead walk by Boba Fett . . . it's not too much to ask!"[138]

The Imperial planet Coruscant, covered almost entirely by an enormous city, was first described by Timothy Zahn in *Heir to the Empire,* the first book in his trilogy. During the mid-1990s it became a staple of *Star Wars* secondary texts and the center of numerous stories about its takeover by the Alliance-turned-Republic and its attempted recapture by various Imperial factions. It appeared in comics, short stories, novels, and role-playing games. Its origin and authorship are a matter of controversy among fans, as I'll discuss in the "Canon" chapter, but the fact remains that it had never appeared in a *Star Wars* film, and so was never canon, until the release of the *Return of the Jedi Special Edition*. Curiously, none of my correspondents note this point—that the geographical center of the galaxy, the planet that served as the home of the Old Republic in *Star Wars* history, the headquarters of the Imperial elite for the duration of the original trilogy, and the base of the New Republic in the novels' projected future was, with a stroke, incorporated into the official mythos for the first time at the end of *Return of the Jedi*. If anything, this may speak to the resonance of the secondary texts and quasi-canon in the collective consciousness of these and many other fans: after reading all the secondary texts and visualizing their internal world, you may well think you've seen something on-screen even if it has never actually appeared.[139]

"Han becomes a nicer guy"

Because every minor alteration affects the canon, it makes sense that these fans pay particular attention to the ways in which the changes shift our

---

[138]Martin, op. cit.

[139]Jay Pennington points out that because Lucas's original *Jedi* script had described an Imperial planet-city, "the core fan base had been well aware of the notion as a semi-canonical Lucas-made concept, even before the Zahn novels had been written. That could explain the mild reaction you describe." Jay Pennington, personal e-mail (July 30, 2001).

perception of the saga's characters, sometimes drawing on seemingly cosmetic details to explain the heroes' and villains' reactions and behavior. Heather, for instance, points out that "the wampa additions"—the fact that we now specifically see Luke cut off the snow monster's arm—"helped make it clear why Luke ran out confused and scared, after it seemed in the original that he had slashed the creature to death."[140] While the original scenes in *Empire* were mainly shot in closed corridors, the *SE* adds glorious sunset backdrops of rosy spires, air trains, and cloud cars; Keara Martin argues that these "opened up" spaces of Cloud City help explain why Han and Leia walked into Vader's trap. "It showed how the Rebels could have been so easily fooled into trusting Lando. After all, who wouldn't be fooled by the seemingly peaceful atmosphere?"[141]

In Keara's reading, the architectural design also enhances our perception of the city's administrator: "We always knew Lando was a bit of a dandy when it came to fashion, but this was perfectly shown when we saw what was outside the windows."[142] We might also note that although Jay Pennington's reference to an extra Chewbacca growl seems trivial, this slight change to the sound track also adds a subtle edge of warning to the scene just prior to Lando's betrayal and indicates that the Wookiee may be more shrewd at this moment than his human friends.

Scott from Michigan comments on another Bespin scene that was ostensibly only added for the purposes of narrative transition. In the original movie, we hear Vader snarl, "Bring my shuttle" as he leaves Cloud City; the *SE* actually shows him striding across a walkway to the vehicle itself, while the line has been changed to "Alert my Star Destroyer to prepare for my arrival." As Jay Pennington points out, the voices and the walk in these amended scenes were not performed by the original actors, James Earl Jones and David Prowse, and the somewhat unconvincing approximations that replace them could be said to detract from the scene's realism. Scott, however, admires the new shot because it confirms to the audience that "yes, Vader did take a shuttle up to the Super Star Destroyer and didn't use some mystical dark side Force power to transport himself there."[143] In this reading, the addition of visual evidence that Vader has

---

[140]Heather, op. cit.

[141]Ibid.

[142]Ibid.

[143]Scott, personal e-mail (July 17, 2000).

to physically travel through space makes an important difference to our perception of his Sith abilities.

As with the unremarked introduction of Coruscant into the official canon, I found it interesting that none of these fans commented on two changes that I consider significant in terms of character. Most obviously, Boba Fett is now shown in a new shot as part of Jabba's entourage in *A New Hope* and again at Jabba's Palace in *Return of the Jedi,* where he playfully strokes a dancing girl's neck. The first appearance places a different slant on his history; Fett now seems to be on retainer for Jabba, following him as a bodyguard on relatively trivial errands, rather than a freelance bounty hunter whose reputation has reached the top ranks of the Imperial forces, as was indicated by *The Empire Strikes Back.*[144] The second is noteworthy for what it implies about Fett's gender and sexuality. Previously seen as a hardened soldier of fortune whose only concern was the financial reward, the new shot suggests that he actually enjoys the louche revels of Jabba's palace, rather than tolerating them as hired security, and strongly suggests that he is indeed a man beneath the mask. As I have already mentioned, Fett's gender has been open to some debate and the notion that he might be female informs at least one feminist website.

More subtle is the insertion of an extended CGI panorama over Cloud City between Luke's departure from Dagobah and the scene where Lando invites Han and Leia for refreshment. On the surface this addition is merely another cosmetic enhancement, a further tour of the imaginary world that Lucas would have shown us in 1980 had the requisite technology existed. However, it also provides a buffer between Yoda and Obi-Wan's conversation on Dagobah and the subsequent scene on Bespin, and so distracts us from making any link between them. In the original trilogy, the last line on Dagobah was Yoda's "There is another," which set up a guessing game about the next potential Jedi: as the viewer wonders, we see Luke's X-Wing depart the planet, cut to a Cloud Car on Bespin, and then cut directly to a shot of Leia, who is, of course, the other Skywalker twin and the second hope for the Jedi. The swooping spectacle that interrupts these scenes in the *Special Edition* makes it far less likely that a

[144]The *Star Wars Holiday Special* of 1978 had shown Fett working for Vader directly after the events of *New Hope*. We can only presume that he managed to juggle Jabba's demands with his occasional employment by the Empire.

viewer new to the story would make the link; but then, as all these fans came to the revamped *Empire* with the knowledge that Luke was Leia's brother, perhaps this was another case where their extreme familiarity with the saga blinded them to alternative perspectives.

There was general agreement that one reinstated scene from *A New Hope,* where Luke meets his old friend Biggs Darklighter just before the attack on the Death Star, was a welcome bonus in terms of its implications for characterization. Scott affirms that "this was excellent."

> Every time I saw the original *ANH* I was curious to know how Luke knew Biggs during the battle. Luke has a TIE on his tail and he says "Blast it, Biggs, where are you?" I thought, "Okay, he knows Biggs because he's in his squadron, but personally I'd be calling for Wedge." . . . it also stresses the loss that Luke must feel after Biggs dies saving Luke from the TIE fighters that are close behind. Personally it made me wish they had added the footage they had filmed of Biggs and Luke on Tatooine as Biggs announces his leaving for the Rebellion.[145]

Chris Foxwell echoes these remarks:

> When Biggs dies, the fact that we know something more about him accomplishes several things: it makes the severe casualties sustained by the Rebels at the Battle of Yavin assume some meaning, it creates more of a feeling of desperation and hopelessness, and it creates a greater burden on Luke, who has just lost one of his best friends and is now all alone in the trench. These changes made by these scenes are evident, and help to streamline the story and add to our appreciation of it.

Most controversial, though, were the slight changes made to the Han and Greedo scene from *A New Hope.* This example is a valuable case study in the way that an apparently minor tweak to the visual effects or sound track can have a major effect on a fan's perception of character. In the original Cantina scene of *A New Hope,* Han slides his gun from its holster while cornered by the bounty hunter Greedo, shooting his antagonist dead with a shot under the table. In the *Special Edition,* Greedo fires first by a split second and misses, justifying Han's retaliation. According to Scott,

---

[145]Scott, op. cit.

> The fact that Greedo fires first has a huge impact on Han's character. Instead of the hardened smuggler who made daring runs to Kessel and back around asteroids and black holes, Han becomes a nicer guy. He was forced to shoot Greedo out of self defense, not to get the stupid green alien off his back. This causes the evolution of Han's character throughout the trilogy to carry much less impact. No longer is it a huge struggle for Han to change to someone capable of love for another being and a belief in fighting a good cause.[146]

Jay Pennington agrees—"It doesn't make Han more heroic, it makes him seem more stupid for letting someone a foot away get off the first shot . . . a totally unwelcome alteration. The scene is ruined"[147]—and Heather is equally vehement. "The only complaint that I had with the *Special Edition* was the terrible change in the scene with Greedo and Han: How could Greedo miss from two feet away? Han isn't the type to 'only shoot in self defense' anyways. That was a terrible change."[148]

Major shifts in characterization, then, can be based on the addition of a single special effect such as a laser blast. Whether the shifts are acceptable or not seems to depend on how they mesh with existing cues in the text. The suggestion that Han's moral scruples would prevent him from shooting first and in cold blood contradicts much of what the rest of the film tells us about his character: he only comes in on the rescue mission for the money, he takes off with his bounty before the Battle of Yavin, and his return to bail Luke out of the Death Star trench is therefore a pleasurable narrative twist. The construction of Solo as someone who only shoots in self-defense seems to be an act of retrospective continuity, bringing him in line with his *Jedi* role as romantic hero, but it weakens the drama of his progression from a cynical smuggler to a rebel with a cause.

It is significant that these viewers refuse to accept George Lucas's conception of the reworked trilogy over their own. Although Paul Ens comments that the Greedo laser bolt was "designed to clarify what Lucas intended for this scene all along,"[149] this authorial intention holds little weight with other fans who, over the past twenty years in some cases, have built up their own firm ideas about what characters would and

---

[146]Ibid.

[147]Pennington, op. cit.

[148]Heather, op. cit.

[149]Ens, op. cit.

wouldn't do. Keara remarks scathingly that "even though we all know that Lucas loves slapstick, we didn't need to see Jabba squirm when Han stepped on him";[150] Scott comments along the same lines that "George thought the audience was not sophisticated enough to understand . . . a small amount of slapstick is bearable when executed correctly, but don't talk to me like I'm an eighth grader."[151] Heather, as we have seen, is disparaging about "a terrible change" and "an utterly pointless change"; Jay, despite his respect for Lucasfilm's attempt to restore the film, has no qualms about expressing where he feels they went wrong or failed to correct an existing mistake.

Keara Martin's attitude towards Lucas—whom she often calls simply "George"—is interesting in its combination of admiration and scorn. She refers to him in familiar tones—"George Lucas must have bust his buttons at this . . . bravo"—and feels free to criticize wherever she thinks her version of the revamp would have been better—"George was sloppy . . . it just didn't fit." But she also retains a measure of respect for his original intention when it fits with her conception: "I think that it added a lot to Lando's character when we were truly able to witness the Cloud City as George has intended."[152]

What becomes obvious from these commentaries is that some fans at least are not about to bow down before a new Lucas creation simply because of its "official" status. It has been well over two decades since *A New Hope* now, and while Lucas has evolved his own view of where the saga is going with the prequels—tidying up the original trilogy to fit along the way—the films have been embraced by and incorporated into the lives of millions of viewers. On one level, *Star Wars* does not belong solely to Lucas anymore; its characters and stories have escaped the original text and grown up with the fans, who have developed their own very firm ideas of what *Star Wars* is and is not about. The next chapter explores what happens when those ideas clash with the way George Lucas himself wants to take the saga.

---

[150]Martin, op. cit.

[151]Scott, op. cit.

[152]Martin, op. cit.

4

THE FAN BETRAYED

Daisy:	So how are you then, you big bloody man?
Tim:	I'm good. I've had a few things to work through, you know . . .
Daisy:	With Sarah?
Tim:	No, with George Lucas.
Daisy:	Tim, it's been over a year.
Tim:	It's been eighteen months, Daisy. And it still hurts.
Daisy:	Well, I didn't think *Phantom Menace* was that bad.

—Simon Pegg and Jessica Stevenson, *Spaced*

After sixteen years with no new *Star Wars* films, the release of *Episode I: The Phantom Menace* was a major event for fans. After such intense anticipation, after such a long wait, it was perhaps inevitable that at least some of them would come away from the cinema with everything from a vague sense of disappointment to a feeling of outright betrayal. Of this group, some would try to rehabilitate the saga, revisiting it over and over again in an attempt to see it in a new light, to celebrate the positive elements and forgive the ones that jarred. Some would physically reedit the film or make their own *Star Wars* digital cinema according to their own conception of the saga; others, on a lower budget, would turn to fan fiction and explore aspects of *The Phantom Menace*'s characters that the film glossed over. Some would take out their fury on discussion boards, debating with other fans who labeled them "bashers" and accused them of ingratitude to Lucas. Simon Pegg, a fan of the *Star Wars* saga since 1977, is probably alone in expressing his betrayal through the script of a BAFTA-nominated British sitcom.

"That kid wanted a Jar Jar doll"

In the second series of Simon Pegg and Jessica Stevenson's *Spaced,* which was screened weekly on Channel 4 during the spring of 2001, comic-book artist Tim Bisley (Pegg) is still dealing with the trauma of *The Phantom Menace* eighteen months after its release. During the conversation between Tim and his flatmate Daisy (Stevenson), we cut to a fantasy sequence showing a funeral pyre in their back garden. Tim, dressed in Luke's black garb from *Return of the Jedi,* solemnly lights the bonfire with a torch. As John Williams' music from Vader's funeral swells on the sound track, we see flames licking around two cardboard boxes, one labeled *Star Wars* Stuff and the other ROTJ. The joke is fairly narrow in its appeal, a personal expression intended for a fan audience; while many viewers will recognize the theme music, the lettering ROTJ is a nod to a more specialist group who will recognize the abbreviation as the sequel to *ESB* and *ANH*.

This dual address continues through the episode. Daisy's holiday videos are tracked by a sinister pair of black-suited agents straight from *The Matrix*; this relatively obvious movie pastiche is underscored in a scene where Tim and Daisy arrive home to discover that their flatmate Brian has let the agents in. "They arrived just before you did," Brian explains apologetically, and Tim accurately identifies the source of the quotation: "You Lando."[153] Again, the joke is directed at the *Star Wars* fan who could recognize key lines from the Bespin scenes of *Empire* in his sleep.[154]

In the next episode, Tim is still nursing his grudge, and it costs him his job at the comic store when he bawls out a kid who tries to buy a Jar Jar Binks doll. His manager, Bilbo, explains, "*The Phantom Menace* was eighteen months ago, Tim."

---

[153]Simon Pegg and Jessica Stevenson, *Spaced,* series 2, channel 4 (2001).

[154]Lando's line, "I had no choice. They arrived right before you did. I'm sorry," comes as Han and Leia discover Vader waiting for them in the dining room.

Tim:	I know, Bilbo . . . it still hurts . . . and that kid wanted a Jar Jar doll.
Bilbo:	Kids like Jar Jar!
Tim:	Why?
Bilbo:	What about the Ewoks? They were rubbish, you don't complain about them.
Tim:	Yeah, but Jar Jar Binks makes the Ewoks look like fucking Shaft![155]

Tim gets another job with a rival store and manages to control his hatred: "Yes, we do stock Jar Jar Binks merchandise. Yes, we've got them in cuddly form, lunchbox, action figure, and keyring." His new boss, Derek, lays a hand on his shoulder: "Well done, Tim. You've just taken your first step into a larger world."[156] Again, the point about Tim's hatred for Binks is broadly made, while Derek's line, a direct lift from Obi-Wan's counsel to Luke in *A New Hope,* is a more subtle reference for the dedicated fan.[157]

Simon Pegg explained to me in an e-mail interview that the dual address was entirely intentional.

> The references to the films in *Spaced* do vary in subtlety, the "Lando" line is definitely one for the fans. The fact is, many of the references in the show are there to be found. The more specific the reference the more gratifying comprehending it will be. Occasionally we include more oblique specificities because those people who do get them will receive great pleasure in doing so.[158]

Pegg's use of his own sitcom as a platform to criticize *The Phantom Menace* is a genuinely heartfelt protest rather than merely a topical in-joke. "I felt that this sacred cow needed to be shot through the head with the bolt of truth and I'm glad I did. I was expressing something felt by a lot of other

---

[155]Ibid.

[156]Ibid.

[1577]The original line comes when Luke manages to "see" a combat remote even with the blast shield of his helmet down. Kenobi praises him: "That's good. You've taken your first step into a larger world."

[158]Simon Pegg, personal e-mail (March 26, 2001).

people and have been rewarded by thanks from many and disgruntlement from a few. I feel qualified to say the things I said and it felt good."[159] His disillusionment—he later uses the term "let down" rather than "betrayed"—stems from a deep-rooted personal involvement and investment in the *Star Wars* saga. I think his account of the films' importance to his life is worth citing at length here, because it echoes so strongly the confessions of my other correspondents in chapter 1 and the playground histories of Tim Meader and his friends in chapter 2.

> *Star Wars* was extremely important in my development as a child. It stimulated my imagination, increased my vocabulary, informed my notion of morality. My friendships were, to an extent, influenced by it at an early age. I mixed with other *Star Wars* fans. Played "it" in the playgrounds of my junior school. It was a social touchstone, an ice breaker, a common ground, shared by so many. Whether it influenced my choice of career I cannot say, although I was giving myself the lead role in *Star Wars 2,* long before *The Empire Strikes Back* came to pass. Perhaps it was just further incentive to pursue something I was already interested in at the age of seven. As for my current relationships, yes I would say *Star Wars* plays a part. It is perhaps not the genesis of my friendships but is certainly a shared ground with many other friends in the same age group. Although, I can pinpoint the moment when I realised that Nick Frost (Mike in *Spaced*) was destined to be my best friend. We were in a Nepalese restaurant in Cricklewood with a bunch of people and Nick made the noise of the little Imperial droid that Chewbacca roars at in *A New Hope*. I heard it, got it, told him and proceeded to bond with him at a geometric rate. I'm not saying that without *Star Wars* we never would have become friends but I can honestly say it was this moment that cemented my relationship with a very kindred spirit.[160]

Again, a story of how the saga not only shaped a fan's career, albeit indirectly, but provided a common bank of references that enabled instant connections and an immediate feeling of shared culture, whether at junior school or as an adult in a Cricklewood restaurant. Although his status as a celebrity fan places him in a different position relative to most people who grew up with the films, and though he is unique in voicing his personal

[159]Ibid.

[160]Ibid.

feelings on the saga so publicly, Simon Pegg's experience of *Star Wars* is far from unusual.

Similarly, his reaction to *The Phantom Menace* is useful here because it shares a great deal with the complaints of my other correspondents and helpfully summarizes many of this chapter's key themes.

> I don't feel betrayed so much as let down by *The Phantom Menace*. It lacks so many of the key factors that made *Star Wars* so affecting. It isn't just the historical, social context. It is as if Lucas thought that what made the original films great was simply the spectacle. What lay at the heart of the first films was a very human story. They had an innocence, a wilful naïvety and a concern for the characters and their motivations. Twenty-three years down the line and Lucas clearly believes it was the fireworks that lined his bulging pockets. Or maybe he just doesn't give a shit. I believe the latter is the more likely, which is why it does feel like somewhat of a slight. He did not make *The Phantom Menace* for himself, he made it for an assumed consumer ideal. When he made *Star Wars*, he was Luke, when he made *TPM* he was Jabba. Go figure.[161]

What we see here is a preempting of the argument that fans were only disappointed by *The Phantom Menace* because they had grown older and expected the impossible—a film that thrilled them in the same way *A New Hope* did when they were seven years old. Pegg is of the same generation as most of my correspondents in this chapter—a group who saw the first film in the cinema as kids and are now in their early to mid-thirties—and in claiming that "it isn't just the historical, social context," he counters the notion that *Phantom Menace* is as equally good a film as *A New Hope* if you view it afresh, unbiased by nostalgic preferences for the original trilogy. This is what internet fan debates identify as the "eyes of a child" gambit: the defense offered for Lucas is that *The Phantom Menace,* like all the other *Star Wars* films, was intended for children and that critics need to give up their cynicism to enjoy its simple pleasures.

Second, Pegg makes a distinction between the "innocence," "naïvety," and focus on character of the original trilogy and the "fireworks" of *The Phantom Menace*. This opposition is common to many fan critiques of the recent film—that Lucas favored CGI spectacle over emotion and relationships. It often goes hand in hand with a specific attack on Tim's

---

[161]Ibid.

nemesis Jar Jar Binks, the computer-generated co-star of *Phantom Menace* who is used as a symbol of this mentality: slapstick over wit, infantile poo-poo jokes in place of adult banter, slick graphic "synthespians" instead of endearingly eager human performance.

Spaced's discussion between two fans, Bilbo and Tim, picks up on another interesting aspect of the *Phantom Menace* backlash: the suspicion, in hindsight, that the rot set in with *Return of the Jedi*. This theory is particularly worrying in its implications that *The Phantom Menace* is merely symptomatic of Lucas's artistic progression over the last twenty years—the cute, clownish antics of the Ewoks were followed by the addition of throwaway sight gags and *Muppet Show* musical numbers to the *Special Editions*—and that *The Phantom Menace,* far from being a blip, is suggestive of where Lucas will take the rest of the prequel trilogy.

We have seen the evidence of Pegg's personal investment in the saga. A frequent result of this immersion in the *Star Wars* mythos is a feeling of personal animosity towards Lucas for spoiling something so precious and important. Of course, this dislike has little to do with the director as a person and is inevitably bound in paradox: the fan's anger towards Lucas has to be balanced with gratitude for his creation of the saga in the first place. But just as fans owe a lifelong debt to Lucas for his founding role in the fantasies that shaped their childhood, so he is perceived as owing a debt to the fans, and to have reneged on it with *The Phantom Menace*. The level of personal criticism in Pegg's comments is testimony to how important all this is to fans who grew up with the saga. To someone like Pegg, Lucas was not just making a summer movie, but was carrying the responsibility for one of the key cultural myths of the twentieth century. And to someone like Pegg, Lucas fudged the job. "Maybe he just doesn't give a shit . . . When he made *Star Wars*, he was Luke, when he made *TPM* he was Jabba. Go figure."[162] This type of accusation, which characterizes Lucas at best as naïve about his own faults, and at worst as a money-grubbing fat slug and gangster, is also common to the anti-*Menace* complainants, or, as pro-*Menace* fans call them, the "bashers."

Research for this chapter was carried out on the "Jedi Council Forums"—the discussion boards of TheForce.net—and, at the recommendation of a Jedi Council contributor, on the specialized *TPM*

[162]Ibid.

Basher Board at ezboard.com.[163] I conducted e-mail interviews with six members of the so-called Basher forum, including its founder, and the following discussion is based largely on their e-mails with supplementary material drawn from the discussion boards.

"Dare to be cute"

The first outstanding characteristic of this basher response was that they all wondered whether their alienation from *The Phantom Menace* was partly due to their age. The issue of how a viewer's generation affects their experience of *Star Wars* will be explored more fully in the final chapter, but it plays an important part here. While these fans suggest that *Episode I* was largely pitched to a younger audience, they stress at the same time that their own lifelong investment in the saga—in most cases, the full 23 years—means they have something of an emotional claim on the mythos. Their sense of rejection is heightened by their feeling that they gave themselves to Lucas's saga, following it loyally for over two decades, only to find themselves knocked back by the director's statement that his new film was meant primarily for kids, not adult fans.[164]

Andrea Alworth, a thirty-five-year-old elementary school teacher, sent me ten lengthy e-mails during July and August 2000, explaining her involvement with the saga at various points in her life. Her first mail explained something of her long-term personal investment and her feelings of bewildered disappointment when she and her friends emerged from *The Phantom Menace*.

> I saw *A New Hope* back when it was simply *Star Wars* in '77, and was hooked. I think it was the scene with Luke gazing at the setting suns that nailed me through the heart. As a young teenager, just beginning to explore the boundaries of my life and the possibilities ahead, I knew exactly what young Luke was thinking and feeling . . . I have invested

---

[163] As far as I can tell, the site no longer exists in summer 2001.

[164] Lucas declared at a press conference just prior to the film's release, "I am fully aware of the fact that some of the fans have sort of put themselves in the situation where they are much older and the film is really for young people." Quoted by Bob Thompson, *Toronto Sun* (May 16, 1999).

> a great deal of emotional energy in the *SW* saga, and entrusted part of my "inner child" to GL. I have read all the EU fiction and numerous fanfic stories, have collected some of the comics and trading cards, have a smattering of *SW* paraphernalia lying about the house . . . I care about the characters in the *SW* universe. In a way, I share a sense of fellowship with them. I know the difference between fantasy and reality, and though the characters in *SW* will never be as precious to me as my "real" friends, I still wish the best for them. Through the years, I have become invested in their lives. From that first moment I felt a bond form with that lonely farm boy on a planet in a galaxy far, far away, I have followed the exploits of the *SW* family, rejoicing in their triumphs and sharing their tragedies.[165]

By contrast, she adds that *The Phantom Menace* "didn't really touch me."

> After my first viewing, I and two friends stood around in the parking lot talking for a long time about our impressions. All of us are long time *SW* fans, and all of us were disillusioned. Perhaps it is our age—having grown up before video games became so popular—but we all would have gladly traded about 5 minutes of pod race for some more intimate conversations between major characters that would have fostered more empathy on our part. And who was GL making the movie for, we wondered? The film seemed to have a scattered quality, disjointed in mood and age appeal—as though Lucas were making two films, one full of sophomoric humor and silliness for the kiddies, and one intense in plot and subterfuge, aimed more at adults. Unfortunately, the two did not always mesh well and left my friends and I feeling discombobulated. As for Jar Jar: we'll get to him later.[166]

Ken West, a thirty-four-year-old corporate attorney, was surprised by his own reactions to *The Phantom Menace*. "I was extremely disappointed in a very personal way—certainly not the response I have for disappointment in a typical movie." His explanation is very similar to Andrea's:

> I saw all the original *Star Wars* films on opening day. My father took me to *ANH* in the summer of 1977, and it was a pivotal experience in my childhood. *Star Trek* made me love science fiction, but *Star Wars* made me love the movies. *TPM* . . . was skewed much more dramatically to a younger audience . . . Lucas' new mantra of "dare to be cute!"

---

[165]Andrea Alworth, personal e-mail (July 4, 2000).
[166]Ibid.

> Another fan described the tone of *TPM* as "wildly erratic" and I think that sums it up. *TPM* is a convoluted tale of political intrigue and military posturing with kiddie elements grafted onto it. This did not work.[167]

Paul Meadows, another refugee from the basher board, also identifies the shift in appeal toward a younger viewer as the main reason for his disillusionment, although he seems sadly to take some of the responsibility for his failure to enjoy *Episode I*:

> I have been a *Star Wars* fan for over 20 years. I'm old enough to have seen the original trilogy in the cinema. I remember the phenomenon that was *Star Wars*. My first reaction to the film that I had been looking forward to for so many years was "I can't believe George Lucas made this!" It was nothing like the original trilogy. It could have been so much better, though. Why did George decide to aim the film at a much larger audience than the original trilogy? The original trilogy had action for the kids, but an appropriate sense of irony for the adults. There was a sense of fun. They were classic adventure stories. Perhaps I'm more sophisticated now that I'm an adult and have higher expectations.[168]

Steve Ash, a thirty-three-year-old computer programmer, offers a melancholy report that vividly contrasts his lasting passion for *A New Hope* against his first experience of *The Phantom Menace*:

> The first time I saw *TPM* I felt totally flat throughout the entire thing. I was about ten when *Star Wars* came out, and feel as if it almost "belongs to" people of my generation. While I can see the flaws in *ANH,* it still reminds me of those times, and the pure shock of delight in seeing things like R2D2 and C3PO, Chewbacca, the Falcon, which no-one had ever seen anything like before . . . Lucas claims that the SW films have always been children's films, yet this is not true. *ANH* and *ESB* were films which appealed to everybody. Additionally, he seems to be deliberately ignoring people of my age. I don't know any children who give a damn about *TPM*. All the showings I went to consisted of about 95% people my age. It just seems idiotic for him to alienate his most committed audience in this way.[169]

---

[167]Ken West, personal e-mail (June 29, 2000).
[168]Paul Meadows, personal e-mail (June 30, 2000).
[169]Steve Ash, personal e-mail (June 30, 2000).

Finally, basher board founder, Darth Derringer alias Alan Cerveny, who is a forty-something university administrator, powerfully sums up the idea that long-term fans in particular have enough of a claim over the saga to feel they can contest Lucas's vision with their own.

> The people like me who have expressed their concerns about *Star Wars* did so because WE LOVE IT! We'll always love it. There was a special spirit with the first films that captured our imaginations and we have developed a sense of ownership in protecting that spirit. You'll see countless discussions in the old [forum discussion] files of "George's Vision Vs What Everyone Else Thinks" but, basically, we felt that some of the cornerstones of the original mythology were cracked by some of the additions of *TPM*.[170]

With no primary texts forthcoming between *Jedi* and *Phantom Menace,* it was arguably up to the faithful longtime fans to become curators of the mythos, to keep it alive, to cherish it, and to sustain it both through their financial investment in all the secondary texts—following the characters though the Expanded Universe—and in some cases, by participating in folk activity like fan fiction or amateur digital cinema. Lucas's return as omnipotent author therefore puts him in the ironic position of reclaiming control over an Empire, stamping his own vision on the *Star Wars* universe and stamping out "rebel" interpretations such as slash fiction or films that infringe copyright.

"Seeds of discontent"

The main complaints from this older audience group about the content and tone of *The Phantom Menace* follow the argument put forward by Simon Pegg. *Phantom Menace* favored CGI over real human emotion—the Jar Jar Binks syndrome—and slapstick over wit. It is interesting to see how many of these respondents also trace the start of the decline, with hindsight, to *Jedi,* and therefore see *Phantom Menace* as a depressingly typical expression of Lucas' current mentality, rather than an anomaly.

---

[170]Alan Cerveny, personal e-mail (June 29, 2000).

"The characters were so boring," writes Paul Meadows. "Where was the banter? The characters were like cardboard cut-outs . . . Very little tension. I wasn't on the edge of my seat even once. Over-reliance on CG animation. There was even a battle that was a cartoon!"[171] Ken West also picks out the imbalance between computer effects and human interaction. "It lacked the wit and chemistry between the main characters that was really what made *ANH* and *ESB* so great. It was a special effects extravaganza and really not much more."[172]

Andrea's complaint again shows a real consistency among this group: "Lack of emotive elements in the film. The characters were too 'stiff' and controlled. There were too few emotionally intimate scenes . . . such an intense focus on the CGI elements that other aspects were overlooked or ignored. The CGI effects were amazing, but without characters you could relate to, it was all so much eye candy."[173] Darth Derringer, meanwhile, directed me to his forum post, which singled out the same key points.

> In the opening sequence of *Star Wars* and the Battle of Hoth, a genuine tension and a sense of danger and dread existed. There was NONE in *TPM*'s battle scene between the Gungans and the battle droids. It certainly would have been harder to create serious tension without human characters, but it could have been done . . . Instead, the battle was played as one giant cartoon. In the original series, Han's wisecracks and cockiness played well off Obi-Wan's seriousness and Luke's earnestness. Without this type of HUMAN character, the movie lacked the playfulness of the original trilogy . . . The movie had no heart and soul. It was a nice summer movie. But that's it. I was very impressed by the special effects but the movie didn't do anything for me otherwise.[174]

Andrea identifies *Jedi*—specifically the scenes with the "Care Bears, I mean Ewoks"—as the film that sowed "the seeds of discontent." In hindsight, she apparently views it as a dividing point between the good "old" *Star Wars* and what she describes as "a new *Star Wars* . . . a sillier *Star Wars*."

---

[171]Meadows, op. cit.

[172]West, op. cit.

[173]Alworth, op. cit.

[174]Darth Derringer, "Top Ten Reasons Why TPM was a Huge Disappointment," www.ezboards.com/official tpmbashersboard (June 30, 2000).

> A *Star Wars* in which Han declares his love for Leia and gives her a kiss that would embarrass a fumbling teenager—let alone a suave lover like Han! A *Star Wars* in which the Rebel assault team is transformed into Larry, Curly and Mo. A *Star Wars* in which teddy bears with sling shots defeat well trained Imperial troops equipped with the latest in weaponry. This was the Muppets meet Othello. The ending seemed confused and disjointed—shifting from serious to comic, as though Lucas couldn't decide if his audience was 7, 17 or 70 . . . I hoped it was a temporary anomaly. I was wrong.[175]

Ken also suggests that Jedi was the beginning of the slide: "*The Phantom Menace* had more kiddie elements than even *ROTJ*."[176] Steve sides with Andrea about the Battle of Endor scenes—"*ROTJ* nowadays frustrates me. Everyone knows that the Ewoks were universally loathed"—yet argues that "the rot set in when the original trilogy was re-raked during the Special Editions and you find out that all the things you loved about the original films were other people's ideas, and were things that GL might have vetoed if he'd had the chance."[177]

What emerges strongly here is a harsh voice of criticism directed personally at George Lucas as director, and a general sense of distrust about his ability to handle the mythos. Not only do these fans doubt his writing skills and aesthetic choices as evident in *The Phantom Menace,* but they are also skeptical about his contribution to the original trilogy, reevaluating *Empire Strikes Back* in particular as a collaborative effort whose merits may have been due more to director Irvin Kershner, producer Gary Kurtz, or the two scriptwriters, Leigh Brackett and Lawrence Kasdan, rather than to Lucas's input as executive producer.[178]

> A lot of the dialogue which makes *ESB* so great (especially between Han and Leia) was made up on set by the actors and Kershner, notably "I love you"/"I know" which GL apparently had serious doubts about. It does trouble me that the saga seems to take a dive at exactly the time Gary Kurtz left because he didn't like what GL was doing. GL needs someone else to keep his creativity within the bounds of good

---

[175] Alworth, op. cit.

[176] West, op. cit.

[177] Ash, op. cit.

[178] There is also debate about Lucas's role in writing the script of *A New Hope*, and how much of Gloria Katz and Willard Huyck's "dialogue polish" was used in the final screenplay.

> taste. Unfortunately, he is now so powerful that nobody's going to tell him anything he does isn't very good. In addition he doesn't seem to care about it anymore.[179]

Andrea Alworth makes the same point, confessing that it inspires in her "no small amount of trepidation for *Episode II*":

> *ESB* (my favorite of the films) was not directed by Lucas. Nor did he write the screenplay. In other words, it was only loosely "his" baby. . . . *ROTJ* and *TPM* are much more likely to manifest his true aspirations. If this is so . . . if he truly wants to appeal to an audience that rejoices in fart humor and dancing teddy bears and bloodless war—then Lucas' *SW* is a mere parody of what I fell in love with all those years ago. Something precious will be lost—a powerful exploration of mythology and storytelling becoming a caricature of itself.[180]

Some of these fans go on to identify specific flaws in Lucas's approach, which they assume his ego has made him blind to. "He has admitted he can't write dialogue," argues Steve, "yet he carried on and wrote a shallow, directionless script."[181] Ken West comments, "I've lost faith in Lucas as a director, but more importantly as a writer. To me, *TPM*'s script is evidence of just how much the writing of *ANH* and *ESB* were collaborative efforts."[182] However, pointing out specific weaknesses does lead to one potential route for salvaging the prequel saga; as Steve adds, "I have totally lost faith in GL and would like to see someone else direct. I think Spielberg, or ideally Kershner, should step in."[183] The next section explores other ways in which these fans attempt to rescue *The Phantom Menace* and the remainder of the prequels.

"I really did enjoy the movie"

One strategy is an attempt to rehabilitate the film simply by watching it repeatedly and trying to adopt a different viewing position, seeing the

---

179 Ash, op. cit.
180 Alworth, personal e-mail (July 6, 2000).
181 Ibid.
182 West, op. cit.
183 Ash, op. cit.

objectionable aspects in a new light, or screening them out, and making the most of the good parts. Darth Derringer notes that "people like me, who enjoyed *TPM* more on repeated viewings, did so because we began to 'tune out' Jar Jar."[184] This approach reached its logical conclusion in *The Phantom Edits,* two revised and "improved" versions of the film that circulated on bootleg video during 2000 and 2001 and which I'll deal with in the appropriate chapter on fan films. However, it is worth noting here that the reedited versions fall into line with many of the basher recommendations: Jar Jar's role was apparently cut out in the more recent tape, while the other makes him more "mature," refining his dialogue and omitting his slapstick "poodoo" scenes.[185]

Andrea Alworth went to great lengths in her second message to draw out points of the film that she did enjoy, confessing "I am admittedly desperate to redeem my *Star Wars*."[186] Some of her comments suggest a real clutching at straws, analyzing incidental moments of performance in the search for "adult" qualities of emotional depth: "I do think Qui-Gon had potential. Neeson may not have had much in the way of hands on directing, but he did manage to talk Lucas into allowing him to put a hand on Shmi's shoulder. And he conveyed a gentleness of personality with his soft gaze and subtle smile."[187]

> I don't want to leave you with the impression that there was nothing I liked about *TPM*. I really did enjoy the movie . . . I just feel it could have been better, and that most of the improvements wouldn't have required much effort . . . Obi-Wan's mischievous, "The negotiations were short!" was perfect, though I would have liked to see Qui's reaction. It was a moment of much-needed levity between the two and hinted at a comfortable level of companionship—as did the scene on the balcony, when Qui tells Obi he still has much to learn. There is a whisper of affection in his admonishment, "I will do what I must, Obi-Wan."[188]

Andrea's focus on the relationship between the Jedi and her informal use of their first names is a clue to her related interest in fan fiction,

---

[184]Derringer, "Top Ten Reasons," op. cit.

[185]Joshua Griffin, review of *The Phantom Edit,* TheForce.net (June 11, 2001).

[186]Alworth (July 6, 2000).

[187]Ibid.

[188]Ibid.

including—as she admitted after a few mails—the slash fiction that explores a homoerotic love between Qui-Gon and Obi-Wan. Reading fan stories and "official" EU novels has enabled her to flesh out the Jedi characters and subsequently return to the primary text of *The Phantom Menace* with a new perspective. "They mean more to me now, because I have taken the bare templates presented in the film and applied layers of 'personality' based on speculation, building multi-dimensional characters with form and substance."[189] Andrea treats *Star Wars* fiction, whether "amateur" or "official," as a means for transforming *The Phantom Menace* into a more subtle and complex text; the brief moments of physical contact, playful banter, or signs of a loving bond between the two Jedi in the film can be viewed as glimpses of their deeper relationship. However, she freely admits that this process is a form of imaginative reconstruction: "perhaps the Qui-Gon I am 'seeing' is more an amalgamation of what I wish for, rather than what is actually on screen."[190]

"Did I say Jar Jar makes me annoyed?"

Steve Ash ended his mail with this remark: "I hope this isn't too long, but it was very therapeutic for me."[191] The act of writing down the things they found problematic with *The Phantom Menace* has obviously given some of these fans a lot of pleasure; after all, they were all part of a bulletin board designed for that very purpose. As a "safe" community of like-minded souls, the basher board enabled Darth Derringer and his online friends to let off steam, often through humor and gleeful satire. Quaff Down Gin responded to my appeal for information in the form of a poem; the first line is an onomatopoeic rendition of Jar Jar blowing a raspberry.

> My "inner child's" reaction to TPM:
>
> PBPBPLLLGGG!! Okeeday?
> Captain Panaka, Ric Olié
> Captain Tarpals, Boss Nass

---

[189]Ibid.

[190]Ibid.

[191]Ash, op. cit.

Space battle, piece o' trash
Neimoidian, what he say?
A trade treaty? WHAT THE HEY?
Just what the hell IS the planet core?
We're supposed to IMAGINE we seen it before?
Qui-Gon Jinn, ahhh, noble one
Uses mind tricks to cheat EVERYONE
Anakin whines about being free
But slavery don't look so bad to me
Our favorite droids are hardly there
There's cartoons running everywhere
I'm SO scared of battle droids
Did I say Jar Jar makes me annoyed?[192]

And so on. The group also took on the challenge of providing alternative titles for Episode I, with the house joker, Quaff Down Gin, again providing the first examples—"*Force Gump, Honey, I Destroyed The Jedi Knights, The Sith Element*"[193]—and other people taking his lead with "*Sleepy Hollow-Eyed Audience,*" "*Eyes Cried Shut,*" and the majestic "*The Man Who Shot Dignity/Balance.*"[194]

Another kind of therapy was provided by the "Basher/Gusher Wars," debates between pro- and anti-*Phantom Menace* factions. Skirmishes broke out when a basher posted on the largely pro boards of TheForce.net or when gushers visited Darth Derringer's community. I even came under attack myself when I requested comments from fans who felt betrayed or disappointed by the movie. "How about you ignore the bashers who have no idea what they are talking about and listen only to the people who have positive things to say about *TPM,*" one fan challenged. "I could write a book about why *TPM* is great."[195] Another chimed in, "You tell em . . . what kind of a book could you possibly get out of basher replies. What are you going to do, just have 100 pages with 'Jar Jar Sucks' written on them? You want to write a *SW* book, you need to talk to the true fans who know what they're talking about."[196]

---

[192]Quaff Down Gin, "Bashers Wanted For Book," www.ezboards.com/official tpmbashersboard (June 29, 2000).

[193]Quaff Down Gin, "Potential Titles for Star Wars Episode I," www.ezboards.com/official tpmbashersboard (June 20, 2000).

[194]Starboard Hair Bun of Leia, "Potential Titles," op. cit.

[195]TPMRules23, "Bashers Wanted For Book," op. cit. (June 29, 2000).

[196]Master Snoopy, "Bashers Wanted For Book," op. cit. (June 29, 2000).

The debates are still continuing on the boards of TheForce.net, although at the time of writing (July 2001), after more than two years since the release of *The Phantom Menace,* they have taken on the sad predictability of a drawn-out war, an ongoing, everyday state of conflict between two stubbornly opposed sides rather than a lively series of rhetorical clashes. Indeed, the current situation on the *Phantom Menace* forum at TheForce.net resembles a hostile stalemate between religious groups. There are approximately as many basher-led as gusher threads—the terms have become accepted as commonly understood shorthand and are no longer resisted or kept at a distance with inverted commas—and every regular knows as soon as he recognizes a contributor's nickname, what that individual's position will be on *Episode I.* The debates are, for the most part, entirely fruitless. Very few people ever change sides, and the arguments pro and con *Phantom Menace*—based on recycling the same key points, backed by the same textual evidence—earn applause from those who were already convinced and jeers from those who feel the opposite. Bashers criticize Anakin's exclamations of "Yippee!" and Jar Jar's clowning. Gushers point out that Anakin was meant to be an innocent child, and that Jar Jar "may seem like cheap comedy relief but he drove the entire third act of the friggin' movie . . . As for all the 'Yippees', that's how little kids talk. I did when I was little, lots of kids I knew did. Kids aren't born talking like Tarantino."[197] Bashers complain about the scatological humor and the wooden performances. Gushers counter that "the poop and the (alleged) fart take up about 4 seconds of screen time. I find it hard to understand how these quick 'throwaway' gags are so bothersome to some people"[198] and maintain that "I thought Liam, Pernilla and Natalie gave great performances as well. Padme's character contrasted well with Amidala's."[199]

There is very little purpose to these discussions; no amount of reference to primary evidence will convince a basher that *The Phantom Menace* was entirely valid and worthwhile, and of course the reverse is true for gushers. Although there is a "Bashers/Gushers Truce" thread on the forum, this is

---

[197]Muke Skywalker, "Gushers Need Some Kind of Media Force," TheForce.net discussion boards, boards.theforce.net (June 30, 2001).
[198]Darth23, "*TPM*: The Good, the Bad and the Ugly," TheForce.net, op. cit. (July 5, 2001).
[199]Ibid.

generally considered an overly optimistic attempt to unite the opposing sides. As one contributor sadly announced, "I fear there can be no true reconciliation."[200] The two factions have therefore formed their own strongholds on the board where they consolidate their own opinions and preach to the choir. Binary_Sunset, one of the most notorious bashers on the forum, opened "The *TPM* Bashers' Sanctuary for Bashers only," a thread where people who agreed with him could "share our stories, feelings, thoughts of the disappointment we felt when seeing *TPM*. Talking with kindred spirits can be a way of taking a load off."[201] The gushers, in turn, started up the "TPM Defense Force," an online gang based on the Rebel squadrons in the original trilogy. Members were given military ranks from private to corporal based on their persistence in arguing the merits of *Phantom Menace* and their heroic visits to basher threads or even enemy boards. "Has anyone been over to http://www.geocities.com/lucasblows? They have some hardcore bashers there that make the ones here seem like nancy boys. . . . "[202] The TPMDF and Bashers' Sanctuary have currently agreed on a treaty—knowingly reminiscent of the Trade Federation agreement in *The Phantom Menace*—whereby they promise not to flame on each other's home threads. Of course, these war-game heroics are slightly tongue in cheek—"It's fun, in a grade 4 kinda way"[203]—and are all the more enjoyable for the way they allow members to play *Star Wars* type roles of mercenary, double-agent, diplomat, or hot-shot soldier within the arena of rhetorical debate.[204]

The arguments, however, are based on genuine, deeply felt belief. To generalize—because of course there is variation within the two main factions—the gushers' main tenet is that bashers disrespect George Lucas as a creator and that his vision of the saga should be accepted with gratitude. One member of the TPMDF states plainly that "the first goal of a *SW* film is to tell a story the way Lucas wants to. It's his story, not anyone else's."

---

[200]Lagniappe, "*TPM* and the Star Wars Fanbase," TheForce.net, op. cit. (July 3, 2001).

[201]Binary_Sunset, "The TPM Basher's Sanctuary," The Force.net, op. cit. (November 15, 2000).

[202]Darth Homer, "*TPM* Defense Force," The Force.net, op. cit. (February 10, 2001).

[203]Darth Maul's Torso, "*TPM* Defense Force," TheForce.net, op. cit. (February 6, 2001).

[204]As a note, it seems that the TPMDF may largely be made up of teens and twentysomethings, while the bashers from Darth Derringer's board seemed to be mainly over thirty years of age.

While bashers question Lucas's role in writing the original trilogy, then, gushers stress his involvement at every stage. "Just because Lucas got some people to help with the dialogue on *ANH* doesn't mean he wasn't the main creative influence. He still created all the characters and plot."[205] While bashers openly criticize his skill at writing and his artistic choices, Gushers are proud of their loyalty to Lucas as a director and, apparently, as a person: "I do not respect people who do not respect Lucas," Go-Mer Tonic declared on the Gusher and Basher Truce thread, putting those talks temporarily into a deadlock.[206] A like-minded fan echoed this firm objection to comments against Lucas:

> Being such a fan of *SW,* and knowing how many happy hours I spend either watching the movies, reading EU or even posting here, it does bother me as well when someone starts posting false garbage about the man who made it all possible.[207]

In fact, a popular gusher interpretation considers the campaign to defend Lucas and his films comparable to the Rebels' struggle against the Empire and the Jedi's pursuit of the Unifying Force over the Dark Side.

> "The Emperor was trying to get rid of Vader, and Vader was trying to get rid of the Emperor. And that is the antithesis of a symbiotic relationship, in which if you do that, you become cancer, and you eventually kill the host, and everything dies." (George Lucas, from *Time* interview)
>
> Now, what part of the fanbase is constantly "trying to get rid of" Jar Jar, or midichlorians, or two headed announcers? Who is trying to get rid of anything? Who is the cancer? Who is the host?
>
> "Fear leads to anger. Anger leads to hate. Hate leads to suffering." Yoda, from *The Phantom Menace*
>
> Now, which side of the *Star Wars* fanbase has expressed fears about the prequels. Which side of the fanbase got angry with, for example,

---

[205]Duckman, "*TPM*: The Good, the Bad and the Ugly," TheForce.net, op. cit.
[206]Go-Mer Tonic, "Gusher and Basher Truce," TheForce.net, op. cit. (July 3, 2001).
[207]CbJedi, "Gusher and Basher Truce," op. cit. (July 3, 2001).

> Jar Jar? (So much so that they called for his death!) Which side of the fanbase expresses hate in these forums?[208]

This clever argument, presented like an evangelical sermon and hailed by its gusher audience, effectively "proves" that the gusher campaign is working in accord with Lucas's wider beliefs about good and evil, with the bashers on the side of the corruptive, self-obsessed, and greedy Sith. Yet as I noted earlier, there is really nowhere for these arguments to go, because their proponents' only aim is to win the approval of those who are already converted. Nobody is going to change their minds in a hurry; and more important, neither side believes they have any power to affect the *Star Wars* saga.

This acceptance of the gross imbalance between the individual viewer and corporate producer in terms of creating meaning is quite unusual in fandom. The *Phantom Menace* bashers have no desire to write letters to Lucasfilm arguing for a remake of the first film or a rethink of the second; they're not boycotting the saga or organizing protests.[209] All they really want, as Binary_Sunset suggests, is a space to kick back and sound off.

> At times I get grumpy about what Lucas pulled. Once in a while it seems positively depressing, and I worry about *Episodes II* and *III*. But most of the time when I think about *TPM,* it is with a shaking of the head, a regret for what might have been. If you need to vent about how bad *TPM* is, do it here. We bashers need a place where we can put our feet up and just talk, without the gushers trying to beat us over the head. Any basher thoughts, feelings, experiences, etc. will be welcomed and sympathized with here.[210]

Although there is some feeling that negative reviews of *Phantom Menace* may lead Lucas to revise his plans for *Episode II,* possibly calling in another

---

[208]Scott2Eyez, "*TPM* and the Star Wars Fanbase," TheForce.net, op. cit. (June 29, 2001).
[209]The classic example of this is the letter-writing campaign that supposedly saved the original series of *Star Trek*; protests in later years apparently led to the incorporation of gay characters and themes into *The Next Generation*. See John Tulloch and Henry Jenkins, *Science Fiction Audiences*, op. cit., p. 9, pp. 237–265. See also my *Batman Unmasked*, op. cit. pp. 299–307, for an account of fan attempts to influence the next *Batman* film and express discontent at Joel Schumacher's handling of the character.
[210]Binary_Sunset, op. cit.

director or other writers as he did with *Empire Strikes Back,* the bashers are under no real illusions that their protests will make any difference. "We fans have the arrogant belief that someone at Lucasfilm is paying attention, that our cries of outrage might be heard, and that *Episode II* might be better as a result . . . this is probably overly optimistic."[211]

Despite their bitterness towards Lucas, the bashers' enthusiasm for the *Star Wars* mythos as a whole—which they now manage to regard as distinct from Lucas's personal project for the films—has not been dimmed. A final point that united my e-mail correspondents in this chapter was a shared optimism for the next chapter in the saga. "I am still a *Star Wars* fan and looking forward to *Episodes II* and *III,*"[212] says Paul Meadows. "My faith has been shaken but I'm going to be in line for *Episode II,*"[213] states Alan Cerveny. Andrea Alworth says simply, "I have hope for the future."[214]

The bashers, of course, are fueled by love for *Star Wars*, although their definition of what "*Star Wars*" means is different—based on their own personal conception established over twenty years of fan involvement, rather than solely on the vision of the original creator—and their loyalties follow a different pattern. For this group of older, jaded viewers who are clinging to their faith, *Episode II* is "a new hope."

---

[211]West, op. cit.

[212]Meadows, op. cit.

[213]Cerveny/Derringer, op. cit.

[214]Alworth, op. cit.

5

CANON

Dr Evil:	You see, I've turned the moon into what I like to call a "Death Star."
Scott Evil:	[laughs derisively]
Dr Evil:	What?
Scott Evil:	Ah, nothing, Darth.
Dr Evil:	What did you call me?
Scott Evil:	Nah, nothing . . . Rip-off!
Dr Evil:	Bless you.

—Mike Myers, *Austin Powers: The Spy Who Shagged Me* (directed by Jay Roach)

"Just what is *Star Wars* canon, and what is not?" asks the introduction to Stephen Sansweet's *Star Wars Encyclopaedia*. "The one sure answer: The *Star Wars* Trilogy Special Edition—the three films themselves as executive-produced, and in the case of *Star Wars* written and directed, by George Lucas, are canon. Coming in a close second we have the authorized adaptations of the films: the novels, radio dramas and comics. After that, almost everything falls into a category of quasi-canon."[215]

Debates over what constitutes an official text in the fictional universe, as opposed to quasi-official or apocryphal material, are not unique to the

---

[215]Sansweet, op. cit. p. xi.

Star Wars community. My 1999 study of internet science-fiction fandom used the network of bulletin boards around the *Alien* films as an example of debating the canon. It cited fans who treated the third movie as "a parallel, overlapping universe" rather than as part of the real *Alien* narrative, or who accepted the Dark Horse comic books as more valid than *Alien Resurrection*.[216] This chapter builds on that earlier work, examining the ways in which contributors to internet discussion boards try to prove their own interpretation of the canonical hierarchy through reference to a range of both primary and secondary texts.

I want to begin by examining the existing definitions of canon and testing them against texts from various levels of the *Star Wars* hierarchy. Sansweet's explanation seems pretty straightforward, apart from the escape clause of "almost everything" and the ambiguity of "quasi-canon." Is the movie *Caravan of Courage: An Ewok Adventure* (1994) a canonical *Star Wars* film, one of the exceptions to the "almost everything" rule? Warwick Davis, who played Wicket in *Return of the Jedi,* reprises his canonical role. Joe Johnston, one of the team who designed Jabba the Hutt,[217] was the production designer. ILM provided the special effects. Most importantly, George Lucas is credited as cowriter. If we agree that these contributions from key members of the *Jedi* creative team qualify *Caravan of Courage* as canon, then we have to accept that between the events of *Empire* and *Return of the Jedi,* Cindel Towani and her family crash-landed on the forest moon of Endor and made friends with the Ewoks, who talked to them in faltering English.[218] This story jars with the Ewoks' reaction to Chewbacca, Han, and Luke in *Return of the Jedi:* in the latter film, the little creatures can only speak their own language and initially treat the humans with intense hostility.

How are we to regard *Shadows of the Empire,* the 1996 Steve Perry novel? While other stories, like Timothy Zahn's "Thrawn Trilogy," operate as a distinct postscript to the films, *Shadows of the Empire* was the first novel that Lucas allowed within the bounds of existing continuity. Perry's novel fits itself into the unrecorded period between *Empire* and *Jedi,*

---

[216]Will Brooker, "Internet Fandom and the Continuing Narratives of *Star Wars*, *Blade Runner,* and *Alien*," in Annette Kuhn (Ed.), *Alien Zone II,* London: Verso (1999), p. 63.

[217]See Joe Johnston et al., *Return of the Jedi Sketchbook,* New York: Ballantine Books (1983).

[218]I say English, but the language spoken by Luke and his friends is apparently Galactic Basic.

explaining how Leia obtained her Boushh outfit and where Luke constructed his new lightsaber. It was also unusual for the way it was marketed: the book formed just one part of a multimedia package that included an original soundtrack, an N64 video game, a line of action figures, even a behind-the-scenes "making-of" book. The cross-platform *Shadows* experience was as close to a new *Star Wars* film as fans were going to get until *The Phantom Menace.* So is it on the same level of canon as the snot vampire from *Tales of Jabba's Palace* and the Great Heep, the giant robot from the *Droids* animated TV special of 1986, or does it occupy a privileged position only one step down from the original trilogy?

Is the *Star Wars Holiday Special* TV show from 1978 canon? It was co-scripted by George Lucas and starred every key member of the *New Hope* cast, including the masked characters: Anthony Daniels played Threepio, Peter Mayhew was inside the Chewbacca suit, and James Earl Jones provided the voice of Darth Vader. If we take these factors as suitable grounds for the show's authenticity and "official" status, then we accept that Chewbacca has a son called Lumpy and a wife called Malla, that Han and Luke battled Imperial troops to be with him for Life Day, that Jefferson Starship perform in hologram on the Wookiee planet Kashyyyk, that Bea Arthur from *The Golden Girls* runs the Mos Eisley Cantina, and that Leia sings a rendition of the *Star Wars* theme. Notably, while Sansweet's *Encyclopaedia* faithfully records the events and characters of *Caravan of Courage* and *Shadows of the Empire,* it neglects to mention Life Day or Malla and only deals with Lumpy because he reappeared in a more respectable secondary text some twenty years later.[219] Yet while the *Holiday Special* seems to be treated as an anomalous embarrassment even by an *Encyclopaedia* that has an entry for the snot vampire, this one-hour TV show also features the first appearance of Boba Fett and a scene cut from *A New Hope* where Vader talks to Chief Bast. Aside from the fact that Lucas and the prime *Star Wars* talent were directly involved in the project, the *Holiday Special* introduces a key character and incorporates canonical material.[220]

---

[219]He apparently renamed himself Lumpawaroo in Michael P. Kube-McDowell's *Tyrant's Test,* London: Bantam Books (1997). Sansweet, op. cit. p. 182.

[220]The *Visual Dictionary* seems to recognize this with its mention of Lumpy, Malla, and Itchy as part of Chewbacca's "Data File." David West Reynolds, *Star Wars: The Visual Dictionary,* London: Dorling Kindersley (1998), p. 17.

If all this seems willfully pedantic and deliberately provocative, consider the ranks that Sansweet proposes as secondary canon, the "authorized" texts based on the films. The Marvel comic book adaptation of *Star Wars*, written by Roy Thomas and drawn by Howard Chaykin in 1977, shows Vader's lightsaber blade slashing down directly through Obi-Wan, electrocuting the older Jedi as he screams and holds his hands up in surprise. "I am the master now!" the Dark Lord shouts. "I—Darth Vader!"[221] This brutal execution is a far cry from the scene in the film, where Obi-Wan smiles peacefully and Vader's deathblow connects only with the Jedi's empty cloak.

The radio adaptation of *Star Wars*, which originally aired on National Public Radio in 1981, expands on the scene where Vader interrogates Leia and unwittingly reveals the truth about their relationship two years before Luke discovered it in *Return of the Jedi.* Here, Vader has the Princess under hypnosis and attempts to draw a confession from her through threats and guile: "Your father commands you to tell us . . . yes . . . don't you wish to please your father? Then tell me what you did with those plans! Say the words! Your father orders you to tell us!"[222]

I should add that Darth Vader is played by Brock Peters and Leia by Anne Sachs and that neither is attempting to impersonate the original performances of James Earl Jones and Carrie Fisher. Yet this scene occupies the upper hierarchies of canon, as part of an authorized adaptation of the first *Star Wars* primary text. Just above it in the ranks is the novel *Star Wars: From the Adventures of Luke Skywalker,* supposedly written by George Lucas himself and published in 1977.[223] This book must surely be within the acceptable boundaries of canon, yet it first introduces us to Luke Skywalker in a concrete station of Anchorhead, where Biggs Darklighter is sharing stories with Deak and Windy, and tells us, bizarrely, that as the Millennium Falcon takes off from Mos Eisley, "Luke was thinking of a dog he had once owned."[224] The reunion between Luke and Biggs was included in the *Special Edition,* but Luke's Anchorhead buddies Deak,

---

[221]Roy Thomas and Howard Chaykin, *Star Wars*, reprinted in the *Star Wars Annual* no. 1, London: Brown Watson (1978).

[222]Brian Daley, "Death Star's Transit," pt. 8 of the *Star Wars Radio Drama,* reissued. London: Hodder (1993).

[223]The author was actually Alan Dean Foster.

[224]George Lucas, *Star Wars*, London: Sphere Books (1977), p. 115.

Windy, Camie, and the Fixer have never appeared in either version of *A New Hope.*[225]

Here we can safely follow Sansweet's rule that the films themselves take precedence over all secondary texts, however high they are in the canon hierarchy. Yet we are faced with more potential problems due to the changing nature of the films themselves. The early Biggs scenes, like the Wampas attacking the Imperial troops on Hoth and the Tatooine sandstorm in *Jedi,* were shot but then discarded. They are, therefore, out of canon and officially deemed not to have happened; but then, the primary texts were altered during 1997 to include other scenes that had never before featured in a *Star Wars* movie, such as Han Solo with Jabba in Mos Eisley, and Luke with Biggs before the Death Star battle. The special editions brought key encounters out of limbo and into continuity, altering the official definition of what really took place. As such, the canon as defined by the primary texts is fluid. For now, though, the sequence showing Camie and the Fixer staring up at the space battle while Luke and Biggs talk in the background does exist,[226] but it didn't happen—unless Lucas chooses to digitally enhance it and incorporate it in a future edition.

As I have already discussed, the special editions have other important implications for the canon and its relation to the Expanded Universe. If the 1997 version of the trilogy, as Sansweet suggests, is now to be regarded as the ultimate reference point, the "one sure answer," then the Outrider is officially within canon because we see it blasting off from the revamped Mos Eisley. So if the Outrider is canon, presumably its pilot, Dash Rendar, is canon; and if Rendar is canon, then presumably the novel he appears in, *Shadows of the Empire,* is canon; and by extension we would have to accept that the scenes where Chewbacca shaves his head as a disguise[227] and Leia is almost seduced by the alien gang lord Prince Xizor[228] are now part of the official mythos rather than the semi-authorized products of Steve Perry's imagination.

Some fan definitions pin down the question of canon more rigorously, and perhaps more successfully, than Sansweet's introduction. Kayla, on

---

[225]These scenes also feature in Lucas's screenplay, *Star Wars: A New Hope,* London: Faber and Faber (1997), p. 11.

[226]See the "Cut Scenes" archive at www.cinescape.com

[227]Steve Perry, *Shadows of the Empire,* op. cit. p. 212.

[228]Ibid., p. 260.

TheForce.net's Jedi Council discussion boards, asserts that the following "is canon": "Movies [not the Ewoks one]. Movie novelisations [where not contradicted by movies]. Radio plays [where not contradicted by movies]. Not anything else."[229] This definition helps to iron out some of the inconsistencies I was picking at. *Caravan of Courage,* despite its pedigree as a Lucas-scripted film involving the *Star Wars* production team and actors from *Return of the Jedi,* is simply thrown out of the equation. The scenes in George Lucas's *New Hope* novel and screenplay where Han Solo unequivocally shoots Greedo in cold blood, not self-defense, are now ruled out by the clause that in the case of a contradiction, the film takes precedence; of course, there could be debate here about which version of the film we are using for comparison, as Kayla's definition doesn't specify the *Special Edition.*

Luke's thoughts of his dog back home, the meeting with Camie and the Fixer, and Brian Daley's inventive but inopportune dialogue about Leia's father still occupy an ambiguous middle ground, as the primary film texts offer nothing to directly contradict them. We may have to assume that the films don't show us absolutely everything and that there is some room for events to happen offscreen. The *Holiday Special* could also feasibly be "possible" according to this framework, as there is no evidence within the primary texts to suggest that Chewbacca does not have a son and wife, that Boba Fett did not meet the Rebels sometime between *New Hope* and *Empire,* and that the Mos Eisley Cantina was not run by Bea Arthur. *Caravan of Courage,* on the other hand, is drummed out of canon by this definition, because its English-speaking Ewoks are directly contradicted by what we see in the higher-level text *Return of the Jedi.*

What this examination shows overall is that canon is a slippery thing. The rest of this chapter is about the ways in which fans deal with it and debate it, particularly as it relates to the Expanded Universe, or EU. It takes as a case study the issue of Coruscant, mentioned in my chapter on the *Special Editions,* but there are many other examples on TheForce.net boards that have proved equally contentious.

As just one additional instance, the novelization of *The Phantom Menace* asserts that "the Sith had come into being almost two thousand years ago."[230] The EU version, as portrayed in the Dark Horse comics, maps

---

[229]Kayla, TheForce.net, op. cit. (October 13, 1999).

[230]Terry Brooks, *The Phantom Menace,* London: Random House (1999), p. 134.

out a far more distant history involving the Dark Lord Exar Kun, who died four thousand years before the events of *A New Hope*. This issue alone has incited lengthy debate on the Jedi Council forums, with some contributors claiming that the Exar Kun stories introduced the concept of the two-bladed lightsaber used by Darth Maul,[231] that Lucas copied Expanded Universe continuity as he had previously with the Asp droids, swoop, and Outrider in the *New Hope Special Edition*,[232] and concluding that "if I ever have to choose between the movies and the EU, I would choose the EU in a heartbeat!"[233] Suffice it to say that if the Coruscant question were resolved to everyone's satisfaction, there would still be enough inconsistencies between the film texts and the EU for the contributors to TheForce.net to continue their debates.

"The current rules of canon"

The Imperial city-planet that was to become Coruscant first appears in the draft script *The Star Wars* (1974) as "Alderaan: Capital of the New Galactic Empire."[234] It reappears in the draft for *Revenge of the Jedi* (1981) under the name Had Abbadon.[235] On this later occasion, Ralph McQuarrie and Joe Johnston drew up preproduction images of the planet, which was to serve as the locale for a final duel between Luke, Vader, and the Emperor, witnessed by the spirits of Yoda and Obi-Wan.[236]

The name Coruscant appears for the first time on page 19 of Timothy Zahn's *Heir to the Empire* (1991). As noted in chapter 3, Lucas's decision to include shots of the planet in *Return of the Jedi: Special Edition*—under that name rather than Hab Abbadon—is an example of the EU's becoming authorized as canon. For fans who maintain that the EU is an essentially meaningless secondary mythos with no bearing on the official characters

[231]Mon Mothma, "This is Canon," TheForce.net, op. cit. (June 8, 1999).

[232]Ibid.

[233]Maxar Re, "This is Canon," TheForce.net, op. cit. (June 8, 1999).

[234]George Lucas, *The Star Wars* (May 1974), reproduced at www.starwarz.com/starkiller/frame.htm

[235]George Lucas, *Revenge of the Jedi* screenplay (June 12, 1981), reproduced at www.starwarz.com/starkiller/frame.htm

[236]These images now appear under "Coruscant" in Sansweet's *Encyclopaedia*.

and narrative, this canonizing of a novelist's invention was a problem. Some of these purists have been struggling to maintain that, somehow, Coruscant was Lucas's invention all along. The following section explores a debate on TheForce.net around Coruscant's ambiguous origins, and the spin-off arguments this conflict threw up within the discussion board community.

"Listen up, EU dudes," Darth Eric announced in July 2000.

> T. Zahn did NOT invent the name Coruscant. I've been listening to the radio dramas and in *ROTJ,* Ep.3, there is a scene right after the Falcon and Luke's X-Wing takes off from Tatooine after rescuing Han. The scene is with Lando telling Han about the second Death Star and what's been going on since he's been 'out of it.'
>
> | | |
> |---|---|
> | Lando: | [talking about the Falcon]: I put a lot of money and sweat into her while you were in cold storage. |
> | Han: | Well, the way I heard it, you almost wrecked her on Coruscant! |
> | Lando: | Oh, relax pal! |
> | Han: | Give me a break Lando . . . lettin' Threepio fly the Falcon? |
>
> So there you have it folks. An absolute canon reference. So no, Lucas didn't use Coruscant because Zahn put it in his book. He thought it up first.[237]

Darth Eric is clearly using this new evidence to discount the influence of Zahn, and by extension the EU as a whole, on the canonical mythos. However, his proof is soon countered by Jediphish:

> The first two radio dramas were produced and aired within the first couple of years after the movie theatrical release. Because of lack of NPR interest in 1983, they did not do one for *ROTJ.* Only after the series became successful on cassette did they go back and make a radio drama of *ROTJ.* So Coruscant is an object of Zahn's imagination. Lucas' names for the capital planet were Alderaan and then Had Abbadon.[238]

---

[237]Darth Eric, "The name Coruscant—not Zahn's invention," TheForce.net, op. cit. (July 24, 2000).

[238]Jediphish, "The name Coruscant," op. cit. (July 24, 2000).

Bib Fortuna then steps in and reminds Darth Eric that "the little conversation" he transcribed—the reference to Threepio piloting the Falcon—"describes one of the scenes from the end of *Shadows of the Empire,* which, according to your logic, is now completely canon."[239] Darth Eric, who had originally intended to trash the EU through his "proof," now finds himself unwittingly providing evidence for the other side. "Bib, what the heck are you talking about, you loon?" he blusters. "*SOTE* is in no possible stretch of the imagination canon. Get a grip on reality."[240] "Does it really matter that much whether Lucas indeed came up with the name, people?"[241] asks Tyrian. Iron Parrot tells him, "YES IT DOES matter, because it's the key to the validity of the EU and its influence on Lucas (or lack thereof)."[242] Darth Eric's piece of trivia about Coruscant has now become elevated into a test case.

The sides are drawn up. Iron Parrot and Darth Eric take the purist view—"it must be thunk up by ol' man Lucas to be canon."[243] Bib Fortuna is arguing for the validity of the EU and turns Eric's evidence against him:

> Yes, Darth Eric, *Shadows* is canon. You know why? The radio drama script you posted at the top of this thread described a very important scene at the end of *Shadows.* According to the current rules of canon, if a higher-level piece of canon uses ANY material from a lower-level one, the lower-level one is elevated to complete canon status. That is a FACT.[244]

This appeal to a transcendent body of "rules" provokes Darth Eric. "Bib, where the hell did you get that crap from? Something does not become canon in its entirety, EVEN IF a small part of it is used!"[245] Iron Parrot backs him up, bringing Coruscant back into the discussion: "Some of them refuse to believe the name came from Lucas even when evidence is stuffed up their noses!"[246] Bib Fortuna simply responds with another absolute law:

---

[239]Bib Fortuna, "The name Coruscant," op. cit. (July 24, 2000).
[240]Darth Eric, op. cit.
[241]Tyrian, "The name Coruscant," op. cit. (July 24, 2000).
[242]Iron Parrot, "The name Coruscant," op. cit. (July 24, 2000).
[243]Iron Parrot, ibid.
[244]Bib Fortuna, op. cit.
[245]Darth Eric, op. cit.
[246]Iron Parrot, op. cit.

> There are two rules of canon that are irrefutable. One of them you have already read. The other is that EVERYTHING in the *Star Wars* universe is canon until contradicted by the movies/scripts/screenplays/radio dramas. Think of it this way. When the radio drama was produced, they indirectly acknowledged a piece of *Shadows of the Empire.* The very act of acknowledging a small part of it means they've acknowledged the whole part of it.[247]

From this point on, the discussion splits into multiple debates. Firstly, the opposing sides, joined by others who support their argument, attempt to prove that either Lucas or Zahn invented Coruscant. The Coruscant theories are always supported by secondary evidence and are taken extremely seriously. "I'm going to reply to this post tonight after I've had a chance to re-read every interview ever published on *Star Wars* since 1983," announces Jediphish.[248] Obi-Wan McCartney refuses to accept an unsupported assertion that "Lucasfilm provided Zahn with a list of planet names to choose from";[249] "does anyone have any actual PROOF of this alleged report where Lucas gave Zahn a list of names? Prove it, someone, please."[250]

To end this skirmish, JediSabre weighs in with an extract from *The Annotated Screenplays,* "since you guys seem to require a Lucas quote to back things up."

> "George Lucas: Of course I had a million different names for the home planet of the Empire, but Coruscant came out of publishing." Definitive proof . . . what does this say? That Coruscant was not George Lucas' name for the Imp Homeworld. Who created the name Coruscant? Timothy Zahn! Sorry, guys, I know you take every shot you can at the EU, but you really should think before you post.[251]

Faced with this textual evidence, Iron Parrot stands corrected, yet debates the second, wider question brought up by Bib Fortuna. This is the issue I raised about whether the *A New Hope: Special Edition* appearance of the Outrider means that Dash Rendar was inside it, which means that *Shadows*

---

[247]Bib Fortuna, op. cit.

[248]Jediphish, "The name Coruscant," op. cit. (July 24, 2000).

[249]JediMasterAlpha, "The name Coruscant," op. cit. (July 24, 2000).

[250]Iron Parrot, op. cit.

[251]JediSabre, "The name Coruscant," op. cit. (July 24, 2000).

of the Empire is suddenly authorized. Iron Parrot challenges Bib's theory that any validation of a single Zahn or Steve Perry invention by a higher-level text immediately moves the entire book into canon. "Just because Coruscant is used in *Jedi* . . . does not mean [Zahn character] Grand Admiral Thrawn is canon."[252]

Bib Fortuna returns to lay down the law again: "It's called consistency."

> If you do something once, then you can do it forever. If you arrest someone for a crime, then you have to arrest EVERYONE who commits that crime or you don't arrest anyone. If you acknowledge one part of a book, then you've acknowledged the entire book. It's really quite simple.[253]

Iron Parrot declines to reply, and as is frequently the case with internet discussion, Bib Fortuna's grand assertion goes unanswered. This second debate, never fully concluded, thus moves into a third, more general discussion about authorship and Lucas's overall control of the secondary texts. Darth Ludicrous points out that the *Return of the Jedi* radio drama has no automatic canonical status, because it was written by Brian Daley and not Lucas, but goes on to argue that "everything is canon" because "Lucas has his hands in everything."

> Lucas is involved in big decisions. Do you really think he is so ignorant of grand events like Luke getting married and Chewbacca getting killed? Lucas has a direct hand in those things. This is one instance where I can comfortably say that I am right, and there's no arguing against it because I'm right. You may not like the EU, but that doesn't change the fact is it as valid as any of the movies.[254]

Unfortunately, the other contributors fail to accept this knock-down argument that Darth Ludicrous is right and that there's no arguing against it because he's right. Jedi Knight Seyrah contests that "Lucas said he doesn't read the EU and he is not bound to it."[255] JediMasterAlpha quotes from a 1991 interview with Timothy Zahn—"All the contact I've had with

---

[252]Iron Parrot, op. cit.

[253]Bib Fortuna, op. cit.

[254]Darth Ludicrous, op. cit.

[255]Jedi Knight Seyrah, "The name Coruscant," op. cit. (July 24, 2000).

LucasArts has been through a liaison. Lucas did read the original outline; I don't know whether or not he's read the final novel"[256]—and when told that this evidence is too old produces a more recent exchange with the author where he states that "as far as I know, George Lucas himself is not involved."[257]

Finally, the contributors already taking part, and others coming to the discussion late, pitch in with their own definitions of what canon means. Primus declares himself a purist: "Canon refers to the body of work by a writer. Therefore, only work written by George Lucas is canon as far as *Star Wars* is concerned."

> EU writers are writers who have been granted permission to play with Lucas' toys, but even if they make up a great game with his toys, he can still take the toys back and play with them in any way he sees fit. Lucas is in no way changing any of his vision to accommodate the EU writers. It doesn't make sense to base speculation of Lucas' work on that of another writer with whose work Lucas may not have any familiarity.[258]

Iron Parrot cites Qui-Gon's line in *The Phantom Menace*—"your focus determines your reality"—to back his point that "my focus is the films. Therefore, to me, that is the 'reality' of *Star Wars*."

> In my eyes, Boba Fett did NOT survive the Sarlacc, the circumstances of Chewbacca's death are ambiguous, and Han may have had a son called Anakin but that is NOT hard fact, but rather a possibility. Same goes for Thrawn or Mara Jade, or, unless something changes by way of the films, Darth Bane.[259]

This approach deems that rather than being true unless contradicted by the films, everything is only potentially true until explicitly validated by the films. To return to my previous examples through this interpretive framework: there is a ship called the Outrider but we don't know for sure who was piloting it; Cindel Towani may have crash-landed on Endor but the events of *Caravan of Courage* remain possibilities rather than fact;

---

[256]JediMasterAlpha, op. cit. The quotation is from wauknet.com/jcwillia/intrview.html
[257]Ibid. The quotation is taken from an interview at www.vii.vom/~jade/intrvew2.htm l
[258]Primus, "The name Coruscant," op. cit. (July 24, 2000).
[259]Iron Parrot, op. cit.

and Jefferson Airplane may have appeared on the Wookiee planet Kashyyyk but we'll have to wait until it's shown in a prequel until we can be sure.

The discussion thread ends with a new proposal. "Canon-ism is an illusion," protests Jedi Knight Seyrah. "As far as the search for the one truth about *Star Wars* . . . there is none, it's all a story . . . Lucas can contradict himself if he likes! Depending on your point of view, he already may have."[260] The final post on the Coruscant issue, then, presents a challenge to previous assertions and once again questions the central terms. Rather than continuing until agreement is reached or one side accepts defeat, these internet debates usually end when nobody posts to them for a while and they are supplanted by fresher, more active threads.

What we see here is an exchange of very different, often contradictory fan opinions with no resolution. The importance of secondary evidence is stressed—proof of Lucas's authorial intention, in particular—as is an attention to dates, sources, and correct citation that approaches academic standards and is valued more than accurate spelling or punctuation. Sometimes participants accept the presented evidence and adapt their position; sometimes they simply ignore their opponent's argument. The overriding impression, though, is of an arena like the Galactic Senate in *The Phantom Menace:* a hubbub of voices speaking in turn but with little agreement save for temporary alliances, and little progression as the participants stick to their deeply-held beliefs. If nothing else, it reminds us that to talk of the fan reaction or the fan viewpoint—in cases such as this, at least—is to impose an imagined consensus on a community that thrives on debate.

---

[260]Jedi Knight Seyrah, op. cit.

6

SPECULATION

Randal:	The first Death Star was manned by the Imperial Army. The only people on board were stormtroopers, dignitaries—Imperials . . . The second time around it wasn't even done being built yet. It was still under construction.
Dante:	So?
Randal:	So a construction job of that magnitude would require a hell of a lot more manpower than the Imperial Army had to offer. I bet they brought independent contractors in on that thing: plumbers, aluminum siders, roofers.

—*Clerks*, 1994 (directed by Kevin Smith)

The last I heard, *Star Wars: Episode II* is going to be called *The Lost Apprentice*. But don't trust me on that.[261] When I wrote a chapter on *Star Wars* in 1997, everyone was telling me the first prequel would be called *Enter the Dark Lord,* and I almost included that detail for publication. I am writing this in July 2001. A lot of what I know about

[261]Less than a month later, on August 6, Starwars.com announced the title *Attack of the Clones,* and the TFN boards went into overdrive; the majority of fans posting to the site were appalled by the cheesy, B-movie tone and preferred their own efforts along the lines of *Rise of the Sith* or *The Darkness Within*.

Episode II at this point is surely wrong, so you should treat this, in part, as a document of historical interest. However, a lot of what I know about *Episode II* is surely right, and that says something for the fan communities' ability to detect, speculate, and piece together rumors from whatever scraps they can get their hands on.

The U.S. release of the second prequel is approximately ten months away, but I have already browsed the film's storyline, read dialogue extracts, become familiar with minor as well as key characters, seen pictures from the set, examined storyboards, downloaded poster designs, and watched video clips of scenes in production. I know what Natalie Portman looks like in her white flight suit and how Hayden Christensen wields his saber. I know about Elan Sleazebaggano, Dex's Diner, and the Kyber Dart. I know about the attempted assassination of Padmé, the duel between Obi-Wan and Jango Fett on Kamino, and the arena scenes with Mace Windu, Count Dooku, and the Reek. I might be wrong about *The Lost Apprentice,* but fandom has been able to provide me with a lot of information, months before the trailer or even the title is released.

Again, guessing-games among fans about forthcoming episodes are nothing new and not unique to *Star Wars*. My 1999 chapter on internet communities looked in on *Star Wars* sites in the summer before the release of *The Phantom Menace,* at a time when nobody had heard of the planet Naboo, but one fan was already working out that it would have to appear in addition to Coruscant and Tatooine: "Classically, if you look to Episodes 4-6, each movie features three different planets."[262] As I indicated in the preface, I was speculating about the possible plot of *Revenge of the Jedi* back in 1981, studying the available evidence and drawing storyboards of the action. My version of *Star Wars Episode VI* had a planet made entirely of jagged rock; George Lucas didn't think of that one until *Episode II.*

In my 1999 research, I remarked that the practice of educated prediction among *Star Wars* fans was reminiscent of the online detection discussed by Henry Jenkins in his article on *Twin Peaks* Usenet groups.[263] Both rely on the instant communication provided by internet boards, which enables

---

[262]Brooker, "Internet Fandom and the Continuing Narratives of *Star Wars*, *Blade Runner* and *Alien*," op. cit. p. 66.

[263]Jenkins, "Do You Enjoy Making the Rest of Us Feel Stupid?" in David Lavery (Ed.), *Full of Secrets,* op. cit.

fans to engage in a swift, sharp evolution of theories through suggestions and rejoinders, trading information and interpretations in an attempt to crack textual puzzles—"Who killed Laura Palmer," of course, but also "Who is Darth Tyrannus?" This kind of rapid-fire exchange of ideas needs a system like the internet to work at all; traditional print fanzines, shipped out every month or two, can carry leisurely correspondence through their editorial pages but are not up to the job of processing new revelations.

Current technology allows developments that contributors to the comparatively primitive, text-based alt.tv.twinpeaks could only dream of—discussion posts illustrated with mocked-up Photoshop images and modified spy photos—but the technique remains the same: treating the chosen text and its related documents "like a manuscript, to be pored over and deciphered."[264] This chapter explores the fans' techniques of deduction and their skills at piecing together information from the unlikeliest of sources in their search for clues about *Episode II*.

"See Things Before They Happen"

Not only can you now read the entire plot to *Episode II* online, you can also find an illustrated version. Roderick Vonhögen's "Virtual Edition" feature at TheForce.net is subtitled "See Things Before They Happen." His rendition of *The Phantom Menace,* completed well before the film's release, is now displayed alongside images and script excerpts from the "real" version: they are impressively similar.

Roderick collects snippets of information from around the internet and collates them into completed scenes, then illustrates them with Photoshop manipulations of existing pictures. February 2001, for instance, shows us Padmé asleep as insectoid robots crawl over her body; the main image is taken from a production still of Natalie Portman on the set, while the bugs are homemade graphic additions. Roderick's conception of the scene is supported by quotations from another fan reporter, T'bone:

> Obi-Wan and Anakin are waiting guard outside of the senator's quarters when they both sense something weird. According to T'bone's

[264]Ibid. p. 54.

Chyren's painting of the rumoured scene

> information, the famous line "I have a bad feeling about this" is said here. "Zam Wesell is controlling a flying droid who tries to get Padmé by sending out little insect like robots to kill her." The Jedi enter Padmé's room; Obi-Wan jumps out of the window on the flying droid while Anakin destroys the insect-like droids. When Padmé is safe, Anakin "gets on his now infamous Coruscant Hot Rod and starts following Obi-Wan, who is dangling from this flying droid"[265]

Roderick's design for the smaller insect creatures is in turn based on a spy report from Chyren, a fan artist who heard about the bug droid from his own personal sources and drew up a full-size painting of it.

As further explanation, Roderick quotes a third fan, Vertical, who offered speculation about this scene on TheForce.net: "So . . . what's a bug? Well . . . THAT is a bug. Obi-Wan is 'riding' it. Why? It tried to kill Senator Padmé in her quarters, but Obi-Wan and Anakin interrupted the assassination attempt before it could finish the job, and it flew out

---

[265]T'bone, quoted on Roderick Vonhögen, "The Virtual Edition," www.theforce.net/virtualedition (February 2001).

the window . . . "[266] Finally, Roderick brings in extra proof to support the speculation about the bug's visual appearance by reminding readers of an official preproduction photograph from starwars.com, the Lucasfilm site. Enlarging and highlighting a section of the image, Roderick points out a model in the background that resembles the creature in Chyren's painting. "Could that be our first glimpse of this 'Bug' droid? I think it's very likely indeed!" He adds a personal note, which reminds us that all this hard work of puzzling, prediction, and creation is undertaken out of fun rather than duty. "This is the kind of stuff I like! Enhancing pictures in search of blurry clues, speculation, mystery, guesswork . . . Just like the good old days!"

While the process of detection is in part a solitary one—Roderick's analysis of the backstage photograph is reminiscent of Rick Deckard's exploration of a snapshot in *Blade Runner*—we can see that teamwork is also important. The bugs image was the result of a collaborative project, with Roderick using the images and reports of Chyren, T'bone, and Vertical to ensure that his picture would be plausibly close to the "real" scene in *Episode II*.

The Virtual Edition became even more reliant on outside contributions in March 2001, when Roderick reported that he had been diagnosed with repetitive strain injury. He posted an announcement—"Send me YOUR pictures, since I'm not able to make them myself"—and since then the site has become a hosting platform for readers' speculative images of *Episode II,* a gallery of Photoshopped artwork. As an indication of these fans' shared interests, most of the pictures show various angles on the bounty hunter Jango Fett, his ship Slave I, and his rumored battle with Obi-Wan in the rain.

Roderick's version of the *Episode II* screenplay itself is also a patchwork of rumor from various sources. The description of the opening crawl and the first scenes of Padmé's return to Coruscant are cited to TheForce.net, the key dialogue "I should not have come back" is taken from Prequelspoilers.com, and her meeting with the Jedi in the next scene is lifted from Aldera.net. Subsequent speculation is based on "call sheets from loresdelsith.unicyber.org"[267] for the appearance of Dar Wac in

[266]Vertical, quoted on Vonhögen, op. cit.

[267]Vonhögen, "*Star Wars Episode II,*" *The Virtual Edition,* op. cit.

hologram, photos from the French *Star Wars Insider* magazine for Anakin's journey to Naboo, and "various sources" for scenes that are so widely accepted, such as the Dex's Diner nightclub on Coruscant, that their absence in the actual film would shock many fans.

Two scenes in particular are described in exact detail: the encounter between Jango Fett and Obi-Wan that caught the imaginations of many fan artists, and the arena battle featuring Mace Windu against a dinosaur-like beast called the Reek. While other exchanges between characters are related in simple, generalized terms—"Amidala wants to go to Geonosis, but Anakin doesn't want to go"[268]—these two fight sequences are accorded lengthy paragraphs, with every move specified.

> Jango suddenly appears, flying towards Obi-Wan. Obi-Wan gets up and reaches for his lightsaber. Jango fires a cable. The cable wraps around Obi-Wan's hands, and he fails to catch his lightsaber. Jango takes off with his rocket pack and pulls Obi-Wan, dragging him along the ground. Obi-Wan rolls to one side and manages to roll around one of the towers. Obi-Wan jumps up and wraps the cable around the tower. Jango crashes to the ground. The rocket pack explodes into the building.[269]

There is a reason Roderick is able, even expected, to describe these conflicts so fully: he, like every other TheForce.net regular who was online in September 2000, will have seen them in storyboard form.

"The biggest scoop of all"

On September 26, 2000, NabooOnline.com published descriptions of two storyboard scans they had received from a fan named Horns. The first was a duel between Jango Fett and Obi-Wan, "the widely-speculated rain battle scene . . . it involves a lot of martial arts and grappling." The second conflict

> occurs in and around a huge arena . . . there is a new major character in this scene and Mace Windu really demonstrates why he is classed

---

[268]Ibid.

[269]Ibid.

> together with Yoda. Take them as certainties or take them as speculation. It don't worry me. But don't come crying when you read them with disbelief and then see them unfold on the big screen in 2002.[270]

"The first battle," Horns wrote in his covering mail, "is pretty much confirmed by a couple of the Select images. The new characters in the second battle have all been made into domain names by Lucasfilm, so they are confirmed."[271] As we have seen before, there is an emphasis on providing proof to back up any theory. In this case, the fact that the storyboards were supported by what had already been seen on Lucasfilm's official "Select" releases—the production photos released on starwars.com—could have worked the other way to suggest that they were based on general fan knowledge rather than revealing anything new. The domain names, as we shall see below, brought their own ambiguities. However, NabooOnline chose to believe that these were the real deal and decided accordingly to restrict themselves to descriptions, in order to avoid trouble from Lucasfilm.

News travels fast among online fan communities. Later that day, TheForce.net had the story via one of its own spies, AL, and announced that this might be "the biggest scoop of all so far, or the most elaborate scam you've ever seen."[272] By September 27, the Jedi Council boards at TheForce.net had over two hundred posts debating whether the boards were genuine. Personally, I thought they were phony, the work of a fan with average talent: the boards were detailed but stilted, far more like an amateur comic book than the rough, fluid lines of the *Phantom Menace* storyboards,[273] and the idea of Fett using all his weapons in one kung-fu action sequence felt like the epitome of fan-boy wish fulfillment.

The board contributors, however, were already asking what this meant for the story line, filling in gaps and connecting the dots with what they already knew of the narrative. The first post was from Wizard of Ozzel:

> Some are speculating that Jango is taking Boba away from the Jedi temple. This is fuelled by the recent picture of a kid (supposedly Daniel

---

[270]Horns, quoted on NabooOn-line.com (September 26, 2000).

[271]Ibid.

[272]Anon., "Spy Report," TheForce.net (September 26, 2000).

[273]Reprinted in George Lucas, *Star Wars: Episode I, The Illustrated Screenplay,* London: Ebury Press (1999).

> Logan) dressed as a Padawan. Logan was previously rumoured to be the young Boba Fett . . . what are all those Jedi doing at the arena? Perhaps the arena is illegal, but would they really go through all that trouble just to end an illegal blood sport? Who is Count Dooku? The name alone tells us he is some sort of nobility. Does he rule a planet? Is he a criminal like Jabba? What, if anything, is his connection to the Sith? Could he be Darth Tyrannus?[274]

While some participants sounded a note of skepticism—"what if that Horns clown is playing you and everyone else for fools like all evidence and common sense dictates?"[275]—the majority of contributors wanted to believe. "The rain battle sounded so cool with the wire wrapped round Obi-Wan," breathed a fan named Q187.[276] The discussion became an exchange of speculative ideas, most of them contradictory although based on the same evidence. "Count Dooku would have Amidala abducted. Jango Fett would complete the mission," John Kenobi proposed, adding, "Don't ask me why young Boba is along."[277] Sense-My-Presence disagreed with Wizard of Ozzel: "I don't think Boba is a Padawan. No proof we do have suggests that Boba had any force powers."[278] Nuche Vader countered John Kenobi: "If Boba Fett was involved with the abduction of Padmé, wouldn't that create tension between him and Vader in *ESB*?"[279]

The storyboards had been accepted as plausible evidence and were used as a new platform for guesswork about *Episode II;* they might not have been proved genuine, but they were the best anyone had. If this makes the board contributors seem slightly gullible, we should remember the quote from Roderick Vonhögen; this online puzzling over clues is a pleasurable challenge, a leisure activity, and while these fans put a great deal of effort into their contributions, the whole process remains an enjoyable game.

Ironically, the storyboard affair turned sour at the moment they were apparently proved to be genuine. On September 28, 2000, NabooOnline

---

[274]Wizard of Ozzel, "What if the storyboards are real," TheForce.net, op. cit. (September 27, 2000).

[275]Darth Impatience, "What if . . . ," TheForce.net, op. cit. (September 27, 2000).

[276]Q187, "What if . . . ," TheForce.net, op. cit. (September 27, 2000).

[277]John Kenobi, "What if . . . ," TheForce.net, op. cit. (September 27, 2000).

[278]Sense-My-Presence, "What if . . . ," TheForce.net, op. cit. (September 27, 2000).

[279]Nuche Vader, "What if . . . ," TheForce.net, op. cit. (September 27, 2000).

published a letter from Lucasfilm's director of business affairs. "It has come to our attention that you have posted images, storylines, descriptions and other material relating to storyboards from the production of *Star Wars: Episode II* on your World Wide Web site."[280] The site swiftly took even its description of the boards down. The discussion on TheForce.net, though, suddenly changed from enthusiastic acceptance to a mixture of panic and stubborn resistance.

"My site is still up," Chyren noted, "and LFL visited it about 6 hours ago. I don't know what is keeping them."[281] Koreynl started to worry—"Mine is also up and running . . . should I close shop, or continue?"[282]—and was told "take them down, if you feel that it gives you peace. But it will only add to the hysteria, my friend, when people start seeing all the dead links."[283] Koreynl protested, "I just don't want them to shut down my message board or pages . . . " and then came close to hysteria himself, even using his real name:

> Problem is, I (Charles) did not post those storyboards on my site—I linked to them. So did I do wrong? I'm no more at fault than anyone who linked to me today. All I did was link to somewhere else, and as far as I know the webmaster of that site is just a little kid. LOL! Hey, dudes, I'M just a little kid. I'm in a heap of trouble, I guess.[284]

"C'mon, Koreynl! Where are your ballzz? Did you lend them or what?" asked another contributor, Blueharvester.[285] The situation had turned into a minor skirmish between fans and Lucasfilm, with Chyren offering to host all the pictures on his site and register traffic as it came through. "Don't be afraid!" Blueharvester comforted Korelyn as Chyren ordered him to redirect his site links, "then in the morning, if nothing has happened, put up the files again. You listenin'?"[286]

---

[280]David J. Anderman, letter posted on NabooOn-line (September 28, 2000).
[281]Chyren, "NabooOn-line has removed their storyboard pics," TheForce.net, op. cit (September 28, 2000).
[282]Koreynl, "NabooOn-line . . . ," TheForce.net, op. cit. (September 28, 2000).
[283]Chyren, op. cit.
[284]Koreynl, op. cit.
[285]Blueharvester, "NabooOn-line . . . ," TheForce.net, op. cit. (September 28, 2000).
[286]Chyren, op. cit.

Literally overnight, the tone had completely changed. While the authenticity of the boards was never to my knowledge fully resolved—although the information they provided is now, as we've seen, treated as reliable by all the contributors to the *Virtual Edition*—the story of their release and immediate censorship provides an illuminating example of the fan relationship with Lucasfilm. While the contributors to TheForce.net appreciate any information they can get and happily gather the scraps that starwars.com feeds them in its "Select" images, they also like to cling to what they have and resent its being taken away.

As soon as Lucasfilm cracked down on the images, regulars like Chyren began to evolve strategies to protect and retain the information. It isn't too far-fetched, surely, to imagine that Chyren, with his advice to do what "gives you peace . . . my friend," is—perhaps even consciously—taking on the role of an older Jedi, counselling his skittish Padawan-learner. The struggle over information gives fans the chance to see themselves as Rebels, and again we see, as we will again in the following chapters, that Lucasfilm unintentionally positions itself in the role of the Empire.

"CLONETROOPERS.COM"

To say that fans piece together scraps is not just a metaphor. On September 18, 2000, TheForce.net reproduced a scan of six paper fragments, rearranged so they formed two incomplete documents. A correspondent called PLG had found them "amongst the leaves of Seville."[287] At the top left of the first page is a partial logo, JA—recognizable as Lucas' production company, JAK—and below it, "STAR WARS: Prod Office: Recce and Production Services, Wardrobe Warehouse/Office. Director: George Lucas. Producer: Rick McCallum."[288] TheForce.net endorsed them confidently as production notes and call sheets for *Episode II.*

The scraps were examined for whatever clues they might reveal. Halfway down the first page, which was ripped across the middle, are the words "dmé Amidala—Sophie Ward," followed by "akin—Hayden

---

[287]PLG, mail to The Force.net, op. cit. (September 18, 2000).

[288]Call sheets for *Episode II,* reproduced at TheForce.net, op. cit. (September 18, 2000).

Christensen," and "D2—digital."[289] Sparse enough, but the editors of TheForce.net seized on the fact that Natalie Portman's character was to be called by her *nom-de-guerre,* Padmé, rather than by her regal title, and confirmation of the rumor that R2-D2 would appear as CGI in some scenes. An instruction on the second sheet provided more fuel for speculation, cross-referenced with an earlier spy photograph of the actors on set:

> When the first pictures arrived from Seville showing Hayden and Natalie in costume with luggage, it was assumed they were going on a trip. Perhaps there's a different angle on that story, as told by these call sheets. Apparently, the Art Department was responsible for "bread, fabric and fruits for the shopping bags" . . . so are Anakin and Padmé going on a shopping trip?[290]

The search for further evidence sometimes takes fans down extremely inventive routes, and the most unexpected areas of the internet can turn up the richest information. In early September 2000, TheForce.net editor, Josh Griffen, working with T'bone and Roderick Vonhögen—collaborating as in the bug case cited above—investigated a list of new domain names with intriguingly familiar connotations. Among them were Greatclonewar.com, a reference to the conflict mentioned by Obi-Wan in *A New Hope;* Beruwhitesun.org, surely the maiden name of Luke's aunt Beru; Sido-dyas.com, a possible variant on Darth Sidious; and Naberrie.com, Amidala's middle name.

Lucasfilm had only recently launched a purge of sites that infringed its copyright—sending cease and desist letters to the likes of Starwarstoys.com and Quigonjinn.com[291]—and this had all the hallmarks of a preemptive strike whereby Lucasfilm registered names some eighteen months before the new film's release and prevented any fans from poaching the trademarks for their own use. Of course, an inevitable consequence was that by making the names public, Lucasfilm was offering up information about the next episode's plot, in disguise and in fragments,

---

[289]Ibid.

[290]Anon., "Call Sheets for Seville," The Force.net, op. cit. (September 18, 2000).

[291]See David R. Phillips, "It's Not Wise To Upset A Wookiee," www.echostation.com./features/lfl . . . wookiee.htm (September 1, 1999).

admittedly, but these fans were accustomed to cracking code and connecting clues.

Prasad, webmaster of TheJediPlanet.com, ran a whois on the domain names and found many of them registered to an individual named John Koenig, whom Prasad described as Lucasfilm's chief information officer.[292] The Wizard of Ozzel, mentioned earlier on the board threads, followed up the name and found Koenig listed as a contributor to the official magazine *Star Wars Insider,* with the caption "This person should never appear in anything."[293] Whatever his status, the enigmatic Koenig had secured some fifty names and variants as dotcoms, dotnets, and dotorgs. As TheForce.net editorial mused, "Is this someone trying to capitalize on a few new *Episode II* domains? Were these supposed to be secured by Lucasfilm and ended up being credited to the wrong person? We don't know . . . ";[294] but whether Koenig was stealing a march on Lucasfilm or simply carrying out its instructions, all the names were treated as reliable pointers to events, characters, locations, even dialogue from the second prequel.

> CLONETROOPERS.COM—What the evolution of the battledroid army will become. An army of clones? Most definitely.
>
> LORDTYRANUS.COM—This is one of the coolest names in the list! Has to be a major character in the movie, perhaps a title for an evil person, even . . . Sidious' new Sith Apprentice!
>
> KITFISTO.COM—We've received emails suggesting that this could be related to *TPM*'s Kitster. Your guess is as good as ours.
>
> AMBUFETT.COM—wow! First Boba, then Jango, now Ambu? Fett must be some type of title, this could again be a relation or another officer in the military.
>
> RISEFORTH.NET—Sounds like a possible title, though it would be very early for that to even have been talked about. Perhaps this is a key line of dialogue in the film.[295]

---

[292]Prasad, "The Truth on John Koenig," www.thejediplanet.com/features/koenig.shtml
[293]Anon., "Who is John Koenig," TheForce.net, op. cit. (September 4, 2000).
[294]Josh Griffin, "A New List of Names," TheForce.net, op. cit. (September 4, 2000).
[295]Roderick Vonhögen, "Virtual Edition," op. cit. (September 4, 2000).

Finally, in the quest for any extra hints on the content of *Episode II,* fans are prepared to go back decades as well as investigate online legal registers. Neil Arsenty mailed TheForce.net in July 2000 after having sifted through all Lucas' drafts of the *Star Wars* screenplays, the earliest of which dates from 1974. "Some of these names have already turned up in *TPM* (Valorum, Mace, Bail Antilles)," Neil suggests, "so who's to say that Lucas won't use more of these unused names in *Ep II* or *Ep III*?"[296]

This was not such a far-fetched idea: indeed, "Clieg Whitesun," a discovery on Neil's archival list, has since cropped up on the domain names, albeit split into Cliegg Lars and his wife, Beru Whitesun. Some names, however, may never be seen outside the original scripts. Along with evocative inventions like the planet Aquilae, present in the rough and second drafts of *The Star Wars* and abandoned by 1976, Neil points out that the character "Dashit" has not yet been picked up from the early scripts, perhaps for good reasons.

"A shocking surprise in *Episode II*"

The fans on TheForce.net may come across like a bunch of monkish scholars, analyzing the most arcane documents for possible rumors; but not every claim of new *Episode II* evidence is seized upon for forensic detection, and anything coming from Supershadow.com is treated with the greatest suspicion.

Mickey Suttle, aka Supershadow, describes himself as "the most famous *Star Wars* fan in the world." His site is decorated with a moody picture of himself, staring off into the distance, biceps discreetly clenched, and a page of photographs sent in by female fans. He has written a book about the saga that weighs in at 943 pages, the first section of which "recounts how Supershadow achieved superstar status on the internet." In March 2000 he claimed to have the script for *Episode II* on his desk. "Lucasfilm," Supershadow announced on his site, "has permitted me to reveal the following to you in order to whet your appetite." There followed a list of revelations, including such specific pointers as "Boba Fett's role and

[296]Neil Arsenty, mail to TheForce.net, op. cit. (July 25, 2000).

identity in *Episode II* are both huge surprises" and "the script provides a very exciting story that raises many, many questions about certain things."[297]

Back on TheForce.net, the regulars were laying the smack on Supershadow: "This is the same guy who claimed *Episode II* would be about the 'Clown Wars,'" pointed out Vertical.[298] Darth Salacious read the predictions and complained, "I want the last five minutes of my life back."[299] StarTours went into a full-blown satire:

> "There will be a shocking surprise in Episode II"—you don't say! I, Criswell the Magnificent, predict that we shall see a sunrise tomorrow . . . you may begin your bowing in reverence now. The biggest surprise will be no doubt experienced by this "Lucasfilm Insider" when he plops his $7.50 down to see it opening day and find out what the movie's really about. Meanwhile, isn't fan fiction fun?[300]

That Supershadow's pronouncements met with scorn reminds us that this community of fans, despite the eagerness for the slightest whiff of *Episode II* news, is shrewd and informed rather than gullible. Although they want to believe and are willing to listen to new theories, they also possess a huge amount of knowledge—impressive in the individual fan, vast in the collective of the discussion boards—against which to test any fresh rumors. In the serious game of speculation, false evidence is worse than no evidence, and the contributors to the Jedi Council are no fools: their network of spies and informants is tight enough to filter out signal from noise. In the process, they had caught enough snippets to patch together virtually the entirety of *Episode II,* months before the film even received its official name.

---

[297]Supershadow, quoted by Leif, "Supershadow Claims Lucas Sent Him Ep II Script," TheForce.net, op. cit. (March 14, 2000).

[298]Vertical, "Supershadow," TheForce.net, op. cit. (March 14, 2000).

[299]Darth Salacious, "Supershadow," TheForce.net, op. cit. (March 14, 2000).

[300]Star Tours, "Supershadow," TheForce.net, op. cit. (March 14, 2000).

7

SLASH AND OTHER STORIES

There are posters for films on the wall. A three-quarters naked woman in a white dress with a very strange hairstyle—it looks as if she had bread rolls in her ears—carrying a science-fiction pistol in her left hand and pointing it very close up in front of her mouth, is advertising a film called *Star Whores*.

—John Lanchester, *Mr. Phillips*, London: Faber & Faber (2000), p. 16

For the most part, the previous chapters have been about topics that, while common knowledge to most *Star Wars* fans, will probably seem arcane to the non-fan, even to one with an academic investment in cult media. Anyone on TheForce.net's boards, including me, could tell you Bib Fortuna's race, the galactic coordinates of Coruscant, and the color of Luke's saber in *Return of the Jedi*: details which will seem obscure to the scholar of *Star Trek* or *The X-Files,* however diligently he or she has researched the fan communities around those TV series. Slash fiction, by contrast—usually defined as fan writing that explores same-sex relationships between the characters—has received a considerable amount of academic attention, yet many *Star Wars* fans seem never to have heard of it, and those that have tend to keep their distance. Terms like "hurt/comfort," "PWP," and "Q/O" may well be more familiar to media scholars than to most *Star Wars* fans.

You will remember that Tim and Mark, my hosts for chapter 2, were wary at the mention of slash fiction once I'd explained the concept, although, ironically, their reading of C-3PO as gay was a form of slash interpretation itself. On the discussion boards about canon, only one contributor, Chyren, mentioned slash in passing as the reason for the rise of the EU novels, and even here the argument is that slash is a *Star Trek* phenomenon that Lucasfilm cannily kept at bay by swamping the market with "official" spin-off fiction.

> Here is the reason for the existence of the EU . . . terrible fan fiction. Lucasfilm learned from the mistakes of the *Trek* franchise. Many of you may know that before the masses of *Star Trek* "official" books began to be released, conventions and fan publications were swamped with fanfic *Trek* novellas and stories, because the fans wanted more *Trek* and didn't care where it came from. Much of this stuff was pure unadulterated horse crap, and indeed some of it was what we know as "slash books"—homosexual stories concerning the major *Trek* characters. All of this served to reflect badly on the *Trek* franchise and was tacky, tasteless and not indicative of the quality the creators of the show wanted to present. Lucasfilm pre-empted this happening with *Star Wars* by allowing chosen authors to write fiction.[301]

Chyren, an influential figure on the boards who posts regularly and authoritatively, is not confronted on this issue, and so his explanation stands to educate any less-informed contributors. Even *Star Trek*, which these fans usually hold in contempt, is degraded by the "homosexual" interpretations inherent in slash books. In fact, Chyren's account suggests that *Star Wars* slash was successfully quashed by Lucasfilm's strategy. If that were the case, it fails to explain the wealth of Qui-Gon/Obi-Wan homoerotic fan fiction currently available online, at a time when there is also a great deal of 'official' fiction about the *Phantom Menace* Jedi being published; indeed, the slash writers actually draw on the secondary mythos of the EU stories to flesh out their own readings.

I had only one more comment on slash from a fan outside the writing community. Rick, a writer of *Star Wars* role-playing material for West End Games, told me

> I'm gay and, quite frankly, I've never come across any gay *Star Wars* fiction. I don't have the time to slush through most amateur writing.

[301]Chyren, "Will Lucas Follow the Books of Zahn?", TheForce.net, op. cit. (October 13, 1999).

> And as for gay *Star Wars* fiction . . . whatever floats your boat. I can empathize with LFL in seeing their franchise tarnished by what most people would call vulgar, obscene and pornographic. I wouldn't like that with my own creations. Secret male societies [like the Jedi] will always be a target of homosexual criticism, sometimes with actual merit. Do I like the idea of gay Jedi? Never really gave it much thought. If it's someone's fantasy, who am I to judge. I would say the episode of *Friends* in which one of the guys fantasizes about going to bed with Princess Leia can be considered base and perverse . . . so is the idea of a "gay" Jedi fantasy untenable to people? Or is it a "perverse" devolution of *Star Wars* characters?[302]

I ended up, then, with only three mentions of slash, two of which I had prompted myself. The attitude of fans outside the fiction community ranged from Rick's mellow indifference to Tim's uneasy bemusement to Chyren's barely disguised disgust. Compare this to the enthusiasm with which media scholars approach and report on slash as a phenomenon and radical writing practice. In a 1991 article, Henry Jenkins discussed *Trek* slash in particular as a creative reworking of the original text, and revisited the subject in a chapter of his seminal 1992 study, *Textual Poachers.*[303] In the same year, Camille Bacon-Smith's ethnographic research around female *Star Trek* fan communities explored the motivations and rewards of slash writing, with a specific focus on the "hurt/comfort" subgenre.[304] Constance Penley's *Nasa/Trek,* as the title suggests, devoted half a book to the practice and pleasures of slash, once more using *Star Trek* as the central case study.[305]

Further articles on the topic can be found online. Sue Hazlett's "Filling in the Gaps," on *X-Files* fan fiction,[306] Su Nact's more general discussion

---

[302]Rick, details withheld on request, personal e-mail (July 4, 2000).

[303]Henry Jenkins, "Welcome to Bisexuality, Captain Kirk," in *Textual Poachers,* London: Routledge (1992). See also the chapter "Scribbling in the Margins" in the same volume, and "Gender and *Star Trek* fan fiction" in John Tulloch and Henry Jenkins, *Science Fiction Audiences,* London: Routledge (1995).

[304]Camille Bacon-Smith, *Enterprising Women,* Philadelphia: University of Pennsylvania Press (1992).

[305]Constance Penley, *Nasa/Trek,* London: Verso (1997).

[306]Sue Hazlett, "Filling in the Gaps: Fans and Fan Fiction on the Internet," reprinted at *X-Files University,* www.geocities.com/Hollywood/Lot/8254/xfuis.html

"Why Women Like Slash,"[307] and AC's "In Defense of Slash"[308] are all academic studies—even if the latter is published pseudonymously—which draw on previous scholarship and add to it through original primary research. On a slightly different level, sites like Slash-Informational[309] host scores of essays, some written by fans—as opposed to fan-academics—and some by journalists. While these take a more personal, even polemical approach, and usually dispense with the conventions of sourcing texts and providing references, Henry Jenkins' work in particular is often noted and his essays are frequently quoted within or reproduced alongside fan articles.

Slash fiction, then, has been extensively documented in both its older fanzine and more recent online form, and with reference to a range of primary texts. Although there is a clear imbalance in terms of the attention *Star Trek* has received compared to other shows, Jenkins' *Textual Poachers* also discusses homoerotic fanfiction based on such diverse series as *Twin Peaks*, *The Professionals,* and *Blake's Seven*. Slash practitioners often experiment with more than one text at the same time, applying the same process of careful study and creative rewriting to *Quantum Leap* as they would to *Buffy*; I was not altogether surprised, then, to discover that *Star Wars* slash follows very similar conventions to those at work in the fiction discussed by Jenkins, Penley, and Bacon-Smith. There is no point in going over ground that has already been covered so thoroughly and thoughtfully in the academic studies of the last decade or in rehashing the work of previous researchers; any readers unfamiliar with *Textual Poachers*, *Enterprising Women*, and *Nasa/Trek* would be better advised to read them in the original.

Indeed, as the heading indicates, this chapter is not exclusively about slash. It is a discussion of the various subgenres of *Star Wars* fan fiction, and it asks what fan writers in all these genres do with the "official" *Star Wars* texts. How do they seize on moments in the films and open them up to further possibilities? How do they support their interpretation by drawing on the Expanded Universe novels or on reference works like the *Encyclopaedia*? What is their relationship with the primary texts: a respectful borrowing, a radical overturning, an indifferent use of the canonical situations and characters for textual experiment? Rather than singling out slash

---

[307]Su Nact, "Two Men Are Better Than One: Why Women Like Slash," reprinted at *X-Files University,* ibid. (April 9, 1999).

[308]AC, "In Defense of Slash," www.chisp.net/~zoerayne/defense.html

[309]*Slash-Informational,* www.fanficweb.net/directory/slash/slash.htm

as a particularly exciting and radical niche of fan fiction, although it is without doubt an interesting form, I am more concerned with what all these types of writing around *Star Wars* have in common.

My core argument here is that *Star Wars* slash fiction plays exactly the same game with the primary texts, on a formal level, as does genfic, its heterosexual counterpart. Stories that do nothing more than fill in the gaps in Luke and Biggs' platonic relationship or expand on Han's evolving romance with Leia are no less radical than slash in terms of their relationship with the primary texts. Slash relies on the films as much as genfic does; genfic departs from the films as much as slash does.

Moreover, I propose that *Star Wars* fan fiction of all genres is involved in the same practice as officially sanctioned EU fiction: extrapolating from the films, filling in spaces, daring to go off on tangents, but always using the primary texts as a baseline. On a formal level, I am arguing that an online fan story about Qui-Gon and Obi-Wan's romantic love does much the same thing with the existing *Star Wars* mythos as does *Shadows of the Empire*, Timothy Zahn's "Thrawn Trilogy," or even Terry Brooks's novelization of *The Phantom Menace*; it makes suppositions, suggests links, and provides background from the cues in the original film texts. Leia and Han kiss in *Jedi*, and Zahn proposes that they go on to have sex and to produce and bring up children. Qui-Gon strokes Obi-Wan's face at the end of *Phantom Menace*, and a host of slash writers propose that the two Jedi had a loving relationship. The process of deduction and invention is not fundamentally different.

That is on a formal level alone, because it would be foolish to suggest that there is no difference whatsoever between a slash tale about Obi-Wan and Qui-Gon, a fan's recounting of an interlude between Leia and Han, and a short story in Kevin J. Anderson's published collection *Tales of the Bounty Hunters*. The slash authors, even the slash readers I corresponded with, all requested that I refer to them only by pseudonyms, for fear that their employers or families would discover their involvement in the genre. On the level of copyright, Lucasfilm draws an explicit distinction between its own authorized texts and fan fiction of all varieties, whether slash, heterosexual, or mainstream action-adventure; while it is most directly opposed to the use of its characters in gay scenarios, the final section of this chapter considers LFL's recent attempts to rein in and control even the less controversial forms of fan fiction.

However, apart from their different positions in the hierarchy of "authorized" *Star Wars* texts, I am suggesting that slash and genfic have the same formal relationship to the canon as EU fiction does: a balance between respecting the established rules of the mythos and providing creative variations, based on personal interpretation, within this accepted framework. Indeed, we could posit that fan fiction of all genres has more fidelity to the official texts than the EU does, as its authors often have more investment in, more knowledge of, and more loyalty to the mythos than professional writers like Timothy Zahn, Kevin J. Anderson, and Terry Brooks.

First, though, I want to discuss the online communities around slash and genfic, asking what pleasures these writers gain from placing *Star Wars* characters in new situations, what support they find in their fellow authors, why the fan fiction networks seem to be predominantly female, and ultimately, what similarities unite the two forms.

"Men are the undiscovered country"

In October 1999, the Master And Apprentice slash site—which primarily features Qui-Gon and Obi-Wan stories—conducted a survey[310] of its visitors and contributors: 95.7 percent were female. This remarkable statistic echoes the situation described by Bacon-Smith, Jenkins, and Penley with regard to *Star Trek* slash, and by Jenkins with reference to fan fiction around other media texts; homoerotic writing about popular television and film characters is an almost exclusively female activity.[311] As one writer told me, "I do know a few gay men that write slash . . . I don't know any straight men that do though. I think that's mostly because straight men don't like to even imagine homosexual situations between males."[312]

---

[310]*Master and Apprentice* survey, www.slashcity.com/sockii/ma/results.html

[311]Jenkins quotes Bacon-Smith's figure of ninety percent for "media fan writers in general"; Jenkins, "*Star Trek* Rerun, Reread, Rewritten," in Constance Penley et. al., *Close Encounters: Film, Feminism and Science Fiction,* Minneapolis: University of Minnesota Press (1991), p. 178.

[312]Katie, details withheld on request, personal e-mail (July 6, 2000). The Jedi Hurtaholics Archive is at www.ktnb.net/jedi/

My correspondents offered various reasons for their involvement in slash fiction. On the most basic level, they admitted that writing and reading erotic fiction is sexually arousing. Krychick's personal story of her introduction to the genre, posted as part of her "Slash Tutorial," is unusual in its frankness:

> I'm just going to come right out and say the reason that others rarely mention: it really turns me on. No shame there—many guys like the thought of two women together. It's no different for women to like the idea of two guys together. Why? This is the best explanation I've heard: to women, men are sexual creatures. We find them attractive. What could be better than two sexual creatures enjoying each other? Makes sense to me.[313]

A handful of the other writers I e-mailed offered a similar explanation, although they were slightly less forthcoming. "Liam Neeson and Ewan McGregor are two very handsome men, which makes the pairing that more delectable," said Katie, webmistress of the Jedi Hurtaholics' Archive.[314] "The implausible stories are just me having fun with two sexy men . . . Most straight men fantasize about two women together, so what's wrong with straight women fantasizing about two men together?"[315]

Kass, who runs the Phantom Menace Lair[316] with her friend Kate—a different Kate—echoed this justification with her observation, "If one hot man is good, two hot men are even better. Three or more hot men require far too much concern about the arrangement of elbows and knees."[317] However, she adds "I rarely write erotic scenes because they arouse me, or because I'm worried about whether they arouse the reader."[318] Fee Folay, a longtime female reader and occasional writer of slash, also suggests a complex relationship with the erotic nature of the fiction.

---

[313]Krychick, "Slash Tutorial," originally hosted at adult.dencity.com/Krychick/slash_tutorial/tutorialindex.html
[314]The Jedi Hurtaholics' Archive.
[315]Katie, op. cit.
[316]The Phantom Menace Lair, www.geocities.com/soho/workshop/3293/lair/q_o.html
[317]Kass, details withheld on request, personal e-mail (June 28, 2000).
[318]Ibid.

> The bottom line is that on any one day I might find that a story entitled *Padawan Takes A Shower* gives me a tingle, and on another day the same story might be dead boring. Thus, I am more likely on the whole to seek out stories that have a broader appeal—that go beyond the sexual relationship and contain an intricate plot, complex character interaction and so on. I do not read slash in order to get titillated and I do not write slash for that reason either. My interest is more in exploring the unfamiliar territory of male/male emotional interaction. If I find a story arousing, it is a pleasant little bonus, but it is not the driving force behind my interest in this genre.[319]

Of course, it could be that even after several e-mails these writers are wary about sharing extremely personal information with a stranger. Be that as it may, the general response was that the appeal of slash lies not so much in its erotic qualities as in its playing with gender roles and liberated treatment of male relationships. Fee Folay writes, "I do read a lot of genfic, but I find the slash is more likely to explore a deeper, more intense relationship between the male protagonists, and that beguiles me."[320] Fee continues

> I've heard it said that one of the reasons that women enjoy slash fiction is that it depicts men (in a general sense) as women wish they were . . . caring, sensitive, romantic, introspective and so on. Deep friendships between men have always fascinated me . . . maybe because of the novelty of it, both due to its taboo nature within our society and because I have never had a relationship like that.[321]

Kass's thoughts on the subject are very similar: "Men are the undiscovered country. I adore men, find them puzzling, fascinating, and much more interesting to explore than my universal sisters. I see human sexuality as a spectrum, not as a universal absolute, not either/or, not yes/no, and I suppose this is one of the ways in which I get to both explore that and express my views of it."[322] This reasoning is entirely in keeping with Jenkins' findings from the early 1990s *Trek* communities that "slash is not

---

319Fee Folay, details withheld on request, personal e-mail (July 19, 2000).

320Ibid.

321Ibid.

322Kass, op. cit.

so much a genre about sex as it is a genre about the limitations of traditional masculinity and about reconfiguring male identity."[323]

Camille Bacon-Smith offers another possible reason behind the fan involvement with slash fiction. She proposes that writing slash—specifically the hurt/comfort genre, which involves assault, abuse and recovery—provides a therapeutic outlet for genuine, deep feelings of emotional pain. "Stories about suffering mask real suffering, sometimes immediate and overwhelming, sometimes remembered, and sometimes only observed."[324]

> I didn't want hurt-comfort to be the heart of the community. I didn't want to accept the fact that pain was so pervasive in the lives of women, that it lay like a wash beneath all the creative efforts of a community they had made for themselves. But there it was, nonetheless, laid out so clearly I could no longer deny it. Shirley Maiewski wrote it without realizing it. Other fans wrote to work through their own problems of personal suffering.[325]

In his 1995 study of gender and *Trek* fiction, Jenkins disputed this theory that slash is built around a core of pain. "Despite good intentions, the focus in Bacon-Smith's account on pain and victimisation comes close to restoring the pathological stereotype of fans . . . Fandom constitutes a site of feminine strength, rather than weakness, as women confront and master cultural materials and learn to tell their own stories, both privately and collectively, through their poached materials."[326] Again, it is perhaps unsurprising that none of my respondents told me they wrote slash to work through personal trauma. Fee Folay gave the notion serious thought.

> I suppose some authors' fanfic and slashfic could be used as a form of therapy . . . however, I have never heard this given as a reason for writing H/C fanfic from those authors I have met or spoken to . . . certainly, in my case, I am not aware of using my fanfic to work out personal problems, even though much of what I have written falls into the H/C category.[327]

---

[323]Jenkins, *Textual Poachers,* op. cit. p. 191.

[324]Bacon-Smith, *Enterprising Women,* op. cit. p. 270.

[325]Ibid. pp. 269–270.

[326]Jenkins, "Gender and *Star Trek* Fan Fiction," in Tulloch and Jenkins, op. cit. p. 203.

[327]Fee Folay, op. cit.

Of course, Bacon-Smith's argument is that emotional pain is at the heart of H/C, and of the slash community in general, whether fan writers realize it or not; any number of denials on the part of my correspondents would not actually disprove her thesis. In any case, her long-term personal involvement with the *Trek* writing community cannot be compared with my relatively brief e-mail correspondences; Bacon-Smith's is a project on a different scale and with a different approach.

However, one thing these *Star Wars* fans would not dispute is that there is a supportive online slash community around the films. The neophyte can choose from a range of portals like the TPM Lair, Master and Apprentice,[328] Sith Chicks,[329] the Obi-Wan Torture Oasis,[330] and the Jedi Hurtaholics' Archive, each of which links to various web rings—ForceBoyz, Prequel Erotica, Pretty Boy Slash—and so provides a variety of different approaches for different tastes. There are tutorials on offer, such as the lighthearted "Fanfic Slasher's Field Guide To *Star Wars*"[331] and Minotaur's detailed Sex Tips For Slash Writers,[332] which includes guidelines on oral sex and diagrams of the male genitalia for female writers of homoerotic fiction.

Many sites feature discussion boards, even chat rooms, where writers can bounce ideas off one another, or lists of beta readers, who volunteer to proof and advise on work in progress. As Katie says, "It is definitely a supportive network. I have never gotten flamed for anything I've written, only constructive criticism. There is a webpage specifically for slash writers that has the whole timeline to *Star Wars*, as well as tips for writing the characters in a believable manner. I have made definite friends through slash."[333]

"Love and that sappy stuff"

Genfic—which as a broad category is used for anything non-slash, although it also shades into many distinctive subgenres—is often kept apart from the

---

[328]Master and Apprentice, www.sockiipress.org/ma/warn.html

[329]Sith Chicks, www.starwarschicks.com/sithchicks/tosith.html

[330]Obi-Wan Torture Oasis, members.tripod.com/~SlashGirls/toto/

[331]Kirby Crow, Fanfic Slasher's Field Guide to Star Wars, members.tripod.com/~SlashGirls/field_guide.html

[332]www.squidge.org/~minotaur/classic/eroc.html

[333]Katie, op. cit.

gay romance and erotica. However, the online communities are markedly similar. *Star Wars* Fanfix,[334] a huge archive of "mainstream" fan fiction, also offers a chat room, beta readers, a message board, and a guide to its various subdivisions from "Old Republic" stories through "Rise of the Emperor" to "New Republic," with a separate category for "Young Jedi Knights." While "Dr. Merlin's Guide to Fan fiction," which is linked under Author Resources from the Fanfix main page, is slightly tamer than Minotaur's sex tips, it serves a similar purpose as a guide and counsel for inexperienced writers.

All of my correspondents from genfic enthusiastically confirmed this sense of a support network. "It might mainly be composed of other fanficers, but it's there," wrote Lilith, a twenty-five-year-old engineering technologist from Utah. "People who read, people who write, people who beta read, and people who do all of the above support each other and encourage each other. It's really quite wonderful."[335] Another author, Kenobi Maul, pointed out that on TheForce.net, "the fan fiction board is one of the biggest, the second-biggest after Community, I believe," and suggested that "the many round robins"—stories that are passed from one person to another on an ever-growing discussion thread—"provide extra proof" of the positive, collaborative spirit.[336] Anne, a Canadian student and one of my youngest respondents at the age of thirteen, added, "This board has been supportive ever since I started to ask questions. I've made friendships with many other *SW* lovers from all over."[337]

In keeping with the earlier findings of Bacon-Smith and Jenkins, the *Star Wars* genfic community, in my experience, is also predominantly female. There is an interesting contrast here between the group of fans who elaborate on the primary texts through digital cinema or computer animation—who are almost entirely men—and the group of girls and women who perform an identical operation on the films, but through fiction. Both are creative departures from the original material, retaining some elements and inventing others; both combine individual work with group activity as filmmaking begins, of course, with a written script

---

[334]Star Wars Fanfix, www.fanfix.com/

[335]Lilith, personal e-mail (July 17, 2001).

[336]Kenobi Maul, no further details, personal e-mail (July 17, 2001).

[337]Anne, personal e-mail (July 17, 2001).

and fan fiction often involves collaboration, assisted rewrites, even joint authorship. Where they differ is in terms of genre. *Star Wars* fan film, as we shall see in the next chapter, is at this stage of its development frequently built around lightsaber duels and special effects trials. That there are more trailers than finished short movies circulating on TheForce.net's cinema forum supports the impression that these films are based far more on spectacle than on character development or narrative; many of them are simply rapid edits of hand-to-hand combat, laser fire, ships swooping toward planets or across cityscapes, interspersed with curt dialogue. *Star Wars* genfic, however—much like slash—is very much about relationships, emotions, and conversation rather than visual splendor and action.

To suggest that the first approach is intrinsically "masculine" while the second is "feminine" seems to buy into the most simplistic gender stereotypes; but it does seem to be indisputably the case that women do one thing with the films, and men do something entirely different. Moreover, it could be argued that the male filmmakers are keeping more within the original tone of the *Star Wars* primary texts, as well as working in the same form. The *Phantom Menace* trailer, for instance, involved a very similar mix of visual fireworks, sound bites, and teasing glimpses of saber clashes, whereas the female authors are expanding on emotional situations that the *Star Wars* movies hinted at or only briefly explored.

Jenkins suggests that "the practice of fan writing, the compulsion to expand speculations about characters and story events beyond textual boundaries, draws more heavily on the types of interpretive strategies common to the 'feminine' than to the 'masculine.' "[338] Drawing on Bacon-Smith, he goes on to suggest that fan fiction of this kind, with its shift from action to emotion, involves a "genre switch . . . the rereading/ rewriting of 'space opera' as an exotic type of romance."[339]

> Women, confronting a traditionally "masculine" "space opera," choose to read it instead as a type of women's fiction. In constructing their own stories about the series' characters, they turn frequently to the more familiar and comfortable models of the soap, the romance and the feminist coming-of-age novel for models of storytelling technique.[340]

---

[338]Jenkins, "*Star Trek* Rerun, Reread, Rewritten," op. cit. p. 179.
[339]Ibid. p. 186.
[340]Ibid. p. 187.

Again, while this theory seems based on a very traditional view of gendered interests, it nevertheless maps onto *Star Wars* genfic with surprising accuracy. While there is some writing on Fanfix that offers pretty straight action sequences of the space-dogfight variety, it is in the minority. As I'll discuss later, most of the stories archived are very much of the type described by Jenkins. Interestingly, a sixteen-year-old writer from Cleveland who describes herself as a tomboy and explicitly opposed herself to this kind of fiction confirmed my impressions of *Star Wars* genfic as a whole.

> You notice that most stories are about love and that sappy stuff. I don't write like that much but that is not the type of stuff that men would write about. They like the action sequences (So do I . . . oh well) and don't seem to go much deeper into the plot and women do and that is what fanfics are about. You can have action sequences but the story can't be a like a Jackie Chan movie. It needs some substance. And think about it, all those movies they call chick flicks (which I hate . . . I'm like a total tomboy) are all that sappy junk that have all this deep plot . . . [341]

"Out of all of the people that I know that write this stuff," confirms Anne, "around 80–90% are girls. It is quite weird, where as in *Star Wars* in general there are so many guys who like it."[342] Julie, a thirty-five-year-old research chemist from California, backs the view that the few male writers find their own niche: "Male fanfic authors seem to skew younger, and toward more 'action-hero' ensemble tales of fighter squadrons and mercenaries . . . it does seem to be the case that most *SW* fanfic is written by and for women."[343] Michelle, a thirty-year-old financial adviser from New Jersey, offered extremely similar conclusions: "I think most women tend to center on the relationship type of fics, while the male writers center on the military type of characters and their adventures. While each ventures into the opposite territory now and again, I find that it still holds."[344] Carol, thirty-four, a technical writer from California, says, "Men tend to want to talk strategy, war games, lightsaber battles and don't seem to talk much about the characters beyond the battle/war setting."[345]

---

[341]Owe-Me-One Perogi, personal e-mail (July 17, 2001).

[342]Anne, op. cit.

[343]Julie, personal e-mail (July 17, 2001).

[344]Michelle, personal e-mail (July 19, 2001).

[345]Carol Jackson, personal e-mail (July 20, 2001).

The one man who responded to my online surveys, a twenty-four-year-old automotive engineer from New Jersey named Dave Pontier, offered a poignant account of his own involvement. While Dave writes mainstream genfic, he finds himself in the same position as the women who write slash, unable to admit his involvement with the genre and even forced to make up cover stories. I want to quote this part of his reply in its entirety, because it is unusual and, I think, quite moving.

> I am not female, so I guess that puts me in the minority. It is at least 80% female. I thought I had been the only one to notice. I don't know if I can come up with a good reason for this that won't sound sexist, but I will try.
>
> I find it very hard to tell people what I do for a hobby. I will walk into work on Monday and they will ask me what I did all weekend. What I did was spend 16 hours writing fanfiction, but I suddenly feel embarrassed about it, and I make something up. I enjoyed *SW* as a kid. I enjoyed cartoons as a kid. I enjoyed Hardy Boys as a kid. I enjoyed GI Joe as a kid. The later three I've grown out of. Something inside me says I should grow out of *SW* too. I'm still amazed when I find out women old enough to be my mom are writing fanfiction. I feel like it is childish.
>
> I know that it isn't childish. I mean is Tom Clancy childish? What about Stephen King? Obviously not. There is no difference between what they do and what I do except they get paid. Writing fanfiction is no different than playing golf with absolutely no shot in the world of making the PGA. It's a hobby, yet for some reason, I still feel embarrassed to tell people. So I guess I did not answer the question: Why are there so many women writing fanfiction? But I did give a possible reason why there aren't more men. Though I hate to say it, we might be too macho to write.[346]

Dave had earlier volunteered that writing fan fiction was best compared to "playing with toys when you were a kid. I had action figures and matchbox cars and stuffed animals when I was younger, and I would set up very elaborate plots for my toys to play through. The evil stuffed gorilla was never easy to defeat, and it took all of my GI Joe and transformers, aided by several Lego creations, to take him down." Writing within the *Star Wars* universe was an adult version of this game, despite his qualms that

[346]Dave Pontier, personal e-mail (July 18, 2001).

the whole practice was shamefully childish, in that "all of the characters are out there for us to play with, and the playground is huge."[347]

Although Dave's perspective seemed specifically male in some ways, his metaphors of play and exploration were echoed by the female writers of genfic. "There's just so much room for growth and creativity without ever coming near the locations that the movies cover. In a setting as big as an entire galaxy there are so many stories that can be told, so many viewpoints that can be considered," said Lilith.[348] Anne suggested that writing within this vast narrative world was a form of wish fulfillment, a symbolic departure from the everyday. "With *Star Wars*, there are so many things you could write about. It revolves around a whole galaxy so there is a whole galaxy of people and things . . . There are times where I wished I lived there and not in my boring life."[349]

Significantly, the slash authors drew on similar images to explain the pleasures of working with the *Star Wars* framework. "I'm playing in my head as a child plays with dolls," wrote Kass. "I'm creating people and events and boy, it's fun, it's free and there are no calories."[350] Katie suggested that rather than improving on Lucas's vision of the text, she was "merely taking the characters in a different direction and placing them in a different world so I can play with them."[351] Kass's writing partner Kate compared fanfic to "creating dolly dioramas in the sandbox. One arranges the dolls in a tableau and then shares it with friends, looks on in satisfaction, then deconstructs it to create another."[352]

Although their chosen genres of fan fiction are usually kept apart and their feelings towards their own work are quite different, Kate's dolly diorama is really very similar to Dave's game with the GI Joe and the stuffed gorilla. Though Dave may not be moving Qui-Gon and Obi-Wan into sexual positions, he, like Kate, is involved in a very personal creative exploration of the possibilities offered by the fictional universe and shares the results online rather than letting them seep into his real life.

---

[347]Ibid.

[348]Lilith, op. cit.

[349]Anne, op. cit.

[350]Kass, op. cit.

[351]Katie, op. cit.

[352]Kate, quoted by Kass, op. cit.

As a final note, if genfic writers seem to lack the edge of lust for their protagonists that was present in the slash response, consider Lilith's explanation for the dominance of women in mainstream fan writing: "Most of the main *SW* movie characters are good looking men. Fanfic would probably attract a large number of females writing themselves into that world to associate with those characters."[353] Michelle's confession, which came at the end of her mail, also has some echoes of the slash writers' declarations earlier: "And ok, if I am going to be totally honest, most women ADORE Han Solo. So, if we can make Princess Leia fall in love with him over and over, that just makes us happy because most of us secretly like to believe we are her."

Krychick, Kass and Katie are, at least in part, arranging their Qui-Gon and Obi-Wan figures in bed together because they think both characters are hot; Michelle is writing romantic scenes with Han Solo, at least in part, because she fantasizes about being kissed by a scoundrel. The gender identification is different, the sex scenes may vary in their degrees of explicitness, but in many ways it seems there is not such a gulf between slash and its more socially acceptable counterpart.

"Partly Angst . . . definitely First-Time"

Slash takes its name from a punctuation mark, the oblique stroke that originally fell between Kirk and Spock in the fanzine stories based on the original *Star Trek*. The same stroke is used to identify all manner of pairings in romantic or sexual fan fiction: Q/O for Qui-Gon and Obi-Wan, but also Lu/H for Luke and Han, Le/La for Leia and Lando, Y/O for Yoda and an "Other", a guest star of some variety. Because the identical slash mark is used to denote Leia and Lando or Luke and Han, I would personally question whether "slash" should always and exclusively connote same-sex pairs; my argument, however, cut no ice with the writers I spoke to, who are clearly happy with the not quite logical convention as it currently stands.

Within slash, there are multiple subcategories. Different sites will break their archives down in different ways, but the key genres would include Alternate Universe (AU), Plot What Plot? (PWP), hurt/comfort (H/C), First Time, Angst, BDSM (bondage, dominance, sadomasochism),

[353]Lilith, op. cit.

Point of View, and Humor/Parody. AU includes crossover stories like Amy Fortuna's *Across the Great Divide,* where J.R.R. Tolkien's Aragorn meets Qui-Gon;[354] but there are also variants on the *Phantom Menace* narrative like Kass and Kate's *Hearts of Darkness,* in which Shmi and Anakin Skywalker are tortured and killed by Jabba;[355] and Maygra's *Faithless,* which is prefaced with the instructions, "Take the film, stop at the 'scene' and turn left. Qui-Gon and Obi-Wan are taken prisoner by Darth Maul." The "scene" here is the duel between the Jedi and Darth Maul; rather than continue with the *Phantom Menace* plot, Maygra makes a deliberate departure and admits "from that point forward it's all AU."[356]

We should note at this point that there is a great deal of hybridization within slash. *Hearts of Darkness* is also listed as angst and "darkfic", a category that indicates particularly graphic violence. *Across the Great Divide* comes with a warning that some might see it as humor, and a cross-listing as "action-adventure." Similarly, *L'Histoire D'Obi,* by Lilith Sedai, is featured on the Obi-Wan Torture Oasis alongside many other examples of BDSM slash—it includes vivid descriptions and illustrations of Obi-Wan chained, collared, and enslaved—but it is also ranked as "hurt/comfort . . . partly Angst . . . definitely First-Time."[357] Lilith even adds the categorization "Alternate Universe—well, if it makes you feel better to say so," implying that the AU subgenre may be seen as a safety valve to keep slashiness away from the official text of The *Phantom Menace.*

PWP fiction, sometimes known as smut, is simply an excuse for a sex scene. *Listen To The Force, Padawan,* by Kass, has Qui-Gon pleasuring Obi-Wan from a distance, using the Force in ways Lucas never intended.[359] The Emu's story *The Offering* has some semblance of a plot about Obi-Wan rescuing his master from a ritual sacrifice; as luck would have it, the religious sect in question can only use a virgin, so the younger Jedi has the duty of deflowering Qui-Gon before the ceremony can take place.[360] Point of View is a self-explanatory approach that can cross over with

---

[354]Archived at Master and Apprentice, op. cit.

[355]In chapter 11, "Medius," archived at the Phantom Menace Lair, op. cit.

[356]Archived at Maygra's Musings, 7parabian.com/Maygra/Musings/swtpm/

[357]Archived at The Obi-Wan Torture Oasis, op. cit.

[358]Thanks for the permission: analise@2cowherd.net

[359]Archived at the Phantom Menace Lair, op. cit.

[360]Archived at The Emu's Feathers, www.zip.com.au/~emu/offer.html

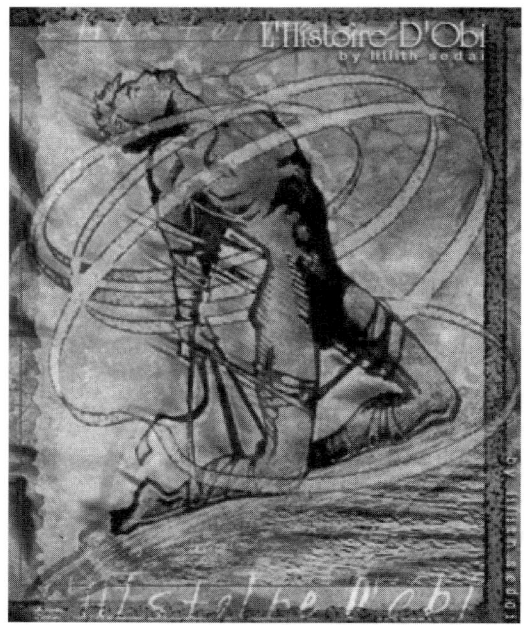

Analise's cover for *L'Histoire d'Obi*[358]

various other subgenres; Kirby Crow's *Stepping to Jonah* is an angst tale about Qui-Gon's realization that Obi-Wan feels more than platonic admiration for him, told elegantly in the first person.

> Now I awake on a winter morning and my joints ache. I gaze into the small mirror in my quarters and I see a grizzled, grey beard. I see small lines at the corners of my eyes. I see old, Obi Wan. I suppose the likelihood of your desiring me had faded to an impossibility in my mind, so that when it finally happened, it seemed like a miracle.[361]

The hurt/comfort formula also features in a great many stories about the two Jedi, but also appears in undiluted form at Katie's Hurtaholics' Archive. "Do you like to read stories about your favorite Jedi being tortured or put through hell? Well then, you have come to the right place. Welcome to the Jedi Hurtaholics' Archive, your one stop shop for Jedi torture and

[361] Archived at members.tripod.com/~SlashGirls/jonah1.html

angst." As this introduction suggests, hurt/comfort also involves angst, but the pain here is frequently of the physical kind in addition to emotional trauma. In Esmeralda's *Lost* and *Recovery,* for instance—the first story dealing with the requisite hurt, and the second with comfort—Obi-Wan is brutally raped and degraded on board a scavenger ship, and slowly comes to terms with the assault through Qui-Gon's support and love.[362] "It is an upsetting topic," Katie admitted in a mail, "but some people like to read about it—we may be 'sick and twisted' but we're not alone."[363]

Finally, while same-sex relationships between Jedi might not seem the most promising subject for a sitcom, there is a seam of humor writing in the *Star Wars* slash community, mainly centered around the Sith Academy website.[364] Run by Siubhan, with a front-page recommendation from Henry Jenkins himself, the Sith Academy is based around the premise that life on Coruscant, the Imperial planet, involves the same mundane annoyances as the daily grind in North America, and that Darth Sidious uses these irritations to train his apprentice in the Dark Side. The first story involved Darth Maul's learning to drive—"Let your hate flow through you, wait for a tiny opening in traffic, then pass her illegally and flip her off."[365] Subsequent tales involve Maul's struggling with an internet connection and discovering faked porn pictures of Queen Amidala,[366] trying out for the Kessel Spice Girls alongside his "twit neighbor" Obi-Wan,[367] and ordering a Tauntaun Hide Outfit on eBay's online auctions with the help of his feline apprentice.[368] Although the Sith Academy is still slash—once an episode had introduced the idea of Maul sleeping with Obi-Wan, the site had to separate nonsexual from R-rated stories—the tone is high camp rather than hard-core.

"Fantasies about his Master"

"A Matter of Control" is a short story by Analise, categorized as "Adventure, Angst."[369] While the preface warns that it contains "smut," this is an

[362]Archived at the Jedi Hurtaholics' Archive, op. cit.

[363]Katie, op. cit.

[364]The Sith Academy, www.siubhan.com/sithacademy

[365]Siubhan, *Life Lessons at the Sith Academy,* archived at The Sith Academy, op. cit.

[366]DarthCleo, *Darth Maul Gets Internet Access,* archived at The Sith Academy, op. cit.

[367]Kaelia and Teza, *Darth Maul vs. the Spice Girls,* archived at The Sith Academy, op. cit.

[368]Shadow, *Darth Maul vs eBay,* archived at The Sith Academy, op. cit.

extended narrative of fifty-five pages, not a PWP. As the story takes place "pre-*TPM,*" it is located within canon rather than in an alternate universe, and so implicitly agrees to follow certain rules and guidelines about character, chronology, and the fictional world of *Star Wars*. Qui-Gon cannot die in this story, for instance; Obi-Wan must be a Padawan learner, not a knight; lightsabers must work through science not magic; and communication is through comlinks and holograms, not telephones or TV. However, the time before the events of *Phantom Menace* is uncharted, so within a certain sketchy framework, Analise can fill it as she likes.

After a brief, enigmatic prologue from the point of view of a native alien, the story opens with Obi-Wan and Qui-Gon on an unfamiliar planet. This is, so far, entirely within canon: we assume that the two Jedi worked together on foreign missions before they took the job of settling the Trade Federation conflict at the start of *The Phantom Menace*. Obi-Wan is musing as we join them:

> Funny how so many of the worlds he managed to find himself on were swamp worlds. The ratio of, say, tropical paradise world to swamp, desert or rock worlds was considerably out of balance in his book. Either that, or the tropical beach planets never had the kind of trouble that called for the Jedi.[370]

This slightly arch internal commentary is in keeping with what we know of Kenobi from *The Phantom Menace*: the young man who asks his master wryly, "Why do I sense we've picked up another pathetic life form?" as Qui-Gon sets off to fetch Anakin from his mother's homestead.[371] The first paragraph also makes a clever swipe at Lucas's habit of setting his action on single-climate planets—Tatooine the desert, Dagobah the swamp, and, although Analise wouldn't have known this at the time, Geonosis, the rock planet from *Episode II*.

In fact, a slightly later passage explains that "planets like these"—that is, swamps—"had an enormous Force-Energy. It was one of the reason so many Jedi had come from these green, damp, slime-covered mud-balls,

---

[369]Analise, "A Matter of Control," archived at Analise's Nest, the-nesting-place.com/analise.html

[370]Ibid. p. 2.

[371]George Lucas, *The Phantom Menace: Illustrated Screenplay,* London: Ebury Press (1999).

Master Yoda himself included."[372] Given that no official source I can find mentions Dagobah as a source of "Force-Energy"—the term itself is slightly unusual—Analise is actively fleshing out the details of canon here, giving a reason for Yoda to be living on the planet in *Empire*. Her sidenote, corroborated to some extent by the EU stories about the cave being strong in the Dark Side, contributes to the mythology rather than stealing from it.

The story goes on to explain that the two Jedi are tracking one of their own, Linia Kwan, a "blue-skinned Noolan," who has disappeared in this quadrant. Noolan, to the best of my knowledge, is not a canonical *Star Wars* species, although there are enough blue-skinned races in the mythos—Sebulba's Twi'lek assistants in *Phantom Menace,* for instance—to make this entirely plausible. Searching for traces of Linia, Obi-Wan "gathered the currents of Force in the air . . . both of them could feel the vague currents in the Force that told them a Jedi had passed by, like eddies on a river."[373]

The idea of Jedi sensing presence in the Force is familiar from the primary texts. Obi-Wan reels with a disturbance in the Force when Alderaan is destroyed in *A New Hope*; Vader remarks, "The Force is strong with this one" as he closes in on Luke in the Death Star trench; Luke senses both Leia and Vader as he clings to the weather vane above Bespin in *Empire*. "Currents of Force" and the extended metaphor of water is a creative addition on Analise's part, although canonical writers use similar devices: Terry Brooks, in his *Phantom Menace* adaptation, has Qui-Gon "becoming one with the Force, disappearing into its flow, searching for Anakin."[374]

In the next paragraph Obi-Wan considers Linia's shared history with Qui-Gon—"he personally thought they had been lovers at some point."[375] In canon, there is no evidence of Jedi having romantic or sexual relationships, except for our knowledge that Anakin Skywalker fathers the twins Luke and Leia and that Luke clearly has a crush on his sister before he learns the truth about his parentage. An eighteen-year-old farmboy who, according to Lucas's stage direction, "looks longingly at the lovely,

---

[372]Analise, op. cit. p. 3.

[373]Ibid.

[374]Terry Brooks, *The Phantom Menace,* London: Century (1999) p. 171.

[375]Analise, op. cit.

little Princess" is not admiring her with objective detachment.[376] In a sense, then, we have already witnessed a canonical example of a Jedi, or Jedi-in-training, falling in love but having to repress his feelings because the relationship is forbidden.

Analise's suggestion that Obi-Wan sometimes found himself "indulging in pointless, selfish fantasies about his Master" may shock some fans, but there is nothing to actively contradict it within the primary texts, and indeed there is some supporting evidence to back up the possibility. We have no idea whether the Obi-Wan of the films is gay or straight, but we know he cares for Qui-Gon; at the same time, we know that training in the Force did not stop Luke from desiring someone inappropriate. At any rate, in Analise's narrative world—unlike that of Kirby Crow's *Stepping to Jonah*[377]—romance between Jedi is frowned upon, and Obi-Wan quickly clamps down on the rogue feelings.

> He turned slightly to see Qui-Gon frowning faintly. It made him want to lean over and smooth the lines out of his forehead.
> With his mouth.
> None of that. Perfect Padawan, remember?[378]

The reader's knowledge that Obi-Wan finds his master sexually attractive gives an edge to the dialogue between the two characters in *A Matter of Control,* but if we isolate it from this context, it is not markedly different from their exchanges within *The Phantom Menace*. This passage is from Analise's writing:

> Obi-Wan grinned mischievously at the older man, trying to lighten the mood.
>
> "Maybe she's taking a vacation on the sly?" he said archly, his brows rising. "What better place than this?" He gestured around the moss-choked swamp, alive with insect life. He was rewarded with a rare chuckle.
>
> He was scoring points right and left.
>
> "Indeed." His Master's voice hinted at more than a little amusement.[379]

---

[376]George Lucas, *Star Wars: A New Hope,* London: Faber and Faber (1977), p. 30.
[377]"Expected, it is, for a Padawan to desire his Master." Kirby Crow, op. cit. p. 3.
[378]Analise, op. cit. p. 5.
[379]Ibid. p. 6.

Although we are invited to read this as flirtation, compare it with this scene from a novelization by Terry Brooks. The Jedi have just escaped the battle droids of the Trade Federation and are about to stow away for passage to Naboo.

> Obi-Wan nodded . . . His mentor glanced at him. "Maybe we can hitch a ride with our friends down there."
> "It's the least they can do after the way they've treated us so far." Obi-Wan pursed his lips. "You were right about one thing, Master. The negotiations were short."
> Qui-Gon Jinn smiled and beckoned him ahead.[380]

The idea that Obi-Wan and Qui-Gon share playful interchanges, that Obi-Wan cracks the odd dry joke and earns a thin smile from his Master, is entirely present in the canonical text: the final two lines of the above conversation are taken directly from Lucas' script. What Analise adds is a way of seeing the exchanges, which by extension changes the way we see the Jedi relationship. Again, it could be argued that nothing in canon actually contradicts her reading, and that this backstory about Obi-Wan's repressed desire in fact gives the characters more depth and complexity than they possess in the original film. Fee Folay takes this view, explaining that she enjoyed watching *The Phantom Menace* far more once she had read a number of slash stories.

> This is especially true of Qui and Obi . . . they weren't very interesting because Lucas didn't give them room to blossom and flourish. Yet despite his best efforts to throttle their personalities at birth by smothering them between layers of Jedi serenity and stoicism, fan fiction authors everywhere recognized the true potential in this Master and Padawan pair. Across the world, fingers flew as authors granted Qui-Gon and Obi-Wan the breath of life. Thus were Qui-Gon and Obi-Wan reborn in the minds of thousands, as fully realized, emotionally complex characters.[381]

Of course, a great many fans would disagree with this perspective and argue that Qui-Gon and Obi-Wan were quite complex enough without

---

[380]Brooks, op. cit. p. 39.

[381]Fee Folay, op. cit.

the addition of a gay crush. Though her implications are quite dramatic, I hope I have demonstrated that in formal terms, all Analise does is build on the structure Lucas has donated to her. She fills out some details such as Dagobah's force potential, works with gaps in the history of the Jedi's previous missions, and keeps with surprising fidelity to the rules of the canon, to the extent that her writing is in some ways similar to Terry Brooks's official novelization. Surprising, not just because slash has a reputation of being shocking and radical, but because Analise states that she was "utterly and totally disappointed with *TPM*. I pretty much loathed it."[382] Her stories are an attempt to rehabilitate the *Phantom Menace* by salvaging its Jedi characters—"the only decent part of the movie"[383]—and creating stories she feels happier with. Again, then, it is curious that in many ways they closely parallel the official fictions.

"I suggest you remove your trousers"

Fanfix was created by a woman named Deborah, who discovered that there was no dedicated site for *Star Wars* fan fiction and decided to set up her own. She now runs the operation with a female friend called Gator. Like the slash sites, its archive is divided into categories; for the most part, though, its subgenres are based around chronology. "Old Republic" is pre-*Phantom Menace* stories; "Rise of the Emperor" stories take place between *Episode I* and the end of *Episode III,* which Deborah sensibly takes to mean "the birth of Luke and Leia." The interim between the prequel trilogy and original trilogy warrants its own category, while the events of *A New Hope, Empire,* and *Jedi* are termed "the Rebellion." Finally, "The New Republic" denotes "stories that take place after *Return of the Jedi,* except for those that center around the Solo children and their peers."[384] This last category is called "Young Jedi Knights."

These subdivisions, unlike those within slash—most of which indicate the nature of the romantic interaction and the type of sex within the story—suggest a strong degree of respect and fidelity for the canon within

---

[382]Analise, op. cit. p. 1, preface.

[383]Ibid.

[384]Fanfix, "Submissions," www.fanfix.com/submis/contents.htm

genfic. The key issue that Deborah wants clarified in her submission guidelines for Fanfix stories is how this new episode fits into the existing time frame; not is this gentle or rough sex, but is it pre- or post-Bespin? While *Phantom Menace* slash also has its basis in the primary text, it tends to use this source as a starting point and then take its characters and narrative in another direction, either before the events of the film or afterward, in which case the rules are shifted to let Qui-Gon escape his death at the hands of Darth Maul.

Genfic romance in particular has a closer relationship with the *Star Wars* canon than does slash. The explanation, of course, is that the official *Star Wars* canon gives authors far more grounds to imagine a sexual relationship between Han and Leia than it does for the equivalent relationship between Obi-Wan and Qui-Gon. While "evidence" can be found within *The Phantom Menace* for the latter reading—a close bond, some physical contact, occasional playful dialogue—we see Han and Leia kiss passionately and exchange declarations of love at several points within the original trilogy. Genfic romance stories of this kind, particularly in the "Rebellion" category, are then able to engage closely with the details of the original films, interweaving themselves between actual scenes from the movie rather than being obliged to take the characters out of the story into other situations where their behavior can be less inhibited.

Moreover, the relationship between Han and Leia is officially sanctioned by the lower-ranking texts in the canonical hierarchy; a score of EU novels from Zahn's trilogy onward supports the idea that the two characters move from flirtatious sparring to committed love, marriage, and bringing up a young family. The Fanfix categories acknowledge this EU extension of the original narrative with their mentions of the "New Republic," a Timothy Zahn invention, and the "Young Jedi Knights," a series of books for junior readers by Kevin J. Anderson and Rebecca Moesta.

Romance between Han and Leia within the "Rebellion" time frame therefore forms a major strand within the Fanfix archive. In fact, there is some common ground between the slash labeling system and its genfic counterpart in this respect, as the romance stories are rated "R" or "NC-17" when they contain explicitly sexual scenes, and many of the interludes between the Princess and Han Solo do go into graphic detail. *Also a Woman,* by Gina Leeds, for instance, has Leia pampering herself in the chambers that Lando offers her at Cloud City, then deciding she deserves a further treat. The story is entirely within canon until the line "almost without thought, Leia's hands rose to her breasts,"[385] and it departs still further from the official storyline when the Princess goes to Solo's room and announces, "I fear there may not be much time left to us, Captain. I suggest you remove your trousers."[386]

The idea that Leia and Han fall in love during *Empire* is entirely within the framework of the official text, and so the notion of their having hurried sex on Cloud City is in some ways plausible within canon. We know they sleep together at some point, because of their three children, but for this reader at least, the juxtaposition of "Leia" with "throaty groan of orgasm"[387] is nearly as shocking as the idea of a love scene between Obi-Wan and Qui-Gon. Again, an explicit story like Gina's, which is not uncommon on Fanfix—Dianora's *Need* imagines that Leia and Han consummated their relationship on Endor; Monique Robertson's *A Matter of Trust* has them becoming intimate on the journey to Bespin; and Angela Jade's *Lost Innocence* details Luke Skywalker's first sexual experience—blurs the boundaries between "mainstream" genfic and supposedly "deviant" slash.

Other categories within genfic deliberately move away from the official version of events, rather than working within it. "Crossover," in Fanfix's listing, means the same as AU in slash terms: the archive includes D. L. Slaten's *Archaeology in Hyperspace,* with Han Solo meeting Indiana Jones; Margo Witkowska's *DuneJedi,* combining the sf universes of George Lucas and Frank Herbert; NYC's *Jade the Jedi Slayer*, and numerous *Trek/Wars* hybrids. While the majority of the stories outside this distinct area of Fanfix engage closely with the canon, there are also scattered experiments in what-if speculation: What if the Rebellion lost at Endor?[388] What if Mara Jade had been on the sail barge[389] or in the throne room on the second Death Star?[390] What if Vader had recognized Leia's Force-sensitivity when he interrogated her?[391]

---

[385]Gina Leeds, *Also a Woman,* archived at Fanfix.com, www.fanfix.com/pages/rebel.htm, p. 1.
[386]Ibid. p. 2.
[387]Ibid. p. 4.
[388]Shadow, *The End of the Beginning,* archived at Fanfix, op. cit.
[389]Karrde289, *Harem Pants and Explosions,* archived at Fanfix, op. cit.
[390]Kelly Kanayama, *Return of the . . . Jade?,* archived at Fanfix, op. cit.
[391]Deanna Kramer, *Reverie,* archived at Fanfix, op. cit.

This subgenre really comes into its own on TheForce.net fiction boards, which due to their format—designed for discussions built out of posts and replies—are dominated by round-robin collaborative stories, with each new reader invited to add the next installment. Perhaps because of the sense that the board works as a space for experiment and instant feedback, as opposed to the online library that Fanfix provides, a great many of these stories are what-ifs, or crossovers, under the general banner AU. Raysa Skywalker asks, "What if Owen and Beru Lars Survived *ANH*?" and describes Uncle Owen reading a news holo about his nephew's destruction of the Empire. AnakinSkywalkerSct proposes a story where Anakin never became Darth Vader. Frostfyre's "Elementary, my dear Obi-Wan" takes the Jedi to Victorian London, while SiriGallia's "Good Day, Mr Kenobi" is a *Star Wars*–Jane Austen crossover:" 'I don't like that Frank Churchill person.' Obi-Wan stated suddenly."[392]

Just as the slash community has its campy, sitcom take on the *Phantom Menace* universe in Sith Academy, so Fanfix has its MSTreatments section. Based on the Comedy Central/Sci-Fi channel's *Mystery Science Theater,* in which Mike Nelson and two robots, Tom and Crow, are imprisoned on a spaceship watching bad old movies, this branch of the site involves one writer scathingly annotating another author's work, using Mike and the robots to banter and heckle as the story unfolds. In this example, Jet Vega is giving the MSTreatment to Toni Carlini's "Can't Run," a Leia genfic story from the "Rebellion" section of Fanfix. The original text is in italics.

> *The Death Star was destroyed, Vader and Palpatine . . .*
> Tom: Plapaltee who?
> Mike: the Emperor, Tom, you dolt . . .
> *. . . were dead, and the Alliance had taken a great step towards freeing the galaxy from the tyrannical iron grip of the Empire.*
> Crow: (as Leia): The tighter you squeeze, Tarkin, the more star systems will slip through your fingers . . .
> *Luke gazed at his friends, and . . . and at his sister.*
> Mike: Uh oh . . .
> Tom: That's a bad sign.

[392]SiriGallia, "Good Day, Mr Kenobi," posted at TheForce.net, op. cit. (July 12, 2001).

Crow: (snickering)
Mike: Crow, if you start . . .
Crow: Oh, chill out, Mike.
It would take him a while to accept that Leia was his sister after the feelings he had had towards her.
Tom: He's in love with his sister who already has a boyfriend. That's two . . .
Mike: Behold the righteous and holy Jedi.
He would have to accept her as his sister . . .
Crow: (starts to say something)
Mike: Crow, please spare us today . . .
. . . and she would have to learn to accept their father.
Bots: GASP![393]

Although Tom pretends not to know the Emperor's name, even this brief extract shows that the three characters are set up as *Star Wars* fans whose knowledge of the Luke-Leia backstory enables them to anticipate any ironic exchanges between the twins. What is most striking about this sequence is its similarity to my transcript in chapter 2—the ribald jokes, the quotation, the constant interruption and commentary on the text, the running gags and group interaction. The MSTreatments essentially give a piece of fanfic the same attention that a bunch of friends would give, say, *Empire Strikes Back,* with the distinction that Mike, Crow, and Tom have no love for the stories they are being forced to sit through. "It's a fanfic," says Mike at one point, "It wouldn't be a *Star Wars* fanfic if it weren't bad."[394]

The second notable point about this parody is that it challenges the idea of an entirely supportive fiction community. While the MSTreatments are funny, they constitute quite vicious swipes at another person's creative efforts, without that author's permission. It is worth remarking that the subjects of the MSTreatments are primarily sentimental and melodramatic Leia/Han romances, which the second author presumably sees as overblown and in need of deflation; as the caption at the top of the MSTreatments section announces, "If you can't laugh at yourself, then we certainly can!" On the other hand, it could be suggested that to write an

[393]Jet Vega, *The MSTreatment of Can't Run,* archived at Fanfix, op. cit., pp. 4–5.
[394]Ibid. p. 3.

extended, jokey commentary on a piece of genfic actually involves a detailed study of the original and a good deal of commitment. If you didn't have at least a grudging affection for "Can't Run," you would surely ignore it or just write a dismissive review, rather than craft a comedy skit around every other line of its prose. It may not seem much of a compliment, but if an author's story is picked up for MSTreatment, it is due for probably the closest reading it will ever receive.

"I'll unzip you to the waist"

"Escape to Yavin," by Marie, is a "Rebellion"-class story from the Fanfix archive. While it stands alone as a short episode, it is also the first part of a story sequence called "Han and Leia Missing Moments," each of which, Marie suggests, "fills in a blank left in the trilogy." Already, then, 'Escape to Yavin' locates itself snugly within canon; unlike *A Matter of Control,* it fits into a tight narrative gap and has to bridge or overlap with existing scenes in the film, in this case the flight from the Death Star on the Falcon and the arrival at the Rebel Base on Yavin IV.

For the author, this is a trickier maneuver than setting a story in the free space before a film takes place; there is only limited room to play around within the brief time frame Marie allows herself. In the original screenplay, Leia has just stormed out of the cockpit, having clashed with Han over her political ideals and his more basic need for financial reward. "I ain't in this for your revolution, and I'm not in it for you, Princess," Han drawls. Leia shoots back coldly, "If money is all that you love, then that's what you'll receive."[395] Marie's story, which opens with the Princess leaving "in a huff,"[396] has therefore set itself tighter parameters than those Analise enjoyed in 'A Matter of Control'. In addition to the obvious rules of chronology—Leia cannot know she is Vader's daughter, Luke has only just begun his training as a Jedi—there are more immediate issues to bear in mind, such as Leia's distrust towards Han following their argument and the fact that she was only recently a political prisoner in a Death Star cell.

---

[395]Lucas, *Star Wars: A New Hope,* op. cit. p. 121.

[396]Marie, "Escape to Yavin," archived at Fanfix, op. cit. p. 1.

The first paragraph leads on closely from the canonical text, giving us Leia's perspective on the quarrel. "What was it about that man? Irritating, irascible, what a mercenary."[397] Lucas's screenplay has Leia passing Luke in the corridor and remarking "your friend is quite a mercenary," so Marie's repetition of the word serves to join her original text onto the end of Lucas's "official" scene. Most readers of her story will remember the dialogue of *A New Hope* well enough for "mercenary" to have a ring of authenticity.

A brief, knowing digression follows as Leia assesses her appearance after her adventures on the Death Star, and finds herself grateful for the "ceremonial double buns" hairstyle, which "looked hideous, but held nicely." The cinnamon-rolls that Leia sports during *A New Hope* are one of the most recognizable visual icons from the film; to Lucas, this is just part of the film's design, no more in need of rationalization than the triangular grille of Vader's mouthpiece, and the authors of the official reference works also fail to provide any comment on the style. In what is perhaps a typically "feminine" fleshing-out, Marie explains the unflattering buns both in practical terms and as a custom from Leia's home planet of Alderaan. "Of course, she had turned eighteen yesterday, so technically she didn't have to wear this hair style anymore."[398] There must be some reason, Marie seems to suggest, that a young woman would sport hairy earmuffs; the style's low maintenance is not quite justification enough, so Marie makes it a ceremonial obligation for good measure.

This observation leads to a memory of her family's palace on Alderaan—"in a quiet, wooded glen overlooking cliffs and the sea"—and, when the Princess realizes her body is still numb and tingling, to the "shock treatments" on the Death Star.[399] Again, these aspects of Leia's story are omitted from official histories. We never see or hear anything of Alderaanian landscape or culture, and while *A New Hope* shows Leia facing the hypodermic needles of a hovering interrogation droid, there is no mention in the film, screenplay, or reference texts of any abuse she suffered on the Death Star. It is left to fan fiction to acknowledge that Leia has not only witnessed the destruction of her home planet, but survived the degradations of being held prisoner by a military enemy.

---

[397]Ibid.

[398]Ibid.

[399]Ibid.

Realizing, now that the drugs begin to wear off, that her physical injuries are worse than she thought, Leia goes back to Han to request first-aid supplies. Most of the treatments he offers—synthflesh, boneknitters—are Marie's invention, although a reference to "bacta gel," deliberately echoing the bacta tank that is used to heal Luke in *Empire Strikes Back,* once more gives her writing the weight of authenticity by linking it to established canon. The author working within this tight a margin, fitting her story between scenes of a film, has to keep touching base with the known *Star Wars* mythos in order to gain credibility for her creative departures.

The dialogue, too, has to match the tone of the previous scene in *A New Hope,* allowing the characters to show some grudging respect and affection while bearing in mind that they have only just met and spent most of their time so far sniping at each other. Without the excuse that this exchange happened years after the original trilogy, Marie has to capture the spirit of their relationship while taking the characters into uncharted territory both in terms of emotional complexity—suggesting subtleties to Leia's character that the film has no time to explore—and in terms of their actual situation. After assessing her physical state, Han tells Leia, "Take off your shirt," and immediately steps outside canon as defined by the films.

> When he turned around, supplies in hand, she was glaring at him.
> "I don't think so," was all she said.
> "Listen, your Highness, you don't have a thing I haven't seen before, and I don't really get off on injured women."
> Leia didn't budge . . .
> "Fine," he said, with measured patience. "Turn around, I'll unzip you to the waist, and I'll wrap you from the back, ok? Trust me."[400]

The image of Solo unzipping Leia's white dress is as radical in relation to the primary texts (that is, as unthinkable) as Obi-Wan caressing the forehead of Qui-Gon Jinn. Although the original trilogy is built around a heterosexual romantic triangle, this is a world where lovers do no more than kiss. However, the nature of this exchange is entirely in keeping with what we have seen during *A New Hope*. Leia's stubborn willfulness

[400]Ibid. p. 3.

has been evident in her encounters with Han, Luke, and the Imperials—when faced with Governor Tarkin's threat to execute her, she remarks "I'm surprised you had the courage to take the responsibility yourself"[401]—and we have witnessed Han's skills of persuasion in the cantina. "I've outrun Imperial starships, not the local bulk-cruisers, mind you. I'm talking about the big Corellian ships now. She's fast enough for you, old man."[402]

So Marie's description of Leia with her dress around her waist, "facing the wall, one arm protectively across her chest, the other pressing the wall for support" as Solo dresses her contusions, occupies a curious position in relation to the official texts. In some respects, it shows a respectful fidelity towards the canon, keeping within its bounds of chronology and character. We know that Leia and Solo eventually become a couple, so their pairing here is based on established truths within the mythos rather than the half-hidden clues from which slash builds its gay relationships.

On the other hand, by choosing to expand upon aspects of the film that Lucas skims over, "Escape to Yavin" adds to and deepens our perception of the characters, and at the same time steps out of those bounds. Although Marie chooses to explore a heterosexual relationship, her implication that Leia has suffered quite horrific torture at the hands of her father's troops, coupled with the physical intimacy between the brutalized teenage princess and Han Solo, goes far beyond what Lucas allows us to see in the official text. Marie's later implication that Leia becomes dependent on painkillers during the flight is particularly mordant given most fans' belief that Carrie Fisher was dealing with cocaine addiction in 1978 and was sedated during the *Holiday Special*.

Like Analise, Marie is bringing figures from a family action-adventure movie into a more adult and emotionally sophisticated world of prose fiction. The whole process is a game of speculation: what if we treated these characters as real people with repressed traumas, sexual urges, deep wounds? Like Analise, Marie retains a balance between canon and invention, keeping within the fences but playing her own game. Although its focus on male-female pairings rather than male-male qualifies it as socially acceptable genfic and excludes it from the more infamous realm of slash, I see no real difference between "Escape to Yavin" and "A Matter of Control."

---

[401]Lucas, op. cit. p. 68.
[402]Ibid. p. 57.

"Leia put on a dark bodysuit"

I have mentioned before that Steve Perry's novel *Shadows of the Empire* (1996) is an unusual case within the EU. It was not only supported by a range of action figures, a video game, audiobook, and original sound track album, but it was also the first spin-off novel to slot its narrative between the events of the existing trilogy, rather than before or after them. None of its events contradict canon, and none ever will be contradicted by canon—unlike, say, the backstory of Boba Fett in *Tales of the Bounty Hunters,* which is knocked out of service by Lucas's *Episode II*. Moreover, some of Perry's inventions, such as the Asp service droids, Dash Rendar's Outrider, and the swoop bikes, were given added credibility within the revamped Mos Eisley scenes of the *New Hope Special Edition*.

Shadows of the Empire is, therefore, as close to official canon as an EU novel can get. It is several places up the hierarchy from an online fan story like "Escape to Yavin," and in a different cultural league from "A Matter of Control," which has to be published under a pseudonym for fear of backlash and would be regarded with contempt by Lucasfilm and many fans outside the slash community. My argument is that *Shadows'* engagement with the primary text follows the same pattern of fidelity and experiment, borrowing and speculating, as did the other two stories.

The novel takes place between the end of *Empire* and start of *Return of the Jedi*. Like Marie, then, Perry has stepped into a rigidly fenced playground and improvises within the framework. Han Solo is out of action, so Perry brings in Dash Rendar, a smuggler "about Han's age" with "that same lazy, insolent look about him."[403] Just as it is impossible for the Rebels to retrieve Han during the course of the novel, so it is impossible for Luke to come face-to-face with Vader or indeed for the military state of play between Alliance and Empire to change before the start of *Return of the Jedi*. Perry therefore introduces a new villain in the form of Prince Xizor, alien mastermind of the criminal syndicate Black Sun, who wants Skywalker dead as part of a personal vendetta against Darth Vader.

The plot cleverly takes the heroes on a tangent away from the battle against the Empire, as Luke and his companions clash with Black Sun on

---

[403]Steve Perry, *Shadows of the Empire,* London: Bantam Books (1996), p. 59.

the city-planet of Coruscant. Vader and the Emperor are largely kept in the background and never come into direct contact with the Rebel characters. However, Perry is able to fill in a number of blanks, to use Marie's phrase: we discover that Luke built his new lightsaber in Obi-Wan's hut on Tatooine and that the bounty hunter disguise Leia wears in Jabba's court is given to her on Coruscant. Most deftly, Perry takes a throwaway line from *Return of the Jedi*—Mon Mothma's "Many Bothans died to bring us this information"—and invents a whole subplot about a Bothan spy net whose members help steal the plans for the second Death Star, thus providing a credible background for events in the subsequent film.

In this scene, Leia has arrived at the headquarters of Prince Xizor on a diplomatic mission. Xizor has the genetic ability to release sexual pheromones from his body, and they are already beginning to affect Leia as she explores her guest quarters. "What had that been all about? That—that emotional attraction that rolled over her like a tropical ocean breaker? . . . What she had felt, what she had wanted to do, well, that wasn't like her at all. Besides, she was in love with Han."[404] Perry is performing the same routine we saw in the fan fiction: touching base with established characterization as he guides it gradually in an unfamiliar direction. We have never seen Leia experience lust for another man, let alone an alien, but Perry's use of her voice is convincing in terms of the Leia we know—stubborn, determined—so we trust his departure from canon.

The next scene is also unusual in that it spends two pages indulging "feminine" details as Leia examines her quarters and in particular her new wardrobe. "This dress was a Melanani original, made of Loveti moth fibre, and for what it cost, you could buy a new landspeeder . . . My. Look at that. It was just her size."[405] It is the more leisurely pace of a novel compared to an action-adventure film that gives Perry room to discuss the domestic arrangements of the *Star Wars* characters. Nevertheless, his description of the Princess in the bathroom, "stretching out in a vat carved out of black marble full of steaming water so hot it turned your skin red,"[406] has more in common with Marie's attention to Leia's hairstyle than it does with anything in the films.

---

[404]Ibid. p. 243.
[405]Ibid. p. 245.
[406]Ibid. p. 248.

"Leia put on a dark bodysuit before she slipped into the nearly transparent green dress," Perry tells us in the next chapter.

> It was probably not the designer's intent that her choice of undergarments cancel out the see-through cloth, but she wasn't interested in letting Xizor look at that much of her. It felt vaguely decadent to be wearing several thousand credits' worth of clothes. She hadn't done that since she'd been a girl on Alderaan.
>
> She went into the 'fresher and looked into the mirror. She had made use of a well-stocked makeup drawer next to the looking-glass, just a touch, and managed to plait her hair and pin it up so it didn't resemble the nest of a crazed ship rat. At least it was clean.[407]

Again, Lucas's films, for all their background detail, have never given any thought to Leia's undergarments, to how much makeup she wears, or to the problems of keeping long hair presentable during interstellar conflicts. However, Perry's writing is prevented from floating off into formula romance territory through his handling of Leia's character: she is a pragmatist who knows others will judge her on her appearance even if it's the last thing on her mind. Perry has already justified her choice of dress in diplomatic terms, having her muse that "if [Xizor] found such things attractive, perhaps she should slip into one of the outfits and use that to her advantage,"[408] and the mention of her girlhood on Alderaan brings us back to the Leia of canon.

In the next scene she is meeting Xizor again and falling under the spell of his pheromones. The strong-willed Rebel leader we saw in the films is still there, but this is a different side of her, a variation on the Leia theme. "Uh, yes, we, that is to say, the Alliance, we have been considering such an alliance," she fumbles.[409] "Leia felt hot all of a sudden. She wished she hadn't worn the bodysuit. She had an urge to excuse herself, find a 'fresher, and take the undergarment off. The cloth of the dress would feel so good against her bare skin."[410] Before the scene is over, Xizor has pressed his advantage and kissed her, and she responds:

---

[407] Ibid. p. 253.
[408] Ibid. p. 246.
[409] Ibid. p. 257.
[410] Ibid. p. 258.

"Delicious. Amazing. She drank him in, enraptured by his touch. He pressed harder."[411]

What we witness in this scene is a familiar character from the primary text behaving as we have never seen in the canon: indulging herself physically, regarding herself as a woman and potential object of lust, and displaying undisguised sexual desire for an alien stranger. The scene is surprising, even shocking, yet it does not contradict anything we know from canon. Leia finds males attractive, she makes sacrifices to achieve political ends, she does not refuse beautiful dresses when they are offered to her on Bespin. In short, it does everything that "A Matter of Control" and "Escape to Yavin" do with the existing *Star Wars* films; it is no more or less ingenious in weaving its own inventions into the established framework, and, I would argue, no more or less radical in its implication that the characters have a sexual life that the films barely explore. However, I would probably be in the minority here. Lucasfilm, the majority of fan readers, and probably most fan writers would see the three stories as fundamentally different, which is why Perry's work is on sale in bookshops, Marie's is allowed, for now, to circulate freely online, and Analise's is under constant threat of censorship.

"An important part of our *Star Wars* family"

Confusing and sometimes conflicting stories circulate around Lucasfilm's relationship with fan fiction. Back in 1977, the company was astonished by the quantity of fan fiction generated by *Star Wars* and chose a reasonable middle ground between banning unauthorized use of its trademarks and letting the zines reproduce freely with no control. Jeff Yorio's online article *Web Wars* explains that "their solution . . . was to set up a no-fee licensing bureau that reviewed material and offered criticism about what might be considered copyright infringement. The ugliness of legal threats was avoided, and fans could still have their say."[412]

According to one of my correspondents, fan author Julie Lim, the situation in the late 1970s was cordial, even friendly; LFL used to request

---

[411]Ibid. p. 259.

[412]Philadelphia attorney Judith Gran, quoted in Jeff Yorio, *Web Wars*, www.houseofboo.simplenet.com/i970517/feature5.html (1997).

an archival copy of each fanzine and store them in its own library. "Early zines do carry reproduced thank-you notes from LFL for having sent them archival copies of previous issues; sometime in the early 80s, this stopped." According to urban legend, Julie goes on, "Lucas received a particularly interesting slash zine in which Vader raped Han, and was so revolted by this that he ordered the entire zine collection to be thrown out, occasioning a midnight dumpster dive to rescue them. I have no idea how much of this is true, but it makes a good story."[413] The collection was salvaged by fans and relocated in the "Corellian Archives" lending library in Santa Barbara: now online, it includes stories like Duncan's "Against the Sith" and Ellen Blair's "Falcon's Flight," dating back to 1978.[414]

Whatever the precise reason, it is generally understood that in the early 1980s, LFL cracked down on *Star Wars* zines and took a particularly hard line on works that violated the "family values" of the original films.[415] Henry Jenkins reproduces a letter sent out in 1981 by Maureen Garrett, director of the *Star Wars* fan club:

> Lucasfilm Ltd does own all rights to the *Star Wars* characters and we are going to insist upon no pornography. This may mean no fanzines if that measure is what is necessary to stop the few from darkening the reputation our company is so proud of . . . since all of the *Star Wars* saga is PG rated, any story those publishers do print should also be PG. Lucasfilm does not produce any X-Rated *Star Wars* episodes, so why should we be placed in a light where people think we do? . . . You don't own these characters and can't publish anything about them without our permission.[416]

Jenkins reports that the adult-oriented stories went underground to be distributed through a network of "special friends."[417] Fanzine editors expressed resistance to this clampdown—"Lucasfilm has said, in essence, 'this is what we see in the *Star Wars* films and we are telling you that this is what you will see' "[418]—but the threat was apparently effective, and

413 Julie Lim, personal e-mail (July 20, 2000).

414 The Fanzine Archives, members.aol.com/fzarchive/home/html

415 Jenkins, "*Star Trek* Rerun, Reread, Rewritten," op. cit. p. 177.

416 Maureen Garrett, quoted in Jenkins, ibid.

417 Ibid. p. 178.

418 C. A. Siebert, editorial from *Slaysu* fanzine quoted in Jenkins, ibid.

webmistresses twenty years later still recall the 1981 censorship as a cautionary tale of what could befall their online slash archives. "Lucasfilm actively pursued publishers of adult fanfic in the 70s [sic], so many of us are a little skittish that he might do the same nowadays if the spirit so moved him," confessed Siubhan, head of the Sith Academy.[419]

According to Chyren's account, the rise in licensed EU novels was a deliberate move to prevent slash fiction. Unless he counts the isolated Lando Calrissian and Han Solo spin-off books published between 1979 and 1983,[420] Chyren must be dating the start of the EU to 1991, the date of Zahn's *Heir to the Empire*. None of these dates really work with the argument that LFL's authorized stories preempted fan fiction or prevented slash. Indeed, the mid-1990s saw fan fiction migrate, albeit not wholesale, from print zines to the internet, where it was immediately able to reach a global audience.

During the late 1990s, LFL seemed largely to turn a blind eye to amateur writing as long as it kept within their 1981 recommendations. The knowledge that they could enforce censorship if they chose, however, seems to have encouraged self-regulation on the part of fan writers and allowed Lucasfilm to take a big-hearted stance. In the view of a Wired.com article from 1997, "Lucasfilm is one particularly reasonable outfit . . . "

> The company simply put up their own official site to counter—and overshadow—the unofficial ones. As Lucasfilm spokesperson Jeanne Cole puts it, "What can you do? How can you control it? As we look at it, we appreciate the fans, and what would we do without them? If we anger them, what's the point?"[421]

This generous and perhaps disingenuous official statement may constitute an exercise in damage control after what Julie Lim describes as "a publicity blunder in dealing with fan websites."[422] Jeanne Cole's conciliatory position dates from 1997; the following LFL notice, posted with reference to a

---

[419]Siubhan, no further details, personal e-mail (July 20, 2001).

[420]Such as Brian Daley's *Han Solo at Star's End,* New York: Del Rey (1979); and L. Neil Smith's *Lando Calrissian and the Mindharp of Sharu,* New York: Del Rey (1983).

[421]Janelle Brown, "Fan fiction on the Line," Wired.com, www.wired.com/news/topstories/0,1287,5934,00.html (August 11, 1997).

[422]Lim, op. cit.

suppressed *Star Wars* fan site, suggests that the company took a firmer line in 1996.

> There has been quite a bit of confusion on the internet regarding Lucasfilm's position on Jason Ruspini's web page. Please let us clarify. First and foremost, we are not "shutting down" Jason's website. We are sorry for any confusion that may have emerged from any miscommunication on our part.
>
> Lucasfilm appreciates *Star Wars* fans' support and we want you to be able to communicate with one another. Your energy and enthusiasm makes you an important part of our *Star Wars* family. As you can understand, it is important, as well, for Lucasfilm to protect the *Star Wars* copyrights and trademarks. Since the internet is growing so fast, we are in the process of developing guidelines for how we can enhance the ability of *Star Wars* fans to communicate with each other without infringing on *Star Wars* copyrights and trademarks and we hope to make these guidelines available in the near future.
>
> As we prepare for the *Star Wars Trilogy Special Edition* which will be coming to theatres next year and as we begin pre-production on the upcoming "prequels," we are now entering an exciting new *Star Wars* era. Many thanks for your support and interest.[423]

For all the talk of a *Star Wars* family, this notice makes it clear that Lucas is still the daddy who can choose to ignore fan activity if it behaves and crush it when it crosses a boundary. The company's power to overlook or to threaten is demonstrated by a further example from 1997. Marc Hedlund, director of LFL's internet development, was reported in that year as confirming the 1981 policy that "the company tolerates the publication of fan fiction, so long as the stories are not for commercial gain and don't sully the 'family' image of the *Star Wars* characters."[424]

If this were the case, it is not obvious why the administrators of the Usenet discussion board rec.arts.sf.starwars refused permission in the same year for a new subgroup dedicated to fan fiction, on the grounds that "the traffic itself would be illegal." Jenkins comments that

---

[423]Web Site Notice, archived at www.geocities.com/jjehrnwa/news/lucas_statement.htm

[424]Marc Hedlund, quoted in Jennifer Granick, "Scotty, Beam Down the Lawyers!," Wired.com, www.wired.com/news/topstories/0,1287,7564,00.html (October 9, 1997).

> Many believe they made this decision based on a series of cease and desist letters issued by Lucasfilm attorneys aimed at shutting down fan-related *Star Wars* websites or blocking the circulation of fan fiction about the films. Throughout the years, Lucasfilm has been one of the most aggressive corporate groups in trying to halt fan culture production.[425]

In this case, LFL didn't even have to show its muscle: the administrators' fear of what could happen was enough to make them quash the fan fiction group themselves.

Lucasfilm's current attitude toward genfic and slash is far from clear. Fully aware of the threat LFL poses to their online existence, slash communities are attempting to lie low, hoping that the company has better things to do than search for archives of Q/O romance. "From what I can tell, their party line is that they wish we wouldn't write it, but I haven't heard of them actually cracking down on any sites or zines. I'm sure the news would spread around the internet fairly quickly if it started happening," Siubhan explains. "We've just been careful not to jump around, wave our arms, and say, 'Hey, lookie what we're doing, George!' "[426] A recent article at Slate.com suggests that the company still makes a distinction between the two forms of fan fiction: "Lucasfilm has suppressed Skywalker slash on the grounds that it harms the *Star Wars* image, but it allows PG-rated fanfic."[427]

However, Lucasfilm's decision in 2000 to offer fans web space in the virtual backyard of its official site, starwars.com, suggests a new strategy toward fan activity of all kinds. On the face of it, this is a generous offer: sixteen megabytes to play with, "dynamic content" borrowed from the main site, and a corporate-sounding URL at fan.starwars.com. The promotion for this scheme is very much in keeping with the notion of the *Star Wars* family, with LFL full of pride for its children's projects and wanting to help them out. "To encourage the on-going excitement, creativity and interaction of our dedicated fans in the online *Star Wars* community, Lucas Online is pleased to offer for the first time an official

---

[425]Jenkins, "The Poachers and the Stormtroopers," online at web.mit.edu/21fms/www/faculty/henry3/pub/stormtroopers.htm (1998), p. 2.

[426]Siubhan, op. cit.

[427]David Plotz, "Luke Skywalker is Gay?", Slate.com, slate.msn.com/Features/fanfic/fanfic.asp (April 14, 2000).

home for fans to celebrate their love of *Star Wars* on the World Wide Web."[428]

"I thought that was a very slick move on their part," admitted Siubhan. "At first, I thought about getting a Sith Academy address there, but then I saw the ToS and thought better about it."[429] Section 8.6 of the fan.starwars.com terms of service states that "you hereby grant to us the right to exercise all intellectual property rights, in any media now known or not currently known, with respect to any content you place on your Homestead-powered website."[430] In other words, everything you put on there belongs to LFL. Lucasfilm had cleverly shifted from repression to containment, drawing fan production into its own fence-ringed area where it could confiscate anything it didn't like—and potentially poach anything it did like.

There was an immediate backlash to the fan sites program, led by fanfic author Elizabeth Durack from her protest site at miscellanies.net. The fan creation of "derivative works" had always, according to Durack, been a legal gray area whereby amateur fiction or art that was not made for profit and that included a disclaimer indicating Lucasfilm's ownership could qualify as "fair use." By offering to transfer this fan work onto LFL home ground, the company immediately translates this ambiguity into black and white. Moreover, as Durack points out, the fan pages scheme solves at a stroke any potential problems of bad publicity. Lucasfilm could seek out and destroy objectionable fan sites with cease and desist letters, but this tactic risks making it look like a tyrannical father; the offer of official webspace puts the company in the role of a kindly uncle.

> The web has been a heck of a hassle for them, as fans cheerfully (and for the most part, innocently) trample all over their precious copyrights and trademarks, and it's bad PR every time they send nasty-grams to webmasters, as they do with some frequency. How much easier would life be for Lucasfilm's licensing folks if all they had to do to shut down an infringing website was pull the plug, without even having to explain?

---

[428]Quoted by Elizabeth Durack, "Fan.Starwars.con," www.qui-gonline.org/features/fanstarwarscon.htm

[429]Siubhan, op. cit.

[430]Terms of Service, quoted by Elizabeth Durack, Starwars.com Fan Home pages Protest Site, www.miscellanies.net/

> Lots. That's the genius of Lucasfilm offering fans web space—it lets them both look amazingly generous and be even more controlling than before (free house in prestigious neighborhood! But after you move in, they tell you what you can and can't do in it and they own all your stuff—and can kick you out without notice).[431]

Durack's campaign earned mention on a range of sites including Slate.com, Slashdot.org, the *Star Wars* zine Echo Station, and TheForce.net. The protest went to the heart of Jenkins' argument about corporate trademarks becoming folk culture. "Legally, it's theirs," said Durack. "But emotionally we feel we have a right to participate in the story."[432] She sees herself not as a rebel or a traitor to Lucas's myth, but a loyalist.[433] "It's bigger than George, and too-strong loyalties may be misplaced. My first loyalty as a fan is to other fans."

> George Lucas will always have sole financial rights to profit from his *Star Wars*. But what of other people's *Star Wars*-es? What of the tens of thousands of pieces of *Star Wars* fanfic which constitute auxiliary myths to complement George's central one? I believe that, in all fairness, they should have the right to share their "product" with the world—yes, even if it competes with George's (which fanfic does only marginally, if at all).[434]

Durack's plea encourages a vision of *Star Wars* as popular myth, belonging to its fans as much as it does to Lucas. While it clearly earned her considerable support, it is important to record that her campaign also met with some dissent. Fern, webmistress of Vader's Mask, explains on her site why she moved it to the fan.starwars.com address with reference to very similar notions of storytelling and the evolution of cultural legends. "Fanfic, as far as I can tell, is part of the natural life of a story. That's how the old myths grew, as a bard swept through town, then left the villagers with new tales to play with and expand to suit their own needs." However, she stresses her respect for LFL's ownership and trusts the company not to steal her own creations. "In the end, they hold the cards,

---

[431]Durack, "Fan.starwars.con," op. cit.

[432]Durack, Starwars.com Fan Home Pages Protest Site, op. cit.

[433]The term is also used by Jenkins in "*Star Trek* Rerun, Reread, Rewritten," op. cit., p. 174.

[434]Durack, "Fan.starwars.con," op. cit.

and I can think of worse hands for them to be in. The fact is, I've been playing with their characters without paying a licensing fee; I have no right to tell them not to play with mine."[435]

Similarly, James Karko's article at Echo Station offered a counterargument to Durack's essay, accepting LFL's ownership of *Star Wars* with grace, even gratitude. His response entertains the idea that *Star Wars* could become popular myth, owned by the fan community, but proposes that this shift is a long way off.

> Lucasfilm does own *Star Wars*, and will continue to do so for quite some time. Maybe 20-30 years from now they will allow it to fall into the public domain, but until then they have the legal and ethical right to do as they see fit with the property . . . should we be attacking Lucasfilm for protecting their interests, or praising them for doing more than any other company in history to include and support their fans?[436]

Karko provides instances of situations where LFL might justifiably exercise its right to censorship: one of them is "when they find content objectionable and damaging to the *Star Wars* name (an example would be a pornographic fanfic using the *Star Wars* characters)." We are, in a sense, back where we started, with a reminder that, to many fans, slash is porn—"only an idiot" would use the fan pages for this purpose, according to Karko—and that there is rarely such a thing as consensus within the broad *Star Wars* fan community.

Henry Jenkins' 1998 article "The Poachers and the Stormtroopers" argues that LFL sees fan fiction very differently to fan film, and contrasts the cease and desist threats sent to fiction websites with Lucas's enthusiasm for Kevin Rubio's amateur film *Troops*.[437] The next chapter examines *Star Wars* fan film, asking—as I did with the various stories cited—what relation it has to the primary texts, and considering whether Lucasfilm really makes such a marked distinction between the two forms of fan production.

---

[435]Fern, "Why I Moved . . . ", Vader's Mask, fan.starwars.com/vadersmask/whymove.html

[436]James Karko, "In Defense of Starwars.com," Echo Station, www.echostation.com/editorials/defendsw.htm (March 24, 2000).

[437]Jenkins, "The Poachers and the Stormtroopers," op. cit., p. 2.

8

FAN FILM

> Like Kurosawa, I make mad films
> Okay, I don't make films
> But if I did they'd have a Samurai
> Like Skywalker, gotta big hunch
> Hey, that's my lunch
> Yoda's a really, really old guy
>
> —Barenaked Ladies,
> "One Week" (1997)

On one level, fan film is simply a branch of fan fiction and has a very similar relationship to the primary texts: a creative departure that stays within a recognizable framework, an experiment that sticks to accepted rules, a filling in of gaps within the official narrative. In the words of Nathan Butler, cowriter of the fan film *Prelude to Hope,* "we all fall under the heading 'fan fiction', whether it is in written or video form." Fan filmmakers and prose writers alike have the opportunity to send their finished work to an online library like Fanfix or TFN Theater where it will reach a potentially massive global audience; both have recourse, through these sites' discussion boards, to a supportive network of peers and mentors. "I do feel that fan filmmakers are part of a cooperative and supportive community," comments Nathan, twenty, from Indiana. "We pool ideas, and often pool talents, bringing people in on projects to allow for more expertise. We often make quite a few friends."[438] While slash writers might ask for tips on Qui-Gon characterization or how to describe a certain type of kiss, fan filmmakers offer online tutorials on rotoscoping lightsabers onto an Adobe Premiere Filmstrip,[439] share extraction utilities to strip authentic sound effects from *Star Wars* computer games,[440] and advise on lighting CGI models of Star Destroyers.[441]

However, as Nathan goes on to say, there are significant differences between the two forms. "Fan films, in my opinion, can be the most difficult of the types, simply because in the written forms of fan fiction, you are only restrained by your imagination. In fan films, unless you have a lot of backing and a great crew, your scope is limited by what you can or cannot do on film and in post production."[442] Making a fan film is a group project rather than an individual venture, and narratives that would have been possible in prose fiction may be ruled out of a film by budget and practicality. On a very simple level, while the majority of fan stories, both slash and genfic, are about the main characters from the *Star Wars* saga, most fan films invent new protagonists or occasionally draw on the EU; dressing your actors in Jedi costume or stormtrooper armor is straightforward enough, but very few filmmakers will have friends who look like Han Solo or Queen Amidala.

As I noted in the previous chapter, there is a marked gender distinction between the fan fiction and fan film communities, and it extends through the creative work in surprisingly traditional, even stereotypical ways; the online tutorials at TFN Theater are almost entirely about technical issues such as CGI modeling, fight choreography, and title crawls, with only a handful addressing questions of story structure and reminding the budding director that there should be more to a film than double-bladed lightsabers. This advice comes too late for many of the short movies already hosted on TFN Theater, which essentially serve as a showcase for martial arts

---

[438]Nathan Butler, personal e-mail (July 3, 2000).

[439]Darel Finley, "Rotoscoping Lightsabers," www.theforce.net/theater/software/premiere/rotoscoping/rotoscoping_finley.shtml

[440]Eric Desormeaux et al., "Sound Effects," theforce.net/theater/postproduction/soundfx/

[441]Darryl Roman, "Lighting in CGI Scenes," www.theforce.net/theater/software/3dstudiomax/romanlighting_tutorial/index.shtml

[442]Butler, op. cit.

technique and saber effects with a few lines of dialogue tacked on; the fact that it needs to be included at all is testament to the mentality behind fan film as opposed to fiction. It would be ludicrous for a site like Master and Apprentice to tell amateur writers that "the kinds of characters you will have depend on the story . . . an Alliance battle might have Rebel soldiers, a Sergeant, some pilots, and Imperials,"[443] but to the TFN community these concerns might be far less important than access to a blue screen and an authentic-looking blaster prop.

Finally, while slash attempts to avoid detection by LFL and genfic circulates within its own networks but rarely breaks through to the world outside its community except in academic studies, fan film actively tries to get itself noticed. Amateur filmmakers increasingly see their projects as calling cards and potential springboards to careers in the movie industry following the success of *Troops,* the fan movie that led its director Kevin Rubio to a professional gig writing *Star Wars* comics; *George Lucas in Love,* which was praised by Lucas himself and is currently being sold on commercial video through Amazon; and *Bounty Trail,* which earned director Justin Dix a place on the *Episode II* team operating R2-D2. Fan efforts like *Troops,* the fake *Episode II* trailer by the "Anonymous Director," and the equally mysterious *Phantom Edit,* which aimed to whittle *Phantom Menace* into something tighter and more sophisticated, were discussed not just on *Star Wars* community sites but on general news boards like Popcorn.co.uk, Zap2it.com, and E!On-line. This kind of publicity quickly attracts attention from studios who could use a promising newcomer, and the Anonymous Director was being courted by production houses shortly after his trailer's release on TFN.

Lucasfilm's attitude toward fan film seems far more lenient than its approach to slash and genfic. The Anonymous Director concludes that LFL's response to his project was "Supportive. In a roundabout way. I hear they enjoy it and appreciate fan efforts such as this—as long as I don't profit by it."[444] Twenty-three-year-old student, writer, and amateur filmmaker Dan Sawyer, of San Francisco, suggests that "the semi-official

[443]Brian Trenor, "*Star Wars* Fan Films for Dummies," www.theforce.net/theater/preproduction/brian_ tutorial/index.shtml

[444]D. W. Dunphy, interview with the Anonymous Director, *Film-411,* www.film-411.com/reviews/interviews/episode2.html

word from Lucasfilm is one of considerable tolerance. The implied policy is that if no money is made, and no original actors or video from the films are used, then it's pretty open. Lucas himself has confessed to enjoying *Troops* and *Lucas in Love*."[445] Other fan directors confirm this impression. A twenty-year-old music student from Sweden says, "As far as I know, no one has ever received any messages whatsoever from Lucasfilm. The only thing they have said is that they will not do anything to stop fan film making as long as there is no profit involved."[446] "I think they encourage this kind of filmmaking, just as long as there is no profit involved. I've never heard of a cease and desist order being issued for a fan filmmaker," adds Jason, a twenty-year-old communications student from New York City.[447] Henry Jenkins, as mentioned at the end of the previous chapter, directly contrasts the censoring of a fan fiction newsgroup with the acclaim for Rubio's film *Troops*: " . . . he is fielding offers from companies like Dreamworks to finance his first feature film. George Lucas . . . has announced his own enthusiasm for the short."[448] Meanwhile, of course, the Usenet bosses were refusing to run a *Star Wars* fanfic group for fear of receiving cease and desist letters; in this respect, "Lucasfilm has been one of the most aggressive corporate groups in trying to halt fan cultural production."[449]

From Jenkins' account, and indeed from all the reports mentioned, it would seem that Lucas smiles on young filmmakers whom he considers to be following directly in his footsteps and paying tribute to his creation, while stomping on writers who dare to explore and expand upon his characters. If this were true, there would seem to be some logic behind the distinction; Lucas, like the fans at TFN Theater, has often been accused of preferring spectacle and eye-candy to human interaction and naturalistic dialogue. From the evidence of the *Star Wars* saga itself, we might expect him to identify more with what we can crudely label the "boy" approach, based on technical achievement with small budgets, fast-paced action and visual splendor, rather than with the "girl" approach of genfic and slash, which uses the stories to examine relationship dynamics and gender roles.[450]

---

[445]Dan Sawyer, personal e-mail (July 4, 2000).
[446]Niklas Oveborn, personal e-mail (July 9, 2000).
[447]Jason Colman, personal e-mail (July 4, 2000).
[448]Jenkins, "The Poachers and the Stormtroopers," op. cit., p. 2.
[449]Ibid.

However, this perspective is not entirely accurate. First, it is not true that fan films escape LFL censorship if they are not intended to make a profit. At least one fan project, Peter Mether's *The Dark Redemption*—which incorporated brief clips from *Return of the Jedi* and featured Peter Sumner, an actor from *A New Hope*—has received a cease and desist and had its dedicated website closed down. Aware of the project from its development stage, Lucasfilm stood back while the movie was being produced for an Australian film competition and allowed its single screening at the US Dragon*Con convention before stepping in. According to one article, "LFL has made it painfully clear that they do not want this film distributed in any manner,"[451] and TFN Theater's continued hosting of the movie actively contravenes the company's wishes. Similarly, videotapes of *The Phantom Edit* were permitted to circulate for a while, within modest limits, before LFL put its foot down and began threatening legal action. Spokeswoman Jeanne Cole once more voiced Lucasfilm's official line that fans are encouraged to play around but only up to a point. "You give the warning. You make the rules really clear. And if they continue to break them, then there are consequences. So that's what we're trying to do here—make it really clear."[452]

Secondly, in addition to these crackdowns on films that directly infringe copyright, the indications are that LFL is now trying the "official fan sites" containment maneuver on homemade *Star Wars* cinema as well as fiction. The November 2000 announcement that Atomfilms.com would host *Star Wars* fan films, allowing its contributors a library of official sound effects and a share in any profit, surely constitutes a further move to rein in fan activity and keep it on corporate ground. As with the Homestead fan sites mentioned in chapter 7, the offer to provide a platform for fan production seems genuine and generous, but again, there is a sting: only "documentaries and parodies" are endorsed. According to a news report, "No attempts

---

[450]We should note, though, that the two films Lucas is known to have approved, *Troops* and *George Lucas in Love,* in fact rely on witty dialogue, wry characterization, and intelligent play with narrative, rather than selling themselves through special effects.

[451]David R. Phillips, "It's Not Wise to Upset a Wookiee," Echo Station, www.echostation.com/features/lfl_wookiee.htm (September 1, 1999).

[452]Jeanne Cole, quoted in Andrew Rodgers, "Lucas Unhappy about *Phantom Edit* Distribution," www.zap2it.com/movies/news/story/0,1259,---7033,00.html (June 14, 2001).

to expand on the *Star Wars* universe will be accepted, ensuring that George Lucas and the company he founded remain the only sources for canonical information and stories about *Star Wars* and its characters."[453] Although the Atomfilms definition of acceptability would include both *Troops* and *George Lucas in Love,* most of the films mentioned in the following pages fall outside these bounds. I shall take up these issues again, but for the moment we should bear in mind that the filmmakers whose work is discussed here may be living, creatively speaking, on borrowed time.

"Before the saga of the Skywalkers . . . "

Like fan fiction, fan films fall into various subgenres. The TFN Theater site categorizes its offerings to some extent, distinguishing "Animation" from "Short Film," "Music Video," "Coming Soon"—which indicates a trailer, rather than the full movie—and "FX Project." I am using these terms to structure my discussion here, and breaking "Short Film" down further to distinguish those that expand on or slot into the existing *Star Wars* narrative, such as *The Dark Redemption,* from crossovers that offer a hybrid between, say, *Star Wars* and *The Matrix*.

The FX Project is the PWP of fan film; the sketchy plot is just an excuse for the creator to get his or her audience excited for a minute or two. These short bursts of action serve two main purposes: producing them is a technical exercise that allows directors to polish their skills or test specific effects; and screening them on the TFN Theater site means they work either as a teaser for a specific forthcoming project or more generally as a vivid display of the director's abilities. Scott Layman says of his *Attack Droids,* an FX short of forty seconds that he filmed entirely alone in a forest, "This was one of many tests I did for a movie I was planning to make called *Star Wars: Jedi Knights*. This movie was going to be about an hour long . . . I did all of my pre-production, but stopped because I couldn't find time to make it."[454]

---

[453]Anon. "*Star Wars* fan films get official home," www.space.com/sciencefiction/movies/starwars_fan_films_001107.html

[454]Scott Layman, "A Word from the Director," theforce.net/theater/fxprojects/attackdroids/index.shtml

Scott Layman's *Attack Droids*

Because it was originally part of a projected longer movie, *Attack Droids* is given some context in terms of narrative and plot. Scott notes that the scene takes place during the extermination of the Jedi Knights and Vader's rise to power; the Jedi protagonist and his forest planet are both named, and the design for the droids themselves takes account of the *Star Wars* chronology. "The style I used for the look of the droid was very Darth Vaderish because the time period the movie would take place was about the time Vader got his mask."[455]

Even a very short piece like this, then, draws on the existing mythos and adapts to fit within the framework laid out by the primary texts. If Scott's film had been set during the period of *The Phantom Menace,* the design of the droids would be incongruous as they would predate Vader's first appearance. Similarly, while Dave Macomber and Mark Thomas's *Duel* is little more than a ninety-second rehearsal for their later film *Duality*—the plot description runs, "As a Jedi crash lands on a desert planet, he encounters an evil Dark Lord of the Sith. Mayhem follows!"[456]—it nevertheless takes care to follow the existing visual tropes and conventions of *Star Wars*. The Jedi character is dressed exactly like Luke in *A New Hope,* while the Sith wears a dark hood like Darth Maul; the desert setting

---

[455]Ibid.

[456]Duel page, www.theforce.net/theater/shortfilms/duel/index.shtml

Dave Macomber as the Sith in *Duel*

and acrobatic fight style are very reminiscent of Qui-Gon's conflict with Maul on Tatooine.

Although the film has only one line of dialogue before "mayhem follows"—"My landing here was no accident . . . inform the Council their assumptions were correct"—the Jedi's observation locates us in the prequel era through the reference to the Jedi Council and consciously echoes Qui-Gon's line from *The Phantom Menace*: "Our meeting was not a coincidence. Nothing happens by accident."[457] Like *Attack Droids, Duel* is backed with John Williams' music from the original films; Macomber and Thomas even recreate a precise sequence from *The Phantom Menace* when a foreboding horn is accompanied by a close-up of the Sith readying his saber.

An equally short but distinct form is the trailer, whose main purpose of course is to arouse interest for a forthcoming fan movie by piecing together clips of action and snatches of dialogue from an ongoing project. It is interesting to note how closely all the trailers on TFN Theater follow the structure and style of Lucasfilm's teasers for *The Phantom Menace,* adapting the official format even in terms of how they sell themselves; the explanation probably lies in the fact that these fan projects aim above all for professional quality, which they equate with coming as close as possible to the "original" LFL product.

The teaser for *Way of the Force,* directed by Josh Taylor, P. J. Tamayo and D. C. Sariti, opens with the announcement that "the following preview has been approved for all audiences,"—added purely for reasons of authenticity rather than necessity—and an animated P. J. T. film logo

[457]George Lucas, *The Phantom Menace,* op. cit., p. 82.

designed to resemble the Lucasfilm device. Over a mournful excerpt from Williams' score, three intertitles appear interspersed with short establishing shots of various locations: "750 years before the saga of the Skywalkers . . . two brothers, one fate . . . a dark force threatens peace in the galaxy." The *Phantom Menace* trailer, by comparison, faded its three titles—"Every generation has a legend . . . every journey has a first step . . . every saga has a beginning"—over its location shots and the same musical theme, before shifting gear into a high-paced edit of pod race, laser fire, and whirling sabers against the familiar *Star Wars March*.

Way of the Force follows an identical pattern. The *Star Wars* title theme suddenly blares out as the trailer kicks into its action sequences, cutting together brief shots of lightsaber combat, swooping ships over cityscape, and a speeder bike chase. Short dialogue extracts pepper the following scenes, including a clip of Yoda and a young Jedi protesting, "Don't patronize me!" At the music's climax, we finally have the title card, and the final shot is a menacing glimpse of the Sith character, Darth H'iver. The trailer content combines enough familiar elements—Yoda, Jedi, a cityscape very much like Coruscant—to locate the action firmly within the recognizable world of *Star Wars*, while introducing new developments such as twin short-bladed lightsabers, an African-American Sith, and speeder bikes racing across a lake; like all the fan fiction in the last chapter, it strikes a balance between authenticity through homage, novelty through creative invention.

The same structure lies behind the Anonymous Director's *Episode II* teaser, which cleverly patches together clips from *Highlander, The Tommyknockers,* Natalie Portman's *Anywhere But Here,* and Hayden Christensen's *Higher Ground*. After an aerial shot from *Dune,* and with the same melancholy Williams theme in the background, we have the three intertitles—"Every general leads in battle . . . every queen discovers her destiny . . . every boy becomes a man"—before the closing theme from *Star Wars* leads us through a quick succession of shots to the finale and the *Episode II* title. Even an extremely short trailer like Maul316's forty-four-second *Episode II* teaser, which simply takes blue-screen footage of Hayden Christensen wielding a saber and jazzes it up with backgrounds and sound effects, uses the same transition from Williams' music—mournful to triumphant—and the same device of intertitles: in this case, "A dream will be fulfilled . . . and a nightmare will begin." Although technical and creative invention is encouraged, there is clearly also a strong instinct among fan filmmakers to stay within an established format and to aspire to the model set by Lucasfilm, rather than attempt to subvert, challenge, or suggest a radical direction away from the original. The Anonymous Director, who strictly speaking only edited and digitally modified, rather than shooting anything himself, is held in great esteem within the TFN Theater community because his trailer fooled news sites into thinking it was a genuine LFL release: the highest praise a fan film can currently receive is that it looks just like the real thing.

"Under Imperial arrest"

Like *A Matter of Control, Way of the Force* is set a longer time ago in the galaxy far, far away; by locating the action seven hundred and fifty years before the familiar narrative, the directors give themselves a great deal of room for improvisation. Films that squeeze into the gaps in the existing *Star Wars* story play a far tighter game. Among these is Peter Mether's *The Dark Redemption,* which takes place just prior to the start of Episode IV, *A New Hope*. Like *Escape to Yavin* and indeed *Shadows of the Empire,* Mether's story makes constant reference to the known world of the primary text as he expands on the narrative, touching base with the familiar to authenticate his own tangential departures. For instance, some of the action is set on Kessel, the mining planet that Threepio and Han Solo refer to during *A New Hope*; the original trilogy never shows us the planet, and Mether's visualization of the spice mines fills out this background detail. The special edition of *A New Hope* showed us Boba Fett working as Jabba's bodyguard, so it makes sense that we find him here working on an assignment from the Hutt, in keeping with Lucas's chronology.

In fact, Mether's creation is less radical than *Shadows of the Empire* in that rather than inventing major new characters like Xizor and Kyle Katarn, it inserts established figures from the Expanded Universe into the prehistory of *A New Hope*. Thus Mara Jade, who first appeared in Timothy Zahn's post-*Jedi* trilogy, appears here as a prisoner of the Empire, suspected of holding the Death Star plans, and Kyle Katarn, a Rebel agent introduced in the *Dark Forces* PC game, cameos as her Alliance contact. Like Perry's novel, however—with its backstory on Leia's Boushh mask and the Bothan spynet—*Dark Redemption* cleverly elaborates on plot details that Lucas chose to skim over or mention only in passing. We see Leia feed the

Death Star plans to R2-D2 in *A New Hope,* but *The Dark Redemption* explains how they reached her in the first place; we know from *A New Hope* that Han Solo was boarded while carrying Jabba's spice shipment, but it takes *The Dark Redemption* to explain that he only got away because of a deal struck between Boba Fett and the Kessel Imperials.

In tone and form, Mether's film follows the *Star Wars* house style so closely as to almost pastiche it. Moments after the text crawl, yellow against a backdrop of stars, we tilt down to the glowing surface of Kessel, and then follow a TIE fighter as it swoops towards a Star Destroyer above the planet. Boba Fett's craft, the Slave I, disengages from the Imperial starship and plots a course down toward Kessel. This opening deliberately mirrors the first few minutes of *A New Hope*—Star Destroyer and Blockade Runner over Tatooine; *Empire*—Star Destroyer and probe droids over Hoth; and *Jedi*—Star Destroyer and Imperial Shuttle over Endor.

As we descend to the planet's surface and see a ragamuffin group of slaves picking out spice from the rocks, an Imperial in the sand-trooper costume from *A New Hope* snarls, "Back to work, Rebel scum! You'll be working the spice mines of Kessel for a long time." The line echoes Threepio's wording from *A New Hope*—"we'll be sent to the spice mines of Kessel"—and the Imperial Commander's jibe at Han and Leia—"you Rebel scum"—in *Return of the Jedi*. Both quotations are surely deliberate, and combined with the expository nature of the dialogue, they give the film a sense of self-consciousness, almost of camp: Mether drops in a knowing homage to the original *Star Wars* films every other minute.

The Imperials dispute the best punishment for Mara Jade, with one officer sourly concluding, "As you wish, Admiral": the line is a direct lift from Vader's exchange with Tarkin in *A New Hope,* which ends with Vader's dry "As you wish." A sleazy Kessel cantina is introduced with a montage cut to jaunty alien music very reminiscent of the Mos Eisley scene of *A New Hope,* and the bar patrons include the familiar creatures Greedo and Walrus Man. An Imperial demands of his soldier, "TX-341, why aren't you at your post?"; the script for *New Hope* has an identical line directed at "TX-421." A stormtrooper strokes the neck of a local floozy, in a precise echo of the shot from *Jedi*'s special edition where Boba Fett flirts with a dancer.

Mara Jade is visited by a Kessel spy who tells her to "trust no-one . . . you're our only hope," a bizarre dual reference to both *Star Wars* and *The X-Files*. Overall, Mether's creation is so relentless in its constant

Cantina scene from *The Dark Redemption*

nods to the original text as to become a parade of in-jokes, a spot-the-reference game for die-hard fans.

The Dark Redemption is to some extent a crossover between the "Original Trilogy" and the EU, bringing characters from novels and video games set in a later period of the saga's chronology into a time frame just prior to *Episode IV,* where they mesh with carved-in-stone canonical elements such as the transmission of the Death Star plans to Princess Leia. Kevin Rubio's *Troops,* usually regarded as a crossover between the TV documentary *Cops* and *A New Hope,* is actually more similar to *The Dark Redemption* than it is to *Matrix Jedi,* which merges the two films in question; or to *George Lucas in Love,* which as we shall see deals with the "real world" of the University of Southern California film school rather than the fictional universe of *Star Wars.*

Troops borrows the funky theme tune ("Bad boys, whatcha gonna do"), the handheld camera style, and the laconic delivery of its stormtrooper protagonists from *Cops.* The rest is from *Star Wars,* from the hardware—Imperial Shuttle, AT-ST, and speeder bikes—to details like the bilingual captions and the troopers' names.[458] However, *Troops* is not

[458]The soldier who discovers traces of droids in *New Hope* is Davin Felth, the captain in *Troops* is Jyanix Bach.

just a clever hybrid of two forms, but also a work of improvisation within a framework just like *Shadows of the Empire*; it interlocks deftly with the events of *A New Hope,* offering an ironic explanation for events that remain enigmatic in the original film. This aspect of Rubio's film may go unnoticed by viewers who are less familiar with *Star Wars*; Jenkins misses the point, for instance, when he describes the troops as "trying to crush the Jedi Knights."[459]

The action of *Troops* takes place between the scene in *New Hope* where Luke leaves his homestead early in the morning to search for Artoo, and his discovery of the massacred Jawas. The troops, Captain Jyanix Bach and his men in the Black Sheep squadron, are therefore reporting to camera at around the same time as Ben Kenobi shows Luke his father's lightsaber and introduces him to the mysteries of the Force. In the original film, Ben and Luke pull up in front of the Jawas' sandcrawler to find it burned out and surrounded by dead bodies. "Why would Imperial troops want to slaughter Jawas?" Luke asks.

The answer is provided in *Troops* as the Black Sheep squadron investigates a stolen droid; Bach interrogates the Jawa suspect while his troops guard a possible accomplice. "Okay, so the, uh, droid belongs to your cousin. Now, if I go over to the sandcrawler over there, and ask to see your cousin, is he gonna have a bill of sale for this? Okay. Well, what I'm gonna do now, sir, is place you under Imperial arrest. . . ." The Jawas make a run for it, and the troops pick them off one by one with rifle fire. As Bach explains the situation to camera—"it unfortunately turned violent"—a shuttle dips into the shot, loosing off missiles at the sandcrawler and reducing the vehicle to a burning hulk.

The discovery of the burned sandcrawler in *New Hope* is a foreboding precursor to Luke's return home, where his aunt and uncle have been slaughtered. Assuming that the Empire has destroyed both the Jawas and his family while searching for Threepio and Artoo, a traumatized Luke resolves to leave Tatooine and learn the ways of the Force; it is a turning point in the young Jedi's life. *Troops* reveals that the death of Uncle Owen and Aunt Beru was nothing more than an unfortunate domestic mishap, which began when Beru blamed Owen for letting Luke run off early in

---

[459]Jenkins, "The Poachers and the Stormtroopers," op. cit., p. 1. His "Darth Vadir" and "Hans Solo" in the same article are presumably typos.

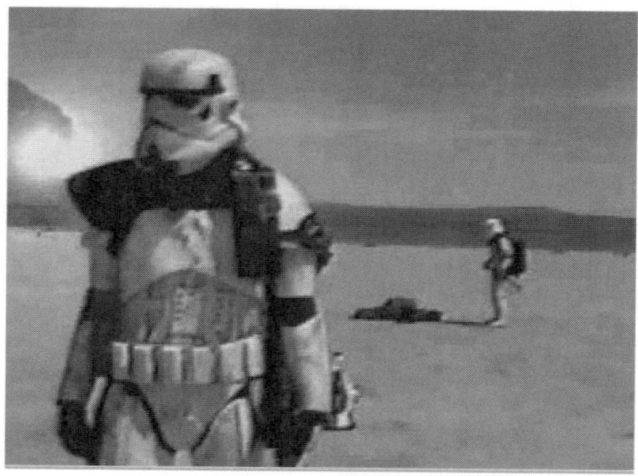

Troops

the morning. Officer Ayches Ram explains to a sympathetic Captain Bach: "See, the wife is under the delusion that their nephew ran away, right . . . and she's blamin' the husband for it. He's saying that the kid left early to fix a couple of condensers, and that the stress of the past week has just, you know, gotten to her." The troopers are taken off guard when Beru produces a thermal detonator, and they have no choice but to retreat as she and her husband go up in smoke.

The film's final shot is of the homestead in flames, an image that in *New Hope* signals personal tragedy and a new direction in the main character's life. In *Troops,* Luke is not even a walk-on part but a casual reference, as the squadron wanders off announcing that their main task is now to look for the nephew "and make sure he's okay." Of course, this is the film's punchline: the Empire is about to spend three films hunting Luke down. More than a hybrid of TV cop documentary and cinema space opera, *Troops* is a perfectly-crafted exercise in dramatic irony.

"Space Wheat"

Joe Nussbaum's *George Lucas in Love* is an unusual hybrid in that it cross-breeds three stories: *Star Wars*, John Madden's 1999 feature *Shakespeare in Love,* and George Lucas's real-life history as a student at the University of Southern California in the late 1960s. The debt to each narrative is fairly equal. *George Lucas in Love* follows the same conceit as Madden's film, that the author in question finds a female muse, then discovers his inspiration in the world surrounding him. Along the way the audience is treated to knowing name-drops and self-conscious textual references.

An early scene of *Shakespeare in Love* shows the young bard crossing a market square as a preacher declaims, "The Rose smells justly rank by any name . . . a plague on both their houses"; Shakespeare ponders to himself, appreciating the rhythm of the lines. He visits an apothecary and complains, "Words, words, words . . . once I had a gift." Assigned to complete the play *Romeo and Ethel the Pirate's Daughter,* Shakespeare now finds his flow blocked, and we watch him angrily tossing scrawled drafts across the room to land in a mug labeled "A Present from Stratford upon Avon."

George Lucas in Love opens with a pastiche of gentle Elizabethan strings and wind instruments, and the title unscrolls not in the spidery handwriting of Madden's film, but in a typewriter font. Lucas is banging away fruitlessly at the keys, flinging discarded efforts into a wastebasket marked "trash compactor." The music segues to a mystical John Williams soundalike theme as Lucas's stoner roommate, sucking on a bong, begins to expand on his drug experiences: "It's like this giant cosmic force, an energy field created by all living things . . . it surrounds us, it penetrates us . . . " They are interrupted by the appearance of their neighbor, a wheezing asthmatic in a black robe—the cue for a take on Williams' *Imperial March*—who taunts Lucas that his own script "is now complete," while Lucas's screenplay *3XR259.7* is still on line one.

Just as the audience to *Shakespeare in Love* is meant to recognize "a rose by any other name" and "a plague on both your houses" from *Romeo and Juliet* and "words, words, words" from *Hamlet,* so Nussbaum's audience is trusted to know Ben Kenobi's "an energy field created by all living things. It surrounds us and penetrates us" and Vader's "the circle is now complete" from *A New Hope*. The novelty mug is the prop equivalent of the 'trash compactor' wastebin, and *3XR259.7* is a spin on Lucas's later movie *THX1138: 4EB,* rather more subtle than *Romeo and Ethel the Pirate's Daughter*.

What Nussbaum's film does, then, is play off both the familiar tropes of *Star Wars* and the jokes from *Shakespeare in Love*; it parodies *Star Wars* by following Madden's model with satirical accuracy, working on two levels and providing dual pleasures for those viewers who recognize both sources. Some of the *Star Wars* jokes are fairly subtle—the use of wipes for scene transitions, for instance—but most are obvious enough to be picked up by the non-fan. A hairy dude howls in frustration as he fixes a hot-rod, and his buddy tells Lucas, "Check her out, kid . . . she's the fastest thing on campus"; a hippy group plays the Cantina theme on pipes and bongo drums; a short guy in blue and white whistles in annoyance, with his prissy yellow-shirted friend pronouncing, "Yes, I thought it was quite rude as well." Some of the gags, like Lucas's encounter with a professor who offers gnomic, fortune-cookie advice—"Search not! Inspiration will you not find"—are almost too labored for a fan audience, but then Nussbaum's film is distributed commercially rather than to the select internet community on TFN.

There is a third level of reference in the film, however, which provides the Lucas aficionado with the reward of spotting more obscure allusions. According to his roommates at USC, Lucas did sport Buddy Holly glasses and plaid shirts, just as Nussbaum's film depicts him;[460] he did grow his trademark beard during his final year at college.[461] His fumbling line in *George Lucas in Love* when he meets his muse, "You're beautiful . . . I'm sorry, I, I don't, uh, normally talk to, to girls like . . . I don't normally talk to girls" echoes both Luke's first response to Leia in *A New Hope* and reports of the director's behavior at college as offered by John Baxter's biography. "Lucas didn't mix much, least of all with women. . . . Lucas was no Lothario."[462]

When Marion enters with her protruding hair-buns and tells Lucas she loves his work, the more obvious comic references are to Leia's distinctive hairstyle from *A New Hope*—and by extension, perhaps, to Rachel's adoption of it in *Friends*—and at a further remove to the audience's familiarity with a similar sequence in *Shakespeare in Love,* when the playwright meets Lady Viola. However, Marion's line, "I loved your student films . . . *1:42:08, 6/18/67*" is not just another spoof on *THX1138*: *1:42:08* was Lucas's 1966 study of a yellow sports car, and *6/18/67* a follow-up from the subsequent year. Nussbaum has done his

[460]John Baxter, *George Lucas: A Biography,* London: HarperCollins (1999), pp. 49–50.
[461]Ibid. p. 58.
[462]Ibid. p. 57.

research, and while there are more than enough jokes along the lines of asthmatic villains, enigmatic mentors, and twin sisters to please the mainstream, it takes a dedicated fan to recognize his more subtle references.

There is a final irony to *George Lucas in Love,* and it prompts pause for thought rather than knowing laughter: it lies in the film's depiction of Lucas's shift from radical shorts like *1:42:08* to the blockbuster epic of *Star Wars*. Lucas did not write *Star Wars* at USC in 1967, but at his home in San Anselemo in 1974.[463] Around the time of *6/18/67,* Lucas was not working on *3XR259.7* (or, as he later calls it, *Space Wheat*) "about a young space farmer who is struggling with a terrible crop," but on a documentary about a Burbank deejay[464] and on the science-fiction dystopia *THX1138 4EB*. Nussbaum's film depicts a turning point for the young director that in fact occurred some six years later, when Lucas followed *American Graffiti,* the feature about his hometown during the early 1960s, with an outline for "The Star Wars."

In *George Lucas in Love,* Marion advises George to "write what you know," and the rest is history as he incorporates his environment into the script that would become *A New Hope*. In fact, the first drafts for *Star Wars*—"the story of Mace Windu . . . a revered Jedi-bendu of Ophuchi who was related to Usby C. J. Thape, Padawaan learner to the famed Jedi"[465]—were, unlike most of his previous films, very far from the world Lucas knew. In 1967, Lucas was an experimental filmmaker who made short movies about the gleaming surfaces of sports cars, adaptations of e. e. cummings poems,[466] and documentaries about local radio personalities; *George Lucas in Love* fictionalizes the moment when he mutated into the director of wide-screen, melodramatic space opera. Even the die-hard *Star Wars* fan can perhaps find something to regret in the loss of Lucas as an avant-gardist.

"Jabba's bitchin' on the dais"

Even a five-minute Flash animation of a *Star Wars* film—like Richard Cando's *Star Dudes* and its sequels, *The Bad Dudes Strike Back* and *Return of*

---

[463]Ibid. p. 153.

[464]*The Emperor,* 1967; no relation to *Star Wars*' arch villain.

[465]Baxter, op. cit., p. 141.

[466]*anyone lived in a pretty little [how] town* (1967).

Star Dudes

the Dude—can have an interesting relationship with the original text. *Star Dudes'* central motif is very simple, substituting "dude" for "man," "woman," "droid," "Jedi" and, with one exception, all proper names. Part of the cartoon's humor stems from the cursory nature with which it treats quite complex dialogue scenes: Luke and Obi-Wan's meeting with Han and Chewbacca is reduced to the four of them in shot announcing "Hi, dude" or "Roar!" and Greedo's encounter with Han consists of the alien's sitting down, taking a laser bolt to the chest, and falling cross-eyed on the table—no room here for debates about who shot first.

However, Cando's adaptation displays certain personal preferences. While key scenes like the lightsaber duel are compressed into five seconds and most individual shots are omitted, the extremely brief scene from *A New Hope* where Chewbacca roars at a tiny droid in the Death Star corridor is retained and lasts about as long as all the Uncle Owen–Aunt Beru scenes put together. Fans have argued for a long time that Mark Hamill forgot his line and yelled "Carrie!" to his costar as he climbed from his X-Wing during the Rebel celebrations; the alleged mistake is included here as a bonus in-joke.

Return of the Dude is even more selective in what it chooses to skim or linger over. Some individual shots, such as the Imperial Shuttle's descent to the landing pad on Endor, are lovingly recreated, while whole sections

Return of the Dude

of character interaction, as Leia's meeting with Wicket, are dropped entirely. Indeed, the Ewoks are included in Cando's version only when absolutely necessary to the story: their heads absolutely pop up in the forest to indicate their involvement, but they are given no dialogue. In the battle of Endor, Cando even introduces a shot where an Imperial Walker stomps directly on an Ewok, turning it to crimson pulp.

Again, some of the cartoon's charm lies in its curt treatment of emotionally charged exchanges; Luke's explanation of his parentage to Leia becomes, "I must face Vader. He's my dad. And you're my sister," leaving her open-mouthed. However, the scenes in Jabba's palace receive far more attention. The scene where Boushh haggles over a price for Chewbacca is reproduced almost word for word, including Jabba's dialogue in authentic Huttese and the subtitles at the bottom of the screen.

As in *Star Dudes,* an individual shot that has no role in the overall narrative is faithfully included: the *Special Edition* of *Jedi* adds an exterior of Jabba's palace where a creature called Bubo sucks up a grub with its long tongue. In the original, the shot lasts perhaps five seconds; in Cando's, it lasts about the same length of time, which is longer than Cando allows the entire "Jedi Rocks" song and dance sequence.

Rather than a straight adaptation, then, *Star Dudes* and its sequels are actually akin to the *Phantom Edit*—reworkings of the original that play down certain aspects and retain, even slightly alter others. Cando's version of *Star Wars* would find favor among a significant body of older fans—like those in my fourth chapter above—who have long expressed their dislike for the Ewoks and "Jedi Rocks" muppetry and who treasure little bloopers like the "Carrie" moment. Remember that Simon Pegg bonded with his best friend Nick over "the little Imperial droid that Chewbacca roars at in *A New Hope*";[467] Cando's preference for these scenes and repression of others identifies him as a certain kind of fan and arguably gives his films a specific address to the viewer who grew up with *Star Wars* in the 1970s.

The Jabba's palace scenes are also revisited in Petch Lucas and Matthew Beal's *Jabba on the Dais,* an example of the music video genre. Lucas and Beal describe themselves as Mississippi rock singers, and their fan film oeuvre to date also includes *Wookiee,* a retelling of the original trilogy from Han Solo's perspective to the tune of Limp Bizkit's "Nookie." *Jabba on the Dais,* less obviously, is a cover of Falco's 1985 hit *Rock Me Amadeus,* and consists of shots primarily taken from *Return of the Jedi* edited to a re-recorded version of the song.

As in Cando's animations, the details that Lucas and Beal choose to dwell on reveal a specific authorial—or editorial—perspective. The opening sequence is a spoken history of the Jabba character's evolution, parodying the original's potted biography of Amadeus. "1977, *Star Wars* debuts to stellar box office receipts . . . 1980, *The Empire Strikes Back* opens to a response most impressive . . . 1983, Jabba makes his film debut in *Return of the Jedi*." As the drawled "most impressive" suggests, Lucas and Beal's version of the Jabba story is along *Bill and Ted* lines—selective, caricatured, and with an eye for the gross or titillating.

The first shot of the story proper shows Bubo spearing fodder with his tongue, and sets the tone from the start: Jabba's palace is treated as something like an intergalactic frat party. Over a montage of Jabba and his cronies, the rapped vocals explain: "Like a two ton slug upon his concrete throne, he swigs his brandy as he tosses the Rancor a bone, springin' trap doors on dancers when they won't put out, this Hutt is vile beyond comparison there ain't no doubt." The next verse tells us that "Han Solo's chillin' on the wall when Chewie's brought before the court of Jabba where See-Threepio's knocked to the floor," and later stanzas

[467]Simon Pegg, personal e-mail, op. cit.

focus on "Boba's macking with that dancing chick" and "Princess Leia's talking smack, but gets chained up instead." In a similar case to Cando's highlighting of the infamous "Carrie!" fumble, Lucas and Beal point out the moment where "Lando tries to be unnoticed though he bumps his head" and insert a cartoonish "bump!" caption over the shot where Billy Dee Williams accidentally hits a low ceiling with his helmet.

Rather than tell a linear story, Lucas and Beal patch together a best-of Jabba's palace sequence that collates the most entertaining shots—from a certain point of view—and adds a wise-cracking spin to less humorous moments, so that characters who originally merely argued, flirted, or were held prisoner are now talking smack, macking, and chillin'. Towards the end, unsurprisingly, Jabba gets irate at the Rebels' infiltration of his palace, and starts "bitchin' on the dais."

Lucas and Beal's approach to retelling the saga in hip-hop slang is echoed in Jason Banning and Chris Crawford's *Star Wars Gangster Rap*. This combination of animation and music video begins with the Emperor's intoning, "It's not the East or the West Side . . . it's not the North or the South Side . . . it's the Dark Side . . . " Vader, clenching his fist, adds "You are correct!" On one level, this is simply a clever musical pastiche with neat lyrics. Vader tells Luke, "Impressive, now release your anger . . . you must have sensed your friends were in danger"; Luke whines "Oww . . . why'd you slice off my hand?" to which Vader replies calmly, "It's imperative that you understand."

More intriguingly, though, the choice of rap as a genre plays up the fact that Vader's distinctive vocal tones are African-American, and the track seems to half-jokingly set up the "dark side" of the Empire as a charismatic and cooler alternative to Luke's white-boy complaining: as stormtroopers wave their hands in the air, the Emperor chants, "We got Death Star!" and offers a persuasive threat "to all you Vader-haters out there . . . we'll blow your planet up." Perhaps most significant of all is a curious sequence in the middle of the video where Luke, flying from Dagobah to Bespin, sips a gin and tonic and muses to Artoo, "Would you mix me up another?" Rather than an approximation of Mark Hamill's intonation, the voice here is unmistakably African-American. In a move comparable to suggesting that Boba Fett could be a woman, Banning and Crawford seem to be pointing out that the son of the Dark Lord should have a little more of Vader in him.

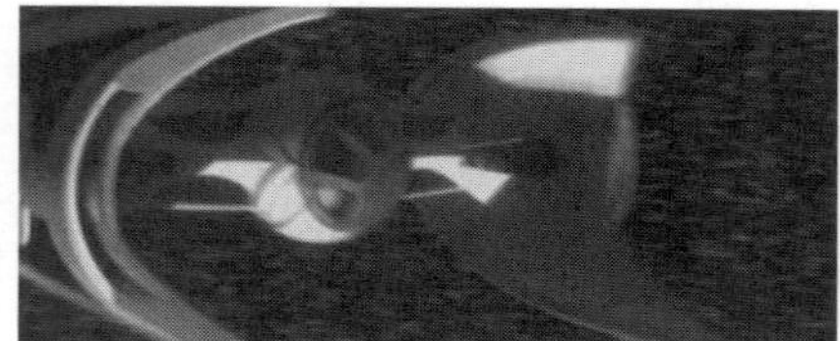

Opening sequence of *Duality*

"163,519 polygons"

At the time of writing—summer 2001—fan films already have the potential to match, if not better, the originals that inspire them. Dave Macomber and Mark Thomas's sequel to *Duel* was *Duality,* a six-minute story about two Sith on the planet Korriban. *Duality* has three actors and two lightsaber props; the rest is entirely CGI, from the first sequences of the Sith Interceptor sweeping toward the planet to the final aerial shot of the landing pad and temple, mounted on the edge of a rocky ochre canyon. It even includes CGI characters, if we count the halt-droid who interrogates the Sith at the door and the remotes that join the warriors in combat.

While Macomber and Thomas approached the project with traditional skills—Thomas has a background in fine art and portraiture, Macomber is trained in both visual and martial arts—the creators had to familiarize themselves with a host of software tools to create the CG effects, learning as they went along. Their production notes combine a sense of aesthetics with an intimate knowledge of the programs' capabilities.

> We wanted the Sith Terminator, like every other design in *Duality,* to be simultaneously retro and modern, with art deco styling. It had to be reminiscent of a classic TIE Fighter, but sleeker, as if it had been designed by an artist rather than an engineer—a ship from an earlier era still concerned with beauty and aesthetics rather than militaristic function alone [. . .] I didn't want the camera to follow the ship perfectly. I wanted a more natural feel to the camera's pan, as if a human were operating the camera, not a computer. I also wanted the ship offset to the left of the frame at the beginning of the shot, not centered.[468]

[468]Mark Thomas, "Sith Terminator" and "The Flyby," www.crewoftwo.com

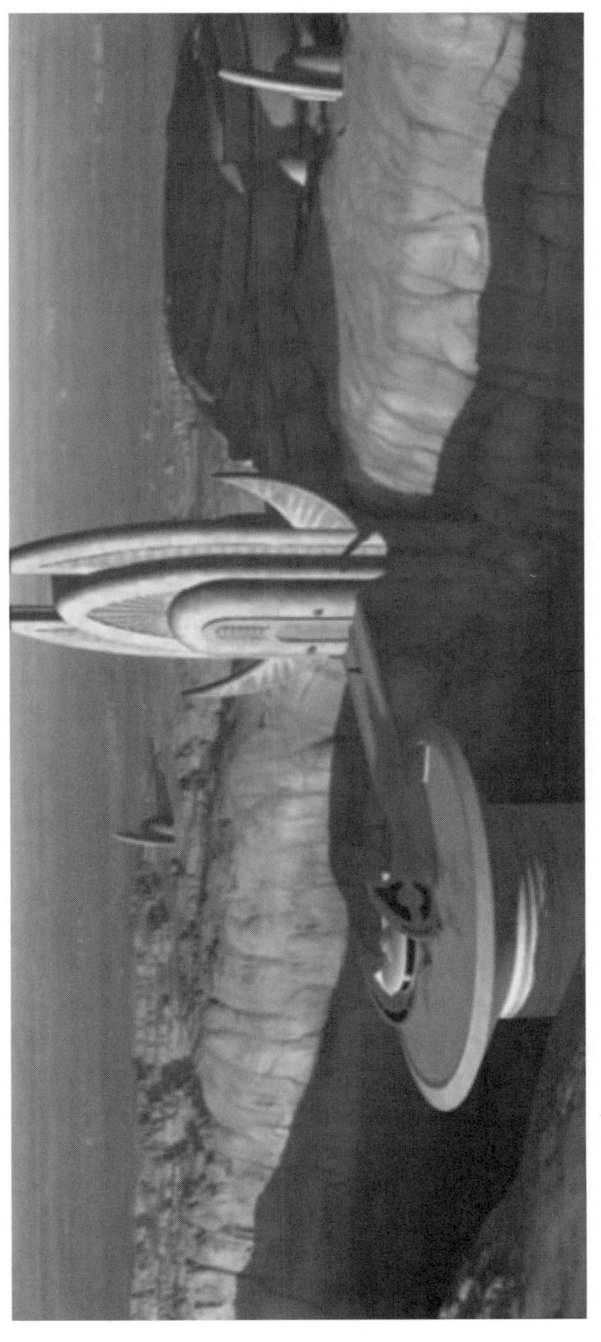

Main establishing shot from *Duality*

Although the ship was built in Electric Image Modeller and composited in After Effects into a shot that "contains 163,519 polygons"[469] and not a single concrete object, the ideas behind the shot, from design to camera movement, are almost reassuringly old-fashioned.

To the untrained eye at least, *Duality* is as visually and technically sophisticated as *The Phantom Menace*. Kevin Blades' *Star Wars Legacy* project is equally ambitious, filming live action against blue-screen and placing its actors in a fully digital environment. Like *Duality, Legacy* tells a story from the outer reaches of *Star Wars* chronology, although this narrative is set in the saga's future, "60 years after the Battle of Endor"[470] The difference between *Legacy* and *Duality*—indeed, between *Legacy* and all the other fan films discussed earlier—is that the former consists of seven thirty-minute episodes, released over a period of months as streaming video on the dedicated website, which will also feature backup material such as interviews, production art, and scripts. *Legacy* is a major, long-term project that will, if it succeeds, tell a three and a half hour original story with professional-quality effects. In theory, fan filmmakers can now equal George Lucas, constructing whole worlds from CGI and reaching a global audience with regular installments of their *Star Wars* vision.

Unfortunately, they are not allowed to. What they are allowed to do is produce parodies and documentaries for Atomfilms.com, using the official bank of sound effects and screening to whatever audience the site attracts. Compared to *Duality,* the Atomfilms archive is not inspiring. The generic restrictions mean that every film featured is either a humorous take on obsessive fandom like *Stargeeks*—"A *Star Wars* fanatic's life is thrown into a tizzy when a beautiful girl asks him out on a date"—or *Mad Magazine*–type spoofs like *Sev Wars*—"The Franchise Menace will squeeze bucks out of anything—including Queen Amidala's hair."[471] There is, of course, nothing wrong with parody or documentary: *Troops* combines both forms. *Duality* already has its own slapstick imitation in Steven Ballew and Roy Thomas's *Two-ness,* and the fan film community would be a poorer place without *Star Dudes* and its sequels. However, a whole cinema that is only permitted to show reportage or spoofs is a perverse and sorry

---

[469]Ibid.

[470]Kevin Blades, *Star Wars Legacy,* www.starwarz.com/swlegacy/story.html

[471]Archived at www.atomfilms.com/

place, and I find it unlikely that the Atomfilms *Star Wars* theater gets more fan traffic than the far more varied archive of TheForce.net.

So far, fan filmmakers have been lucky; far luckier than slash writers, although they are taking the same creative liberties with the official texts and, as Jenkins points out, pose a far more obvious threat to Lucasfilm in their attempts to emulate the original *Star Wars* films.[472] To date, Lucas seems to be adopting the strategy of incorporation and containment, drawing outstanding fan directors into his own team and offering a platform for others to show their work, if it fits certain guidelines. The case of *Dark Redemption* has shown that if LFL wants to stamp out a film's home on the web, it can do so; and yet, the corporation seems to have overlooked *The Dark Redemption*'s continued existence on TFN Theater.

It is not clear why LFL would choose to turn a blind eye to explicit copyright infringement on the part of semi-professional filmmakers who use the *Star Wars* properties as industry calling-cards. Perhaps Lucas simply identifies far more with twentysomething men who pay tribute to his creation through cinema than he does with thirtysomething women who write stories about his characters' gay relationships. The makers of *Legacy* in particular, however, are playing a dangerous game with their plans for a continuing, web-based *Star Wars* serial, and there must surely come a point where Lucasfilm draws the line. If and when the fan film community witnesses a corporate crackdown and is driven underground like the slash network, its nature will fundamentally change: instead of the proud display we currently see on sites like Macomber and Thomas's Crewoftwo.com, *Star Wars* fan filmmakers will, like their counterparts in prose fiction, have to keep their heads down and constantly hope to fly under the radar.

[472]Jenkins, "The Poachers and the Stormtroopers," op. cit., p. 3.

9

STAR WARS CHICKS

The names roll out importantly, joining other incantations around the table: "Darth Vader . . . Chewbacca . . . Han Solo . . . Luke Skywalker . . . Death Star . . . " No story receives more attention from the boys or gives greater pleasure in the telling. Sometimes a girl is drawn in, though her facts may differ from the boys'.

"Princess Leia is Luke's sister," Charlotte notes.

Andrew rejects the idea. "Uh-uh. Princess Leia is the boss of the good guys."

—Vivian Gussin Paley, *Boys and Girls: Superheroes in the Doll Corner* Chicago: University of Chicago Press (1984) p. 22

Star Wars combines two traditionally male genres—science fiction and war—in its title alone, and in its content combines them with the Western and the Saturday-morning adventure serial. In the original saga, eight of the nine main characters[473] are male—Artoo and Threepio are referred to as "he" rather than "it" throughout, as is Chewbacca. In *The Phantom Menace,* the ratio is one primary female character to three men, a boy, a Gungan, and an Iridonian Zabrak Sith Lord. The main roles for women in the *Star Wars* saga are, of course, Princess and Queen. The princess and queen will dress either in elaborate ceremonial robes with matching hairstyles or in tomboy fatigues, except when they get captured and show a little skin: Leia notoriously wears the slave bikini

[473]I am taking them to be Luke, Han, Obi-Wan, Vader, Lando, Chewbacca, the two droids, and Leia.

as Jabba's prisoner, and photos from *Episode II* show Padmé wearing a ripped shirt when she is held captive in the arena. Other women will fill the roles of mother—Shmi Skywalker, Rebel leader Mon Mothma; handmaiden—Sabé, Cordé; or floozy—Jabba's dancing girls Oola and Greeata, the Twi'lek twins who service Sebulba in *The Phantom Menace*.

The spin-off merchandise that extends the *Star Wars* experience from the cinema to the home is based around action figures and toy spaceships, console games and CD-ROMs, encyclopedias, trading cards, and reference books. The range of large *Star Wars* dolls, as opposed to little plastic figures, never caught on; plush Ewoks and dress-up Queen Amidala models are rare novelties, unrepresentative of the trend. On the face of it, *Star Wars* would seem to have little to offer a female fan, young ones in particular. Even if she found a way into the films, the whole culture surrounding them is traditionally male, and she would either have to join in the boys' games of action figure combat or—unless she could find some other girls to share her enthusiasm—create her own solitary fandom. "Well, it's not *Titanic,*" George Lucas is reported to have said. "This is the boy movie."[474]

Nevertheless, women and girls are into *Star Wars*. Online, female-run communities attract thousands of hits per week. The webmistresses of sites like Star Wars Chicks have loved the saga since they were young and found ways to explore it in make-believe games and fiction during their childhood, despite pressure to ditch *Star Wars* and conform to more traditional gender roles. This chapter examines the ways in which young female fans managed to negotiate these gender stereotypes to pursue their investment in a "boy's film"—and the extent to which that negotiation continued when they grew up, yet retained their loyalty to the saga. Do women fans experience a process of identification different from men, pinning their interest on Leia or Amidala as a role model? Do they imagine themselves in the position of Luke or Qui-Gon, or are these characters merely desirable set-dressing, objects of lust? Based on the evidence of female-run websites, are women's extended pleasures in the *Star Wars* films different from those of men—are they more focused on storytelling

---

[474]George Lucas, quoted by Mike Antonucci, "Leia With A Blaster: An Icon For Women," *Mercury News* (May 13, 1999), www0.mercurycenter.com/justgo/story/docs/063266.htm

than technology, for instance—and are female *Star Wars* communities distinct and different from a more male-oriented online network like TFN?

"Cute and sexy looken"

One distinct strand of female *Star Wars* fandom is represented by Kristen Morrisson's site, Always Luke.[475] Kristen's little community is based solely around the adoration of Luke Skywalker; it includes select sounds and images, debates about Luke's relationships with Callista and Mara Jade, fiction with Luke in the central role, and even a page of Luke action figures. The guestbook is crammed with girls' names—Rebecca, Taylor, Cassie—all of whom salute Kristen, telling her that her site rocks and Luke rules. "Mark Hamill is totally the best, and Luke Skywalker can rescue me any day!"; "Mark is so cute and sexy looken. Wonder if he still looks that way. Bye"; "I finally got my own Lukey stand-up, and he's so cute! My birthday was on Tuesday this week, and I wish Mark (Luke) was with me, but that dream didn't come true."[476]

The nearest real-world equivalent of Kristen's site might be a girls' slumber party in a bedroom plastered with Luke Skywalker posters, with the contributors passing notes or whispering from one sleeping bag to another. While it seems remarkable that these young women are drooling over an actor who was born in 1951—the comment "wonder if he still looks that way," sounds a little mournful—the overall sense is of a traditionally male film saga appropriated for traditionally female purposes. Instead of discussing the internal workings of lightsabers or the call signs of Red Squadron, Kristen's guests debate whether Luke was better suited to Callista, the love-interest from Barbara Hambly's novels *Children of the Jedi* and *Planet of Twilight,* or Mara Jade. "I didn't like Mara, because of the way she treated him on Myrrkr"; "Mara does not AT ALL strike me as one to get married or even fall in love."[477] In the "Creative Corner," Kristen and her colleagues expand or improve on the "official" stories of

---

[475]Kristen Morrison, Always Luke, www.geocities.com/Hollywood/Academy/5952/index2.html

[476]books.dreambook.com/kaywookiee/alwaysluke.html

[477]www.geocities.com/Hollywood/Academy/5952/maracallista.html

Luke's relationships: every single story in this section, from *Tears of a Jedi* to *The Engagement,* is a romance about Luke. "Luke meets the perfect girl: Dilaaana"; "Mara and Luke, the perfect couple?"; "A story about a girl who only has one important thing to live for: Luke."[478] This is one fiction archive with no need for sub-categories; the whole collection is generically pure and single-minded.

Based on the previous chapters, we might expect that a female *Star Wars* community would focus on EU novels, with the extra space they offer for characterization and relationships rather than relentless space adventure, and that fan fiction would be an important part of the shared activity. What is perhaps surprising is the page for *Star Wars* toys—not the larger dress-up figures that manufacturers intended for the female market, but the Power of the Force mini-action figures originally released in 1985. These are not dolls or decorative figurines, but crudely-jointed characters designed for shuffling around on dioramas while making laser gun noises. However, they are apparently important fetish objects for Kristen and her friends: the "hall of 3 1/4 inch Lukes" is full of loving descriptions of Luke in his warm Hoth parka, cute black Jedi robes, and garish X-Wing bodysuit: "I'd say orange is his color, wouldn't you?"

"Why and what if"

While Kristen's site gives a friendly femme twist to a boy's film saga—drawing out the romance and ignoring the galactic war, pointing out that a Jedi Knight can also be a gorgeous hunk—Victoria Hoke's site is an explicitly feminist project that works along the same principles of shifted perspective, casting a new light on familiar characters. "The best and only goal I could have for the website," Victoria told me, "is to get its readers to look at what they take for granted. If I can compel a reader to wonder 'why' and 'what if', I have achieved my goal."[479] Victoria's site name reveals its purpose: The Campaign for a Female Boba Fett.[480] Her manifesto is worth quoting at some length.

---

[478] www.geocities.com/Hollywood/Academy/5952/corner.html

[479] Victoria Hoke, personal e-mail (July 3, 2000).

[480] Victoria Hoke, The Campaign for a Female Boba Fett, www.hostmaker.com/femalefett/

> The character of Boba Fett is an ideal candidate to counteract *Star Wars*' female role rut. Fett is a potent and popular figure in the series, offers no evidence of being either gender within the films, and unlike Leia or Amidala has enough of the dark side to be interesting. In addition, such an interesting and strong female character would attract the viewership of women who otherwise would experience *Star Wars* only in the company of more enthusiastic boyfriends, brothers and sons. *Star Wars*' story is appealing and accessible to women; it is only its characters that are not.
>
> The force of female exclusion from *Star Wars* is reflected in the paltry proportion of its female fans. The casting of a female actor in the role of Boba Fett would demonstrate that women are not a forgotten or negligible demographic, as well as provide evidence that women can serve a cinematic purpose other than romance and reproduction. The fact that a female Fett would win female fans without alienating male fans begs the question why, instead of asking why Fett should be female, audiences aren't asking, "Why not?"[481]

The purpose of Victoria's campaign, then, is to remodel Fett as a strong female character who would both give a boost to the meager selection of female role models in the *Star Wars* saga and, in turn, encourage more women and girls to become fans. The site makes its arguments firstly by responding to reader criticisms, as detailed below, and secondly by providing historical examples of female warriors in drag—Mary Read, Joan of Arc, Hua Mulan—to support the notion that a bounty hunter could keep her gender undetected and perform to the highest male standards. This latter plank of Victoria's argument is supported with references to other sites: one link to the full poem-story of Hua Mulan at China the Beautiful, another to the National Archive section on Union Army officer Sarah Emma Edmonds.

"I do consider the site a feminist project," Victoria explained to me. "I attempt to stun a reader into questioning his or her convictions. I wish to present a fresh perspective—I'm afraid most of what there is to say about Leia or Amidala has already been said." Her manifesto complains that "Although Leia and Amidala wield weapons and kick enough ass to keep the plot moving, they prefer planning to acting, require protection and rescue, and serve primarily to continue the Jedi bloodline. Their royal privilege and youth make them difficult to take seriously."[482] Rather than

---

[481]www.hostmaker.com/femalefett/essay.htm

[482]Ibid.

attempt to rehabilitate these existing female characters, Victoria brings a character usually thought of as male—without any conclusive proof either way—over to the other side.

Although she knows she is only defending a hypothetical position and retains a sense of perspective—the site has won a number of online humor awards—Victoria sticks to her guns in the face of criticism through sharp and imaginative manipulation of the official evidence. Boba Fett flirts with dancing girls in Jabba's palace? She was just showing solidarity with their servile position. Fett's costume has a codpiece? She stole the armor from a Mandalorian warrior, whose outfits were probably designed for men only. The Campaign is a superb example of a speculative interpretation defended to the death: it will be interesting to see how Victoria's arguments survive after *Episode II* details Boba Fett's childhood as a boy.

"The little girls who wanted to pilot an X-Wing"

There is more than one site devoted to the saga's female characters. Helen Keier's Women of Star Wars[483]—with its slogan "Think *Star Wars* is just about a bunch of fly boys? Think again"—goes some way to countering Victoria Hoke's argument by listing approximately three hundred and fifty female characters from the mythos, from Amidala through Cindel Towani to Aurra Sing and Jaina Solo. To be fair, many of these girls and women are confined to the EU novels, and some of the examples from the original films are extremely minor parts: Torryn Farr was glimpsed for a moment in the Battle of Hoth, Saché is one of the less remarkable handmaidens. The inclusion of the Millennium Falcon is perhaps especially tenuous.

The site is important, however, not just for its listings but for its role as a linking hub for a host of other similar sites and for its concerted attempt to help build a community of *Star Wars* webmistresses. "These following are all female run web sites," announces the link page. "Check out what The Women of *Star Wars* can do!" The site's title shifts its reference here from the heroic characters of the saga to the pioneers and architects of the female *Star Wars* network; there is a sense of pride behind the mentions of Sisters of the Force—"a much needed and very

---

[483]Helen, Women of Star Wars, www.geocities.com/Area51/Cavern/3920/index.html

commendable effort to build a community of webmistresses"—and the "dedicated, talented, female" Jedi Grrls.[484]

Star Wars Chicks, which is "dedicated to all of the little girls who wanted to pilot an X-Wing when they grew up," bypasses this transference stage by concentrating directly on the female audience. Tamela Loos, one of the webmistresses behind the site, explained: "I wouldn't say that at SWC we are trying to draw the focus onto the female characters—I think our focus remains more with female fans. We are encouraging others to see the fans differently, to see that the *SW* films are multigenerational and that they cross gender lines as well."[485] The exercise in shifting perspective is in itself very similar to the idea behind the Campaign for a Female Boba Fett, with the same progressive intentions; Tamela adds, "I would say that our attempting to make the female *SW* fans known and recognized could definitely be seen as a political act."[486]

The site itself aims to offer the same variety as TFN, but pitched by women for a female audience. As we might expect, there is a section on EU fiction and separate archives of both genfic and slash. "Traditionally," Tamela offers, "I think women have always been more focused on written word as opposed to men."[487] The "multigenerational" aspect of fandom is shrewdly addressed by dividing the archive into Star Wars Chicks for genfic and SithChicks for over-eighteens. The same distinction applies to the mailing lists, with SithChicks reserved for "darker," NC-17 discussion. Significantly, only seventy-five percent of the content, in Tamela's estimation, is about *Star Wars*, an indication of a broader community whose conversations no longer revolve solely around the films but also deal with relationships, careers and family issues.

Star Wars Chicks includes topics that usually would be thought the preserve of male fans—role-playing games, collecting—and almost stereotypically "feminine" areas given a *Star Wars* twist. The recipes section includes Darth Maul Loaf and Kenobi Cutlets, while the fashion page offers a reading of a *Star Wars* comic entirely in terms of the characters' outfits.

> I would have to say that my vote for worst dress was this young Twi'lek female who was on the arm of Senator Viejer from Tynna. I was like

---

[484] www.geocities.com/Area51/Cavern/3920/main/links.html

[485] Tamela Loos/"Miss Jedi," personal e-mail (June 28, 2000).

[486] Ibid.

[487] Ibid.

> girrrl! This is a wedding, not casino night at the Corelian Hyatt. The Senator must be staying there and didn't have himself a date, so picked up one of the showgirls . . . I've seen more clothes on a Wookiee than she was wearing . . . whew. . . . [488]

The site's most notable feature, however, is its "Fight for the Cure" breast cancer campaign, which had raised more than eight thousand dollars within its first year through sales of Star Wars Chicks T-shirts. Remarkably, Lucasfilm Licensing gave its permission for the T-shirt design, which features a cartoon woman very much like Leia wielding a pink lightsaber. "I think it tends to build up their image in being more female friendly," Tamela guesses; an interesting example of fan activity being sanctioned by the corporate producers for mutual benefit. The webmistresses claim, perhaps disingenuously, that the logo is simply "a characterization of the female fan,"[489] but the familiar white gown and hair-buns surely imply that this is a Leia Organa who, within a female fan community, has finally been allowed to graduate to Jedi Knight.

"Fighting . . . so they can love one another"

Becky Mackle is twenty-seven and works as a senior library assistant. In her spare time she is the British news correspondent for Star Wars Chicks, and runs the Sith Chicks mailing list. Becky has been a *Star Wars* fan since 1982, when she first saw *A New Hope* on video; she started writing *Phantom Menace* slash in 1999. I met her on November 25, 2000, in a London pub: I recognized her by her Yoda backpack. We talked for three hours, with a tape recorder running.[490] She didn't drink.

Will: Do you think that women enjoy or experience *Star Wars* differently to men, and if so, how?

Becky: I think it's a case of we enjoy the story, the

---

[488]J'an Streems, "The Marriage of Luke Skywalker and Mara Jade," Star Wars Chicks, starwarschicks.com/galleria.htm

[489]Loos, op. cit.

[490]Many thanks to Fiona Graham for transcribing the entire interview, from which the extracts are taken.

action, the adventure. There might be aspects we enjoy more than men do, say for example, in *Empire Strikes Back,* one of my all time favorite scenes where Leia goes "I love you" and Han says, "I know." When I first saw that, I was there wiping my face, and my then partner was like, "Are you alright?" Some blokes might find that a bit, "Eugh, can't we just get to the bit where they go for the escape?" but I thought that it was just so perfect. To me it's a case of . . . that is what *Star Wars* is about. It's not just about action and adventure, it's also about emotions as well, it's about fighting for something you believe in. Yes, they're fighting to overthrow evil and everything else, but the reason they're fighting is so they can love one another.

Will: Are there any other moments that you feel women might place an emphasis on? Or which men might enjoy more, and women less?

Becky: Men might enjoy the scenes with the bounty hunters and things like that. There's on the Star Destroyer, when Vader says, "No disintegrations" and "As you wish" and all that sort of thing. They might enjoy that more, whereas a woman would most likely choose the scenes, say, where Luke is talking to Leia about Amidala, about their mother. I find those some of the most beautiful scenes in the trilogy. They're very, very quiet, and the emotion . . . those scenes are going to become more laden with meaning as we go into *Episodes II* and *III* because we're going to be finding out more about Amidala, about why the twins were separated, what happened to Amidala. We haven't found out yet, though we assume she's dead. I think the reason that the twins were separated is because Vader wanted to prevent both of them being turned to the Dark Side, because Sidious would have realized.

Will: You say that, but Palpatine didn't know about Leia . . .

Becky: I think that's because . . . I think he only really found out . . . I think there's a story, *Vader's Quest,* that deals with that. I'm not quite sure how they explain it away, but they do. I think if the young Luke had showed any Force skills, it would be a case of his Aunt and Uncle saying "don't do that," even though they did live in the back of beyond, they would have worried that someone would notice.

Will: Then again, though, we know that Anakin can see things before they happen, and his mother knows that. We don't know that Luke had done anything out of the ordinary at all. Then again, he's good at flying a T-16 isn't he, so maybe he does, he's a good pilot isn't he . . . right, let's move on.

I would have liked to excise this last pointless ramble on my part, but I think it illustrates some important points. Although Becky suggests that her reading of the saga, as a woman, might be markedly different from that of a male fan, my engagement with her is very similar to the conversations I had with Tim Meader and his posse in chapter 2. We might note that the exchange Becky singles out to illustrate her point—"I love you"/"I know"—did indeed prompt a stereotypically "feminine" reaction from Emma Mepstead during the group screening; but in general Becky and I are connecting as fans just as I did with Tim, establishing a common knowledge and then slipping into what almost amounts to a subcultural language.

Ten minutes before this exchange, Becky was a stranger, but she and I are immediately able to draw upon a universe of references that would seem arcane to a non-fan: I know who "the twins" are without Becky's having to specify Luke and Leia, and don't feel any obligation to explain that a T-16 Skyhopper is a light Tatooine spacecraft, while Becky, despite her theory that women have different preferences, can effortlessly quote

Vader's dialogue from *Empire Strikes Back*. The reference to an EU text, *Vader's Quest,* to explain gaps in the official narrative is very similar to Tim's falling back on *Tales of the Bounty Hunters* or *Enemy of the Empire* to support his arguments. The division between non-fan and fan, I would suggest, is more significant in this kind of exchange than the division between male and female fan.

"People would have thought it strange"

Will: How did *Star Wars* relate to you as a child? Did you play *Star Wars*, hang out with boys . . .

Becky: No, no, I was very much a girly girl when I was younger, didn't have any *Star Wars* toys or anything like that. It was a case of "this is for boys, I don't want anything to do with that." I enjoyed the movies and everything else, but if I had asked for a *Star Wars* toy as a child, I very much doubt my parents would have bought me it, as they didn't think it was for girls. But I don't think it made me hang out with boys over girls.

Will: Were the girls you hung around with into it at all?

Becky: No, no, we were very much into Sindy and things, it didn't really come up in conversation at school, it was all Care Bears, girly things. You didn't say you liked *Star Wars* because people would have thought it strange, and at that age you want to conform, to be like everyone else. But as I grew older, I realized that it was important to be true to yourself.

Tamela Loos and Andrea Alworth, who shared their memories of early *Star Wars* fandom with me by mail, felt less constrained as little girls. "As a child I played with and collected the action figures and ships same as my male cousin," wrote Tamela. "When we were bored of that, we would use the tractors around the ranch as X-Wings . . . on rainy days his bunk beds became the Millennium Falcon." In her teens, things began to change.

> As you become older it does become unacceptable for you, especially as a female, to indulge in fantasy/adventure. It's seen throughout society that men are allowed to be "boys" all of their lives. People refer to "boys and their toys" and everyone seems to comment that men are just little boys with more expensive toys. People expect them to be involved in role-playing, video games, movies and so on. While women are taught when they are young to mature, to grow up, have a family and be a mother and wife. If, as a woman, you try to explain to people that you like toys and video games and role-playing just as much as any guy, people tend to regard you as if you are some strange, unexplored phenomenon.[491]

Andrea, despite the fact that her liberal parents "never tried to shove me into any 'gender peg holes' . . . they let me negotiate my own way without the dictates of what girls should do instead of boys," nevertheless found herself isolated in her fandom during her teens.

> I did begin to notice in junior high that most of the girls my age were reading romance novels while I was working my way through Tolkien, Steven R. Donaldson, Larry Niven, *Trek, Galactica* and *Star Wars* novels. In high school, there were sci-fi clubs, but I avoided joining because all the members were boys and I felt a mite intimidated. For the most part, my love of sci-fi has been a solitary pursuit.[492]

The choice open to these teenage female *Star Wars* fans was either repression and compromise or stubborn resistance and isolation. However, while Andrea chose not to associate with organized male fandom, Becky found solidarity in a male group, although she found that her own response to the films was seen as "typically female," and seems to have responded by maintaining and emphasizing this position rather than trying to adapt to a "male" perspective.

> Will: When you started watching the films at university with other people, were these people male or female?

---

[491]Loos, op. cit.

[492]Andrea Alworth, personal e-mail (July 6, 2000).

Becky: Male. For the longest time, I was the only female *Star Wars* fan I knew. I was the token female, although I still saw it from a very female point of view, looking at the costumes and stuff. I made the mistake of pointing at Leia's gold bikini, commenting that I'd really like to try it on, and . . . don't put this down, but I actually did that for a fancy dress competition for my twenty-first birthday. A friend of mine made it; I hope no one finds the pictures. Remember when Rachel in *Friends* dressed up like that? After that was aired, I just couldn't hold my head up in public!

Will: Do you think women are particularly into the costumes and so on?

Becky: From a personal point of view I would say yes, but I have an interest in fashion, and I don't know about other female *Star Wars* fans. Amidala's costumes are interesting, like peacock feathers. "Look at me, I'm important, pay attention."

Will: When you were younger, did you wear you hair like Leia's? I don't mean in the buns, but perhaps in the more simple styles?

Becky: I did when I was younger, seven or eight, I had really long hair, and I had it plaited, the Nordic plaits, wrapped over the head. And the style from the end of *A New Hope,* one plait twisted into a bun, one going down the back.

Will: What were the men in your group into?

Becky: The ships. My ex-boyfriend was very into Han Solo, that was his hero, the epitome of cool. Most of the guys thought that, Luke was okay, but everyone wanted to be Solo with the cool ship and everything.

While Becky admits that her interest in the characters' dress and hairstyles may be personal to her rather than a typically female response—it is, we should note, echoed in J'an Streems' wedding feature at Star Wars Chicks—her description of the male fans' specific interests tallies closely with what we saw in chapter 2: for instance, Tim's "That's a Nebulan B Frigate. I like my ships." I would venture that none of the men in Tim's group would know what a Nordic plait was, or be able to describe Leia's hairstyle at the end of *A New Hope*.

"A brown-haired little girl"

Will: Do you think you, as a woman, identify with female characters?

Becky: Yes. I've always been into Princess Leia, right from the word go. She had the look, she had long dark hair, she wasn't at all passive, and she fought every step of the way, right from when we first see her. She stands up for herself when she meets Vader instead of going, "Help me!" She was no shrinking violet. Heroines in storybooks that I had met previously tended not to be proactive. Here was a heroine who broke the stereotype in terms of looks and behavior. And she came out with all the lines: "This is some rescue," "Aren't you a bit short for a stormtrooper?" Later on, I got into the Jedi. I think because of my Catholic education, the Force made more sense than this patriarchal deity in heaven. It didn't coalesce into a specific being; it was all around us, as opposed to God, a single entity. I was pig sick of religion and having it rammed down my throat. So it made more sense than conventional religion, because it didn't make rulings like the Catholic Church, against contraception and abortion and things, it was just good and evil, and you could interpret that in whichever way felt right to you. It wasn't that if you looked at things in a certain way you were good, and in another way you were bad, it was a case of you made up your own mind. It was more of a guide than a set of rules; it just seemed more right. I know that sounds nebulous, but it felt more right to my mind.

Will: So that gives you identification with all Force-sensitive characters, even if they're male. So, in *Phantom Menace,* that would be the Jedi.

Becky: Yeah.

Will: More than Amidala?

Becky: As much as Amidala. I could understand her point of view and why she was doing what she was doing, that she'd been trusted with the ruling of the planet, and knows what she has to do.

Aside from her affinity with the Jedi from a religious perspective—her view of the Force as an alternative to Catholicism provides interesting comparison with the Christian sites mentioned in chapter 1—Becky has always identified closely with Leia as a female role model who went against dominant stereotypes.

> She was, and still is, a heroine of mine. Here was a character who was no fading flower at the first sign of trouble, and she was beautiful. She was a leader and fought alongside the men. Not only that, but she was a brunette and a princess. All the images of beauty I remember as a child were of blonde-haired, blue-eyed princesses with the wicked witch or stepmother being dark-haired. Now, you can imagine what signals that would send to a brown-haired little girl who was a bit of an ugly duckling, can't you?[493]

Interestingly, Andrea felt the same way about herself and the lack of fictional heroines who actually resembled her physically, but found her likeness in a different text: "In fourth grade I read [Madeleine l'Engle's novel] *A Wrinkle in Time* and was both surprised and gratified to find the protagonist was a girl—an intelligent misfit with mousy brown hair, braces

[493]Becky Mackle, personal e-mail (November 24, 2000).

and glasses. She was me, I remember thinking."[494] Andrea, accustomed to identifying with male characters through years of reading science fiction, put herself easily in Luke's position.

> I identify with personality more than anatomy . . . in *New Hope* it was Luke, the naïve farmboy longing for adventure, the one looking away to the horizon . . . oh, that was me alright! Besides, I must admit that in my adolescent eyes, Mark Hamill was absolutely adorable—though I'm sure that had nothing to do with my strong interest in the character![495]

"The bad boy"

Will: Right. Objectification, fancying basically. You would think there would be a clear gender divide here, although I haven't come across many men who watch it for the women, who say "I really fancy Leia."

Becky: I think with me it was a case of, the cute guys were second from bottom of my list of reasons for liking the film, or the icing on the cake, an added bonus. Like if you're going shopping and you see an absolutely gorgeous outfit; it goes with everything, it looks wonderful, makes you look like a million dollars, and it's cheap.

Will: When you were younger, did you think differently?

Becky: It didn't really come into it. It was something I grew into as I got older, rather than an original reason for liking *Star Wars*. But, thirteen years on, I think Han Solo is an absolute sex god! You suddenly realize why Leia likes him so much.

Will: So, it was Han rather than Luke?

---

[494]Alworth, op. cit.
[495]Ibid.

Becky: Definitely. Quite a few of my friends are into Luke, and I can see why, but it's always been Han for me. But all these cute men are just icing really. I wouldn't be so enamored with them if I didn't like *Star Wars* in the first place.

Will: So you're not into the technology or anything? I know men who are.

Becky: Not really, it's more of a case of, I can differentiate between an X-wing and a Y-wing sort of thing, but I'm not like these people who know which shipyard they come from, or which company produced that model.

Will: Do you know how to make a lightsaber, for instance?

Becky: No!

Will: People do, you know, all that stuff about crystals and alignments . . .

Becky: Well, I know the basics.

Will: Are you into Darth Maul, at all?

Becky: Oh, yes I am! But it's very much more, of a—

Will: It's not fancying him is it? A lot of women do.

Becky: Yes! I'm sorry. [laughs]

Will: I suppose he's powerful—

Becky: He's cute!

Will: How can you say he's "cute" in the film?

Becky: Well, basically, it started with the scene in the second trailer, which was the first time I heard him speak. "At last we will reveal ourselves to the Jedi, at last we . . . "

Will: One of his two lines!

Becky: Yeah, and I remember sitting on the floor and going, "Whoa, that voice," and then seeing him move, with the lightsabers and stuff, it was like, "Wow! That's nice." I'm strange, forgive me.

Will: No, it's not just you, is it. I don't get it though; he looks so abnormal, with horns and stuff. To me, it's like fancying Watto.

Becky: It's the air of mystery, and also the fact that he's very focused. I get the impression that if he focuses on you, you end up either dead with a saber in the chest, or sexually exhausted!

Will: One way or the other, you wouldn't be walking.

Becky: Exactly. [laughter] It sort of turned me more to the Sith. Before then, the Sith were evil, we didn't like the Sith, but then there was Darth Maul. But it was also that in between watching *Star Wars* and watching *Phantom Menace,* I'd also grown up a hell of a lot, and been exploring different sides of sexuality. At university, it was all the guys that hung around with the rock society, grew their hair out, wore leather jackets, bunked lessons, smoked, drank, dabbled in substances you're not supposed to, that sort of thing.

Will: And that's what Darth Maul represents, the bad boy.

Becky: To an extent, the bad boy, definitely.

Clearly, I am unable to comprehend Becky's reading of Maul as a sex object, and our little verbal scuffle is, I think, a telling sign of this key distinction between heterosexual male and female readings of the saga. Despite her insistence that the good-looking male actors are "second from bottom" in her list of priorities, Becky's one comment about her experience of watching the *Empire Strikes Back: Special Edition* with a group of female friends was that "the heckling of 'get your kit off' to Han Solo was most enjoyable."[496] Mark's recommendation of *Return of the Jedi* from chapter 2—"you get to see what's-her-face in a bikini!"—is perhaps comparable, but this is a rare example of a salacious response from a male fan, whereas unashamed female desire for the men of *Star Wars* fuels a whole fictional genre and several online communities, from Master and Apprentice to Always Luke.

[496]Mackle, op. cit.

Of all the male fans in my study—the filmmakers, the *Special Edition* analysts, the TFN contributors, the men who became cops, soldiers, programmers, or Straight Edge because of *Star Wars*—Mark was the only one who made anything like a lustful remark about Princess Leia. Desiring the male characters, however—in Qui/Obi slash or on the Always Luke guestbook—seems to be a significant and undisguised factor in female engagement with the films. I only had one response from an openly gay male fan, and Rick, quoted in chapter 7, made no mention in his mail of any sexual feelings for the characters. There probably exists a community of gay male *Star Wars* fans, but I am unaware of it; it would be interesting to see whether such a group celebrates fantasies about or crushes on Han, Qui-Gon, and Maul with the same openness as straight women fans.

"We're not alone"

Will: How important is the Star Wars Chicks community to your enjoyment of *Star Wars*?

Becky: It adds validation, as in, I'm not alone, I'm not a freak. I think one of the most wonderful things that happened to me in 1999 was finding the Star Wars Chicks. And this was the year that I finished my exams and got a job, saw *The Phantom Menace*. I felt not alone any more. I had people to natter with about Amidala's costumes, Maul's saber, who didn't think I was being stupid.

Will: Is it important that they're women, or do men feel the same way?

Becky: It is. You do find men who feel the same way, but it's also a case of I could talk more about the costumes. I went to the *Art of Star Wars* [exhibition] with a couple of female friends, and was really able to talk about the costumes in detail. With a bloke it would have been, "Look at Boba Fett's blasters, blah, blah, blah." That is one of the reasons I'm glad of having female fans as friends. You're the first man I've been able to talk to about *Star Wars* in years.

Will: You have real life fan friends too . . .

Becky: About four or five.

Will: How did you meet them?

Becky: Through the Master and Apprentice site. Some of them are based in London. Also one who I met through Star Wars Chicks based in Boston . . . the people who run the site don't meet because we're too scattered. Angela and I are based here, Lori—Jedi Girl—is based in Boston, Tamela—MissJedi—is based in Missouri . . .

Will: How many people are involved with Star Wars Chicks?

Becky: On the Sith Chicks mailing list, about three hundred, and a good amount of lurkers.

Will: All female? Do you have to be female?

Becky: Oh, you're allowed to be on it if you're not female! But the way we talk, you wouldn't want to be! [Laughs] We don't prevent men, but . . . they can't put up with us.

Will: What about the numbers on Star Wars Chicks in general?

Becky: Per week, about fifteen thousand. We're not up with TFN or Jedi.net, but we're holding our own. They're more news based, and we do absolutely everything. We also specifically deal with women, and we're gathering a good lot of female fans, who can think "we're not alone."

Will: How many full-time staff does the site have?

Becky: About seven or eight of us.

Will: With no profit? How do you manage it?

Becky: Basically, [webmistress] Mary Jane's other half pays for our service space. But it's getting to the point where we might have to consider sponsorship; it's growing too big.

Will: To what extent do the message boards move away from *Star Wars*, and what other topics would they cover?

Becky: I would say with Sith Chicks, we try to keep it on topic for seventy-five percent of the time. But we discuss people's lives, people's problems, with jobs, family, or if they want to get things off their chests.

Will: What about the use of Star Wars Chicks for the breast cancer campaign? Presumably it was chosen as a female issue?

Becky: Yes. It was chosen because it affects all women, I think it's one in twelve. Jedi Girl and MissJedi went to Lucasfilm and said this is what we want to do; this is what it's in aid of . . . Lucasfilm said yes you can, but limited it to five hundred. We put it up online, and the t-shirts went so quickly. We managed to give five thousand dollars to the University of Kansas Medical School. We aimed at ten thousand, but it was still bloody good going . . . we handed over the money in May.

Will: And what real life commitment is there, for you?

Becky: Star Wars Chicks is my weekend . . . it's what social life I have.

To cynics, Becky's final comment might reinforce the stereotype of science fiction fandom as desperately pitiful: grown women giving up all their free time to run a website about men with laser swords and "talk" to "friends" they'll never meet. Her admission brings to mind William Shatner's put-down to the *Trek* fans on *Saturday Night Live:* "Get a life, will you people?"[497] But to Becky, and clearly to thousands of women like her, Star Wars Chicks is a very important part of life. The site offers a genuine sense of support and belonging, allowing women to feel that a passion

---

[497]Quoted in Jenkins, *Textual Poachers,* op. cit., p. 10.

they may well have repressed or abandoned for much of their lives can be validated and shared.

Over time, the community has evolved to the point where it is about more than *Star Wars*, although the films are still at the core of its network, forming the common ground that unites all its members. Women who may originally have bonded over a shared memory of dressing like Leia at age seven can go on to discuss career changes or family problems on the same mailing lists. The image of a Jedi girl launches a campaign that raises thousands of dollars for a specifically female charity; again, the starting-point is *Star Wars* but the sense of shared motivation ripples out into other areas that have no direct relationship to George Lucas's saga.

There is nothing illusory about the pleasures and rewards of a community like this. A female-dominated network in particular, by providing a meeting ground for fans whose views are often marginalized and who may never have met another woman with the same enthusiasms, is not a substitute for "normal life" but an enhancement of it. In very real terms, the breast cancer campaign's Jedi Chick, smiling wickedly as she wields a pink lightsaber—in Tamela's words, the "characterization of the female fan breaking out of the 'rules' of society"[498]—has already helped to save lives.

---

[498]Loos, op. cit.

10

GENERATIONS

> In the back there is a guy putting out a magazine called *Star Wars Generation*—no explanation necessary.
>
> —Dave Eggers, *A Heartbreaking Work of Staggering Genius*
> London: Picador (2000), p. 149

For the most part, this book has given a voice to a specific generation of *Star Wars* fans: my own generation, the kids who saw *A New Hope* in theaters on its first release. This group of fans tends to treasure the original trilogy as a nostalgic relic of childhood and to view the prequels with wariness or disappointment. There is frequently a degree of possessiveness about their relationship with the films. Steve Ash, born in 1967, admits

> I feel as if it almost "belongs" to people of my generation. I get sad when I hear people who were only born in 1980 claiming to be "the *Star Wars* generation." I genuinely think there is a dimension missing if you don't know a world where there wasn't a *Star Wars*, just as I sometimes wish I could remember a time when man hadn't landed on the moon.[499]

Marc Schlaf also saw *Star Wars* in 1977 and suggests that fans who first encountered the saga in the 1980s or 1990s "really missed out. Seeing

---

[499]Steve Ash, personal e-mail (30 June 2000).

the films when they first came out made it a whole new experience. I had no idea what would happen next and that made it all the more exciting."[500]

Six years can make a lot of difference in terms of perception. Matthew Stein, who was drawn into the saga in 1983 when his dad took him to *Return of the Jedi,* agrees that his experience was different to that of the fans who were there from the start. "They saw something that was a new frontier in movies. The effects that I saw as old-fashioned were brand new and revolutionary to those who were around for the original releases."[501] However, he distinguishes himself in turn from a younger generation whose first experience will be the prequels, rather than the original trilogy. "I think that those who are growing up with *The Phantom Menace* are actually going to accept and understand the movies better than those who saw 4-6 first. Those who started on *TPM* will get to see it all through with no preformed ideas about it."[502]

Similarly, Andrew Meadows, born in 1982, regrets the fact that he missed the original trilogy's first release—"I would have loved to have been alive to see them . . . I did get to see the Special Edition on the big screen, but that isn't the same"—yet counts himself lucky in comparison to the younger kids who came to the saga in 1999. "I do think they're missing something and in a way I very much feel sorry for them. Whilst *The Phantom Menace* is the beginning I feel it can only be fully enjoyed after having watched 4, 5 and 6."[503] For Marc Schlaf, the experience of the younger generation is more immediate, as he takes on the task of guiding his baby niece through the saga.

> Her experience will be somewhat different in that she'll be seeing *Episode II* and *III* in the cinema, and 1, 4, 5 and 6 at home. I'm still debating with myself which I should show her first, the original trilogy, *TPM* and then *Episode II* or some other order. Given that she's 9 1/2 months old right now, I'm not gonna give her much in the way of *Star Wars* merchandise yet, but I'm thinking she might enjoy a stuffed Jar Jar toy when she's a bit older.[504]

---

[500]Marc Schlaf, personal e-mail (June 29, 2000).

[501]Matthew Stein, personal e-mail (June 28, 2000).

[502]Ibid.

[503]Andrew Meadows, personal e-mail (March 6, 2000).

[504]Schlaf, op. cit.

Clearly, these fans feel that age plays an important factor in shaping interpretation of the *Star Wars* saga. This final chapter explores the idea that age may place viewers in a specific interpretive community, giving them a different perspective to fans of another generation. In contrast to the rest of the book, which recorded the views of people aged fifteen and older, this section is based around an interview with an eleven-year-old fan, Frazer Bowdery. Frazer's initiation into the *Star Wars* mythos, like that of Marc Schlaf's niece, was guided by a close relative. His uncle, Martin Hutton, aged thirty-one and a fan since 1977, had introduced Frazer to the saga in 1997 and consciously shaped his nephew's experience of the films by showing him videos, taking him to the cinema, and buying him selected toys and accessories for Christmas. The relationship is irresistibly reminiscent of a Jedi apprenticeship, with Martin as the teacher and Frazer as his Padawan learner.

Martin e-mailed me, having read of my research on an online message board, and arranged a meeting with Frazer. I carried out the interview in Frazer's bedroom, tape-recording our conversation and taking notes. The resulting transcript cannot, of course, be treated as representative of an entire generation, but Frazer's views, as I suggest below, are in keeping with the online contributions of fans his age, and they make intriguing, suggestive reading. While this is only a single case study, it has the advantage that I was able to talk to a dedicated young fan in his own environment, surrounded by his *Star Wars* toys and videos: any interviews on a broader scale would have had to take place outside the subjects' homes, and I think the responses would have been far less rich.

My comments on the interview place Frazer's responses in a wider context, indicating that his uses and interpretations of the saga are far from unusual for his generation. I draw this contextual material from online sources. Both the official Star Wars.com site and TheForce.net have little brothers, junior versions of themselves designed for preteens. Examining these sites, StarWarsKids and Rebel Friends respectively, I was asking the questions that informed my interview with Frazer. Do fans aged twelve or younger exhibit the same levels of creativity as we have seen with the older generation? Do they make any distinction between the original and prequel trilogies? Very broadly, in what ways are they the same as their older counterparts, and in what ways different?

Woolwich is a notoriously shabby part of southeast London—I grew up there—but Frazer and his brother, two half-sisters, and parents live in a tall, spacious house on a quiet street. His dad is a chauffeur and his mum sells antiques. Frazer's bedroom is large and he needs a ladder to reach his shelf of *Star Wars* toys. He offered me a seat, his mum brought me coffee, and we began.

Will:	When did you first see a *Star Wars* film?
Frazer:	I went round Martin's . . . he gave me them on video when I was quite small, but I was afraid to watch them because I didn't know what they were, and then I went round my uncle's, and he had *Return of the Jedi* on, and I thought, "Hm, this is good."
Will:	Do you remember how old you were?
Frazer:	About seven.
Will:	So you just saw *Return of the Jedi*?
Frazer:	. . . and then I watched the others. Oh, I went to see *Return of the Jedi,* the Special Edition one, at the cinema.
Will:	Who did you go with?
Frazer:	Martin. Hardly anyone else in my family likes *Star Wars*.
Will:	Did you watch the others on video?
Frazer:	Yeah, I thought that I should see what they're like, and I thought they were good, and so I started watching them lots.
Will:	How many times do you think you've seen the films in total?
Frazer:	I've watched them lots, I can't . . . a wild guess . . . fifty-nine times, altogether.
Will:	Which is your favorite out of the original trilogy?
Frazer:	I'm not really sure, probably *Empire Strikes Back,* or it might just be *Return of the Jedi* because it's like the latest of that trilogy.
Will:	When did you start getting toys and stuff?
Frazer:	When I'd watched them a couple of times, then I started getting them from Martin. At the time I didn't know that they're more valuable if you keep them in their packages.

Will:	So, did you start asking for them for your birthday and Christmas presents?
Frazer:	Yeah.
Will:	Do you talk about *Star Wars* with Martin?
Frazer:	Yeah, sometimes.
Will:	Do you think that if Martin didn't like *Star Wars* you wouldn't?
Frazer:	Yeah, because if he hadn't liked it, I never would have seen it in the first place.

The notion of fan apprenticeship—an adult guiding a young viewer to a text that means a great deal to them, and that the child might otherwise not have discovered—is central to Frazer and Martin's story. It is also explicit in the parents' guide attached to Rebel Friends, which stresses the idea of passing *Star Wars* down a generation like a cultural heirloom.

> For a long time TheForce.Net has wanted to do a *Star Wars* website geared towards younger *Star Wars* fans. After all, most of us on the team became fans when we were under 10 years old. Now, all of us have young friends, nieces and nephews, or brothers and sisters we'd like to share *Star Wars* with, but this site [TheForce.net] is a little over their head or boring. So we've created a kid friendly site with features and cool stuff geared toward our younger friends and fanatics. So drag the munchkins to the computer screen and get ready to let them explore this new corner of the *Star Wars* Universe![505]

Notably, the suggestion is that the adult will "drag" the younger viewer into their own fandom, forcing them into the *Star Wars* mythos for their own pleasure as much as that of the child. The official Star Wars Kids site also encourages young fans to engage in repeated viewing and close reading of the films, similar to that carried out by the adults discussed in chapter 3; a guide points out things to look for in the background of *The Phantom Menace* "whether you've seen it one time or one hundred times."[506] Frazer's estimated fifty-nine times falls respectably in the middle of this range.

---

[505] *Rebel Friends,* www.theforce.net/kids/

[506] www.starwarskids.com/enter_the_saga/tpm_funguide/index_ yes.html

I wondered next whether the order in which Frazer had seen the films would affect his understanding of the story. Viewers of my generation, of course, were thrown in with *Episode IV* and were only given the first installment, *The Phantom Menace,* twenty-two years later. Frazer saw *Return of the Jedi: Special Edition* first and had only two years to wait before *The Phantom Menace*. His experience of the saga was therefore very different from mine. In 1980, I refused to believe that Vader was really Luke's father—he was a villain after all, why shouldn't he lie?—but Frazer saw Vader unmasked in *Return of the Jedi* before he watched *Empire Strikes Back,* and the question of Luke's paternity had been resolved before Frazer even knew it was a cliff-hanger.

My experience of the films encouraged a strict distinction between "original trilogy" and "prequels," due to the gulf between their respective releases, which marked a huge change in my personal history. When *Empire* came out, for instance, I was still at primary school; when *Phantom Menace* reached cinemas I was finishing my PhD. Frazer had moved up two years at school between his first viewing of the two films, and has no reason to draw such rigid boundaries between *Episode V* and *Episode I*; they are both texts of his childhood.

Generations

Will: If you saw *Return of the Jedi* first, did you understand the story?

Frazer: Well, I didn't understand it, the part I saw, was in Jabba's palace, and it was the part when he drops the Rutian twin into the Rancor pit, and I thought that this looks good . . .

Will: That's Oola, the Rutian twins are Sebulba's assistants.

Frazer: Oh, yeah.

Will: But, if you saw *Jedi* first, you knew the end really, didn't you, before you saw the beginning. When you watched *Star Wars*, you knew that Darth Vader was Luke Skywalker's dad didn't you?

Frazer: Yeah, it came up to the part that he said that,

and then I didn't see the rest, but I thought, "I should watch them all" and then I did.

Will: Do you think it's strange that when you saw *Return of the Jedi* and Vader takes his mask off, it's Anakin, and then you saw *The Phantom Menace* and he's a little boy. Is that strange to see him as an old man, and then a little boy? Like, when you saw little Anakin in *The Phantom Menace,* did you realize that he was going to become Darth Vader?

Frazer: Yeah, because I was told before I watched it, otherwise I wouldn't have known. I didn't believe them, but then I watched *Return of the Jedi,* and Luke says, "You are Anakin Skywalker," and I thought this is strange, and then I worked it out, and I knew it was true.

Despite the differences in our understanding of the saga, note that I immediately fall into the same sense of community that I observed in my conversations with Becky Mackle and Tim Meader: when Frazer states that one of the Rutian twins falls into Jabba's pit, I unhesitatingly correct him, and he instantly understands what I mean. There is twenty years' age difference between us, but we are both *Star Wars* fans, and we share a language.

It is significant, as a sidenote, that Frazer's mistake stems from confusing two characters of the same alien race who appear in both the prequel and original trilogy: Oola is a Twi'lek like the Rutian twins, but she appears in *Jedi* and they in *The Phantom Menace*. Frazer jumps between the two films far more readily than an older fan would. Likewise, the fans who contribute to StarWarsKids.com are encouraged to see both trilogies as part of the same six-part story, rather than separating them as many fans of my generation tend to do. The site's "Skywalker Family Album" is representative of this approach; it helps viewers like Frazer who may have come to the story haphazardly, going back and forth between *Episodes I* and *VI,* to understand the relationship between characters, emphasizing that the films are interlinked chapters.

> Anakin loved to fly fast his whole life. Here's Anakin flying in the Boonta Eve Podrace . . . later in his life, after he turned to the Dark

Side, he still loved to fly fast. Here he is piloting his curved-wing TIE during the Battle of Yavin.[507]

The fact that Anakin is Darth Vader—a revelation that shocked the first generation of *Star Wars* viewers and kept millions of kids guessing between *Empire* and *Jedi*—is now given away from the start, in picture-book format. Vader's pursuit of Luke in the Death Star trench, which audiences of 1977 booed pantomime-style, is repackaged as a grown-up version of young Anakin's pod race triumph. The galactic villain becomes the kid gone wrong, and the shift in perspective will surely affect young viewers' perception of Vader in the original trilogy, giving them a more sympathetic and perhaps more complex view of the tyrannical Dark Lord.

Similarly, the young fan is offered pictures of young Obi-Wan next to his older incarnation, linking Ewan McGregor's character of 1999 to Alec Guinness's of 1977; Anakin's meeting with the young Jedi is compared to Vader's final clash with the same man on the Death Star, and Luke's home on Tatooine with Anakin's dwelling on the same planet. "Father and son both loved to fly from an early age. Anakin built a high-speed podracer. Luke owned an old model landspeeder."[508] The next screen reveals that "Father and son, as pilots, shot torpedoes that ended critical battles,"[509] effectively giving away the ending to both *Phantom Menace* and *A New Hope* at a stroke.

There may be no surprises for the kid who reads this guide, but he or she is encouraged to gain a sense of the thematic and visual echoes between the prequel and original trilogy, making links between them and seeing them as equal parts of a whole. The gulf between 1977 and 1999 is cleverly bridged, and the young fan is urged to make no distinction between episodes released twenty years apart.

Unbetrayed

Will: So what's your opinion of *The Phantom Menace*? You like it?

---

[507] www.starwarskids.com/enter_the_saga/album/2.html
[508] www.starwarskids.com/enter_the_saga/album/7.html
[509] www.starwarskids.com/enter_the_saga/album/8.html

Frazer: Yeah . . . I like the special effects.
Will: Out of all the films, is that your favorite?
Frazer: Yeah, probably. It's a bit . . . more modern.
Will: Did you like it straightaway?
Frazer: Yeah.
Will: What is it you like about it?
Frazer: The lightsaber duel is good, the pod race is, because it's all computer graphics, but like, really good ones.
Will: Do you think the effects are better in that than the originals?
Frazer: Yeah . . . Who's your favorite in it?
Will: Han Solo probably, or out of *The Phantom Menace*? Obi-Wan Kenobi, but out of all of them, Han Solo. I quite like Qui-Gon Jinn. What do you think of Jar Jar Binks?
Frazer: He's very clumsy. I like his accent, I can do his accent.
Will: Do you want to do it now?
Frazer: Nah, I only do it when I'm with my friends, I do [in accent] "meesa Jar Jar Binks, meesa think you are stupid."
[laughter]
Will: So, you think he's a funny character?
Frazer: Yeah . . .
Will: But he's not your favorite in that film? Who is?
Frazer: I actually like Darth Maul.
Will: He's not in it much, but his fighting is good.
Frazer: Yeah, that's why I like him.

In contrast to the older fans of chapter 4, Frazer has no prejudice against *The Phantom Menace;* indeed, he prefers it because of its sophisticated effects and fight choreography. The online communities for young fans also exhibit a lack of distinction that edges into a preference for *Episode I.* Rebel Friends includes a letters page where readers can ask questions of the saga's characters: young Obi-Wan replies alongside Luke Skywalker, and Amidala is as popular a correspondent as Leia, while several mails are addressed personally to the older fans' bugbear, Jar Jar Binks. Meanwhile a poll on StarWarsKids asks visitors for their favorite character, and Obi-Wan Kenobi trumps Han Solo; clearly, voters automatically considered the name Kenobi to refer to the dashing Jedi of *The Phantom Menace* rather than the haggard old Ben of *A New Hope*.

Speculation

Will:	Let's see, *Episode II,* what have you heard about that?
Frazer:	I've got a magazine that shows you what Obi-Wan looks like in the film.
Will:	Have you heard the title?
Frazer:	No.
Will:	It's *Attack of the Clones,* it's going to be about the Clone Wars. What do you think of the title?
Frazer:	It's good, yeah. It fits *Star Wars* pretty well.
Will:	So, if you just heard the title, would you want to see the film?
Frazer:	I would, yeah, even if I didn't know it was *Star Wars*.
Will:	Are you going to see *Episode II* in the cinema?
Frazer:	I'd like to, if someone will go with me . . . There's something else I heard.
Will:	What's that?
Frazer:	I heard that Darth Sidious from *Episode I,* his son is Emperor Palpatine, and he becomes the emperor later on, Palpatine does.
Will:	Where did you hear that?
Frazer:	Martin told me . . . and I heard that in *Episode II* Jar Jar Binks gets killed.
Will:	What else have you heard about *Episode II*?
Frazer:	Obi-Wan becomes a Jedi . . .
Will:	What about Anakin?
Frazer:	Anakin becomes as young as Obi-Wan was, and he looks like . . . nearly as big as Obi-

> Wan, and he's got that braid that Obi-Wan had, and I think his lightsaber color is crimson . . . Anakin actually dies, but the Empire brings him back, but he's still dead, and that's why he has to have the mask and everything.

Frazer does not have regular access to the internet, and so has remained untouched by the furious online fan reaction to the *Episode II* title, which was announced more than a month before this interview. His immediate response is very far removed from the disgust of older fans posting to TheForce.net message boards; rather than associate it with corny B-movies, he presumably accepts *Attack of the Clones* as a title in keeping with *The Empire Strikes Back* and *Return of the Jedi*. Again, it is interesting that Frazer seems to view *Episode II* as an integral part of the six-part saga—"it fits *Star Wars* pretty well"—while many older fans attempt to keep the original trilogy separate and distinct in their minds from the supposed childishness and cheesiness of the prequel movies.

Frazer's information, then, comes not from online sources but from magazines and from his mentor, Martin; and of course, in this case, from me and my unashamed spoilers. Clearly, the urge to speculate about forthcoming episodes is not confined to older fans: Frazer's need to work out what will happen is extremely similar to the online detective work of chapter 6. Drawing on rumor and available material—a magazine illustration, the knowledge of what must happen by the start of *Episode IV*—Frazer pieces together a possible narrative about Anakin's fall to the Dark Side.

Due perhaps to his comparative lack of solid evidence, and the misinformation passed down by his uncle, Frazer's speculation is likely to be proved incorrect. Palpatine is in fact the same person as Darth Sidious, rather than his son, and it is generally accepted that Anakin will be severely injured but not actually killed before he becomes Darth Vader. Be that as it may, it is evident that predicting the future of *Star Wars* is important to Frazer just as it is to Chyren, Roderick Vonhögen, and their colleagues on TheForce.net boards for *Episodes II* and *III*.

Community

Will: So, are your friends into *Star Wars* too?

Frazer: Yeah, at my old school. My new school, it's a bit more posh, and I think that there was more people at my old school that liked it. I don't like the new school so much.

Will: Did you ever play *Star Wars* games?

Frazer: Yeah, in my old school we used to act them, and it was always me ending up as Han Solo, always.

Will: Lucky you. Were you playing with figures, or acting it out?

Frazer: We didn't play with the toys, we acted it all out ourselves.

Will: Were you acting the stories from the films, or your own?

Frazer: Our own, but using the characters from the films.

Will: Have your friends only seen *The Phantom Menace?*

Frazer: I think most of them have seen *The Phantom Menace* in the cinema, and some have it on video, but they've all seen all the films. And I've got two Playstation games. One is really old, and one is new. My brother Max has got another one, but he won't let me keep it in here.

Will: Do you play *Star Wars* with him?

Frazer: Yeah, because some of these games are for two players, and we play together.

Will: Do you know any girls that are into *Star Wars*?

Frazer: No, I think it's a boys' thing.

You will recall that Duncan and Phil, Tim Meader's friends, remembered playing *Star Wars* in a big group at school, acting out the stories; there is something reassuring about the fact that, twenty years later, a generation brought up on Playstations is still hanging around the playground doing the Rebels in different voices. Again, while Frazer entertains his friends with an impression of Jar Jar Binks, the group performances put him in the role of Han Solo; his schoolmates obviously draw on both trilogies indiscriminately for their games.

Further research could investigate Frazer's suggestion that social class might have something to do with a child's involvement in *Star Wars*; whatever the reason, though, something is lacking from his school life now that he has left the solidarity of his old fan-group and failed, so far, to find a new one. Note that, in keeping with the evidence of my last chapter, any *Star Wars* chicks of Frazer's acquaintance are keeping their love of the films very quiet.

Star Wars Kids actively encourages a sense of online community among its young visitors, organizing a "*Star Wars* Summer" of friendly competition based around its puzzles and games. Kids who play the site's "Garbage Masher" quiz, for instance, earn points according to their knowledge of *Star Wars*, but, significantly, they are not allowed to enter their score in the heats unless they join a team. The site therefore nurtures a sense of group bonding in younger fans, structured according to the films' internal alliances: the teams are named "mentors," "royalty," "pilots," "apprentices" and "leaders." The focus is not on individual achievement—indeed, such solo efforts are not even recognized—but on helping your chosen community. Forty percent of the visitors polled say they "definitely" felt a special connection with both their teammates and the site during *Star Wars* Summer; a better training for running a fan-group, whether real life or online, could hardly be imagined.

Creativity

Will: Do you draw pictures or write stories about *Star Wars*?

Frazer: Not really, once I have a printer I will. There is a game that I tried to turn into a story. It's called *Star Wars*: *Shadows of the Empire,* on Nintendo 64. You have to verse [*sic*] different things. There's this rare robot, a bounty hunter, not Boba Fett—you have to verse him anyway and he's really hard—1G-88, that big robot thing. There's a person called Dash Rendar—

Will: Hang on. *Shadows of the Empire,* isn't that a book?

Frazer: Oh, yeah, it's a book too.

Will: Did you write the story?
Frazer: I started it, at school, but it was so hard, I didn't finish it.
Will: Have you drawn anything?
Frazer: Yeah, I found it difficult though. There's this ship that Dash Rendar has—
Will: The Outrider.
Frazer: Yeah, I couldn't draw it. It looks really like the Millennium Falcon, but the cockpit, there are two of them . . .
Will: You know this from the game, what the ship looks like?
Frazer: Yeah, from the game, and this picture I saw of it. It showed Dash Rendar holding his arm up high, Boba Fett is in the background, and the Outrider is there, and you see this strange Empire, and some TIE fighters, but it was too hard to draw.

Frazer's use of Playstation game graphics and their cover artwork as the basis for fiction is surely specific to his generation; although kids my age had the *Star Wars* arcade game at fairgrounds or seaside amusement parks, and home computers from 1982 onward, the vector graphics of the arcade machine and the crude color-schemes of the ZX Spectrum were unlikely to inspire us into writing short stories. However, though the source material has changed, the creative process is surely no different to that of the *Star Wars* digital filmmakers or even the slash authors: continuing the pleasures of the primary text by copying some elements and expanding on others.

At the moment, Frazer finds that his own drawing skills lag behind his imagination, and that writing stories will be pointless without the hardware to print them out, but he is apparently on the same creative route as the older fans we encountered in chapters 7 and 8. Unlike some of TheForce.net contributors from chapter 5, however, he seems to make no more distinction between canon and non-canon than he does between original trilogy and prequels: the computer game of an Expanded Universe novel, rather than an actual George Lucas film, was the text that fired his creativity.

Neither Star Wars Kids nor Rebel Friends has space for stories by their young visitors. However, Rebel Friends does feature the "Alderaan Museum of Beautiful Artwork," where contributors exhibit their drawings of *Star Wars* characters to a wide audience. While a good portion of the pictures are inspired by *The Phantom Menace*—Matt Homer's "Darth Maul Rocks," James Heirman's portrait of himself with a Padawan braid like Obi-Wan—the image that currently has pride of place is Princess Leia, by five-year-old Emma. Under the portrait of a beaming face, huge white dress, and blobby brown hair-buns is a caption telling us that Emma "drew this picture for her little sister Hannah who wants to be Princess Leia when she grows up."[510] Clearly, *Star Wars* is catching them young.

Like Frazer's *Shadows of the Empire* story, the creative inspiration behind these drawings is taken from a range of primary and secondary texts far beyond that available to the kids of 1977, and it crosses the boundaries of canon. One picture of a female Jedi knight "from Bakura" refers back to Kathy Tyers' Expanded Universe novel[511] rather than any of the films. However, while some things change, some aspects of junior fan art remain the same. Emma's *New Hope* Leia would easily fit next to the young fans' illustrations reprinted at the back of *The Art of Star Wars*. Here we find eight-year-old Trey Fitz-Gerald sketching Vader in black pencil, with the helpful speech balloon "Hi, I'm Darth Vader"; Steve Mandich, also aged eight, shows the Dark Lord cutting down Obi-Wan Kenobi while a sound effect caption explains "Poof." Three-year-old Anne Olney and seven-year-old Richard Davis' portraits of Princess Leia are very much along the same lines as Emma's picture.[512] The *Art of Star Wars* drawings, however, are relics from 1977: Anne Olney would now be twenty-seven, and Richard Davis thirty-one. The mythos has expanded in the last twenty-four years and has provided more source material, but the creative impulse *Star Wars* fires up in its young fans seems unchanged.

"I'll probably like it forever"

Will: Would you ever want to make films or anything when you're older?

[510]Rebel Friends, op. cit.

[511]Kathy Tyers, *The Truce at Bakura,* London: Bantam Books (1994).

[512]See Carol Titelman (Ed.), *The Art of Star Wars: A New Hope,* London: Titan (1997), pp. 168–175.

Frazer: Yeah, I would. I like computers . . . I'd like to be a DJ, like Martin.

Will: What other things are you into?

Frazer: I like James Bond, and I really like *Final Fantasy,* and that's a film now. I like fighting games and TV shows. But not like *X-Men,* real powers. I like music—

Will: Is music more important to you than *Star Wars*?

Frazer: No, *Star Wars* is definitely more important, I like it more than anything else. My sister's boyfriend told me that there's going to be a third trilogy, with Luke versus Mara Jade. I saw on this game that Mara Jade has got a purple lightsaber. I might make a book about it.

Will: About what?

Frazer: About Boba Fett, before he dies and stuff. Because you know how he's in the pit, and they get digested over a thousand years, and he's just down there, and he presses the button on his jet pack, and it works, and he gets out.

Will: So do you think you'll always like *Star Wars*, don't you think you'll think it's babyish?

Frazer: No! Never.

Will: Do you think you'll still like it when you're, like, fifty?

Frazer: Yeah, definitely. I've already liked it for a long time, four years. I'll probably like it forever.

When four years is a long time, it is easy to be certain that you'll like a film forever; but then, Frazer had the evidence before him of a fellow fan who had stayed loyal to the saga for twenty-three years. In a decade or two, Frazer will have his own nostalgia about the period from 1997 to 2005, just as I still fondly recall the battle-damaged Creature Cantina and painting gold bracelets on my Hammerhead action figure. He may have found a job that allows him to express the creative impulse *Star Wars* sparked in him, or he may devote his spare time to it; he might publish a Boba Fett novel, or run a CGI modeling site, building three-dimensional ships for digital cinema. He may create his own fictional worlds, or come into conflict with a younger generation that insists on seeing the saga in the correct order or champions *Episode III* over his favorite, *The Empire Strikes Back*. His passion, as I hope my book has proved, will not make him a geek but an author, a producer, a director, a debater or a campaigner. Above all, like so many of the fans discussed here, he will be not just a consumer but a creator.

Star Wars as a franchise may finally dwindle, as it did in the late 1980s before it was rekindled by novels and the promise of a new trilogy. It may be continued by fans, becoming an online folk culture as amateur producers extend the *Star Wars* saga beyond *Episode VI,* their work attaining a professional quality that makes them indistinguishable, visually at least, from the Lucasfilm originals. Without new primary texts from "above," the fandom itself may thin out, retreating to a specialist hardcore that continues to celebrate the films for their nostalgic value; *Star Wars* may truly become a cult, cherished by a minority as the dominant cultural myth of a specific historical period.

One thing, I think, is fairly certain: in twenty years time, Frazer will meet a man his age who wears a Jango Fett T-shirt or quotes Padmé Amidala or whistles the Imperial March, and something will click between them as Frazer points out the reference. There will be at least one more *Star Wars* generation after his—the children who grow up with the prequel trilogy—and when *Episode III* is history they too will meet again and recognize one another, finding they can talk in an old language, unearthing their shared past and establishing new alliances.

My greatest pleasure in researching this book was meeting a twenty-five-year-old from a solicitor's office, a twenty-seven-year-old senior librarian, and an eleven-year-old schoolboy—not to mention the scores of correspondents who shared confidences with me by e-mail—and discovering within moments that we were bonded, that we knew the same people and places intimately. This is the lasting gift that *Star Wars*, as a hugely popular yet deeply loved film series, sustained across three decades, offers its fans: a community, worldwide and possibly lifelong, grounded in a common heritage and united by a fictional universe.

Epilogue

POST BELLUM

There is a moment at the start of every new *Star Wars* film, after the cyan of "a long time ago . . . " has faded to black, that seems to stretch. The screen is dark and silent. In an instant—surely the whole pause can't be more than five seconds, however long it feels—the familiar yellow logo will flare up onto the screen with the first horns of John Williams' march; but for that moment, it's just darkness and the friends next to you, and the hundreds of people in the cinema, and the millions of fans you imagine across the world who have been waiting years for this, a new episode of *Star Wars*. At that moment, at the top of the roller coaster when everyone around you holds their breath, you can truly believe in a Force that binds, penetrates, and unites.

I walked out of the AMC in Chestnut Hill, Massachusetts, unable to speak for the lump in my throat. This had been heavy stuff for a space opera—a mother dying in her son's arms, a father killed before his son's eyes, a young couple declaring love in the face of death—but what choked me up was the feeling of sheer relief that *Attack of the Clones* hadn't let me down. It had been a good film, thank God, and the mythos was saved. I wanted to find George Lucas and throw an arm round him, murmuring "It's alright . . . it's alright." Embarrassingly, I had become an *Episode II* gusher.

Over the next few weeks my opinions mellowed, fortunately, until I evened out at broadly enthusiastic rather than weepily ecstatic. Crucially, though, the main reason for my reevaluation of the film was the experience of reading and responding to other fans' online opinions. This epilogue charts and explores the initial fan reaction to *Attack of the Clones* across most of the bases covered in previous chapters, revisiting the same sites and many of the same people. Almost all the data were gathered in May 2002, in the month following the film's release, while reactions were intense and traffic on boards like *TheForce.net* was peaking. Even by the time of writing, August 2002, online activity around *Star Wars* has settled down into a lull, a ticking-over in preparation for the serious detection and debate that will build momentum when meaty scraps from *Episode III* start coming in.

Balance of the Fan Force

The most immediately striking aspect of the response to *AOTC* on the *Jedi Council* boards was its unanimity and sheer lack of debate. Of 5,390 fans on *TheForce.net,* 54% voted it either the best or the second-best film in the saga; in a second poll of 6,729 visitors, 83% felt it was "excellent" or "very good," with only 0.65% going for "poor."[513] The basher-gusher wars were virtually ended with a stroke in mid-May, as hardly anyone, it seemed, had a bad word for the film. More than a truce, this was a merging of camps and a closing of ranks, and it led one poster, GreedoCMZ, to ask, "Is *AOTC* reuniting the fan base?"

> I really wanted to start a thread called "Bashers and Gushers Unite" because it seemed like *AOTC* was welding the fan base back together . . . it seems to me that overall we are agreed that *AOTC* is a great movie. Everyone seems to have their own minor complaints but there doesn't seem to be any one theme (such as Jar Jar) that bashers can rally around.
>
> Basically, *Episode I* got most of the fan base divided into two camps: those who loved it and those who hated it and there was a lot of emotionally charged debate going on here over it. I guess I leaned toward the gusher side but I could see where the bashers were coming from . . . I hoped that *Episode II* would solve a lot of that problem. And it seems like it might be solving it.[514]

The replies confirmed this feeling of relief and newfound unity.

> I agree with you GreedoCMZ. I'm a *TPM* basher and I loved *AOTC*. From what I've seen and read and witnessed myself, many more fans

---

[513]"Now That You've Seen *AOTC,* Where Does It Rate?" and "What Did You Think of *AOTC*?" *TheForce.net,* op. cit. (31 May 2002).

[514]GreedoCMZ, "Is *AOTC* Reuniting the Fan Base?" *TheForce.net,* op. cit. (21 May 2002).

> liked *AOTC* than *TPM*. Thank God really. If George made two *Star Wars* movies that bad it might have brought down the whole saga.[515]

> I have indeed noticed an overall change of attitude around the boards over the last week. Fans are beginning to forget about *TPM* and are enjoying the fact that *AOTC* kicks some major tail! I'm glad to see that balance has been restored to the Fan Force.[516]

Some *Phantom Menace* gushers made friendly enquiries in this new spirit of peace—

> I'd be most interested in hearing if there are any hard core *TPM* bashers who have been so disappointed in that one that they almost left the series, what brought them back. What aspect of *AOTC* brought you back in?[517]

—while others, less forgiving, took the opportunity to chastise fair-weather fans who had deserted the saga during the *Phantom Menace* period.

> The bashers even set up their own forum to bash *TPM* undisturbed. I lost faith in the fans, many of whom seemed like disturbed individuals pretending to be fans while harbouring utter contempt for all things Lucas. It is only now that I truly accept that these people are not fans. Someone who watches *Clones* and still has something negative to say is certainly not a fan of *Star Wars*.[518]

> This flick really is separating groups, and giving the bashers a good reason and opportunity to just LEAVE. What are you holding out for?[519]

> I agree that the bashers should just beat it. If after these two films you guys are still bitching and moaning, LEAVE!!![520]

As the preceding posts suggest, some TPM gushers saw the general agreement about *Attack of the Clones* as a triumph for their side. The fact

---

[515]Gorilla, ibid.
[516]DarthGunray, ibid.
[517]Jumbo_Fett, ibid.
[518]Jedi3167, ibid.
[519]Meatypants, ibid.
[520]Hitchikinggalaxy, ibid. (22 May 2002).

that *AOTC* had won over many of those who disliked the first film seemed to prove the value of the Prequel Trilogy as a whole, and through a flawed, retroactive extension of this logic, demonstrate that *The Phantom Menace* was a decent film after all. Taking advantage of the overall positive feeling towards *Episode II,* these gushers circled their wagons against the minority who dared to comment on its flaws, and tried to bully them out of the community with the argument that a *Clones* basher could never be a "true" fan. In the following post, a contributor quotes a tentative voice of dissent, then immediately slams it:

> I admit, there's a lot I liked about *Episode II,* but as a whole it didn't work for me. The—Stop right there. Not a *Star Wars* fan.[521]

Although there was a genuine, overwhelming approval for the film then—as the *TF.N* polls surely indicate—this shift in support was seized upon by those who had previously defended the Prequel Trilogy, and parlayed up into a dominant gusher hegemony where the notion that *Clones* had restored faith in the franchise became "common sense." Unsurprisingly, complaints were voiced cautiously; as we have already seen, they were brutally policed.

> Anyone checking my profile can see that this is my first post . . . however I have been visiting the forum for about 5 years and been a *Star Wars* fan all my life. This could be construed as a negative post but don't think I'm a simple basher.
>
> I really enjoyed *AOTC* . . . there are of course moments in the film that you wish had been different but after watching the movie 3 times you begin to see the film for all the wonderful things it is . . . many times during the film the audience started laughing at the wrong moment but I stayed firm and stayed with it . . . HOWEVER . . . there is one scene that is so AWFUL that it completely ruins it for me . . . it's the scene at the end when Padmé arises after falling from the Republic Cruiser . . . one minute she is in agony . . . the next she's running across the sand dunes . . . the acting was atrocious.[522]

The reaction to this post, even with all its disclaimers, was hostile.

---

[521]Meatypants, ibid.

[522]RichieSm, "Worst Scene in History," *TheForce.net,* op. cit. (24 May 2002).

> Well if it takes something that small to ruin a film for you there's not much hope.[523]

> You're insulted by something like that? A life, you need.[524]

> How can you visit a forum for 5 years, that's only been in existence since 1998? Busted.[525]

Note that in the last retort, the complainant's integrity as a fan is undermined; if he's lying about his long-term commitment to the board, his comment doesn't even deserve a proper response.

This instant shields-up defensiveness in the face of criticism was typical of the *Jedi Council* during late May. A mocking observation about Obi-Wan's cheesy line "Good call, my young Padawan" earned nothing but contempt—"Ugh, bash bash bash. What did you want him to say?"[526]—and every whisper of disapproval was prefaced with reassurance that the poster was a true, long-term fan.

> Don't get me wrongo [*sic*], I loved AOTC . . . the characters and story are perfect. Even the dialogue is mostly quality (mostly). But there are a few little things that bothered me that I feel Lucas could have improved.[527]

> Please don't get me wrong. I'm a huge *SW* devotee . . . have been since 1977. And I think *AOTC* was amazing. But, I just saw *Lord of the Rings* again today, and, well . . . *AOTC* just didn't come close. I feel kinda dirty for saying it . . . but it's true.[528]

If the latter post wasn't apologetic enough, with its wringing of hands and confession of a sullied conscience, the title pleaded "Almost . . . But Just Not Good Enough . . . And Don't Get Mad at Me!"

---

[523]Slave2, ibid.
[524]TheBiggerFish, ibid.
[525]Shine, ibid.
[526]1stAD, "Good Call My Young Padawan!" *TheForce.net,* op. cit. (31 May 2002).
[527]Duckman, Little Things That Would Have Improved *AOTC*. *TheForce.net,* op. cit. (31 May 2002).
[528]JermaineRogers-com, "Almost . . . But Just Not Good Enough . . . And Don't Get Mad at Me!" *TheForce.net,* op. cit. (25 May 2002).

In place of the old debates, the aggressively united community discussed less controversial matters, such as how many times they had seen the new film. "I'm on showing four now and plan on seeing at least six times," IronParrot remarked nonchalantly, three days after *AOTC*'s official release. "On my third and fourth viewings I was able to sit back and enjoy the picture for what it was, rather nice"[529] On the back of these multiple viewings, the *Jedi Council* fans quickly launched into close analysis to pick apart the visual and narrative detail. As most contributors had no access to illegal video, DVD, or downloaded versions of *Attack of the Clones,* the only way for them to reach an adequate level of expertise was to keep going back to the cinema; and this they did willingly, even travelling to theaters with digital screening in order to get the highest level of visual quality.

> 3 times, might see it today, have tickets for tomorrow, and next weekend driving up to San Fran to see it on the digital projection.[530]

> Twice on the first day, will go again and again, hopefully every weekend. Got to find all those Easter eggs.[531]

"Easter eggs" is a term often used in PC and console game discussion, meaning an accidental or deliberate cheat. Applied to cinema, it means a little bonus for the eagle-eyed or repeat viewer, a treat inserted by the filmmakers for the fan to hunt down. Bloopers—accidental errors—offer very similar pleasures, although in this case the thrill comes from catching the producers out rather than spotting a wry in-joke. Both involve a playful I-Spy contest between fan and filmmaker, and the competition extends to other fans because of the challenge to discover a new detail before anyone else does. Note the dates on these posts—the close analysis began on May 16th, the day of the film's release, based entirely on fans' memory of their most recent screenings—and that the observations range from the obvious through the trivial and obscure to the tenuous.

---

[529]IronParrot, "How Many Times Have You Seen *AOTC, TheForce.Net,* op. cit. (19 May 2002).

[530]Darth_Hater, ibid.

[531]Keokiswahine, ibid.

Anyone catch a sound clip from *Raiders of the Lost Ark*. When Anakin and Padmé are in the rickshaw, you can hear what appears to be the dialogue of beggars from that film (from the basket scene).[532]

After the lines "Anakin! Anakin! Noooo!" . . . you hear Vader's breathing. Listen for it.[533]

When Anakin and Padmé board Padmé's ship to transmit Obi-Wan's message it appears that the ship itself is pretty cold because Padmé is certainly showing under her tight white bodysuit.[534]

Did anyone notice when Padmé and Anakin were talking and the camera pans across to see their shadows that Anakin's looked a lot like Vader's?[535]

Did anyone see stunt coordinator Nick Gillard as a Jedi in the arena towards the beginning of the battle, he is in the far right corner. I noticed him by his short blond hair.[536]

Can we have a vote on whether or not you heard Vader's breathing? I was listening for it and I swear I didn't hear it![537]

When Anakin and Amidala leave the ship at Naboo and Artoo tries to follow—there are steps down from the ship that Artoo can't take so George boy just does a quick cut instead and Artoo is already down on the concourse.[538]

Lucas' fat daughter appeared as a "tweliki??" [Twi'lek] in the bar scene, I mean you could tell the camera stayed there for a second too long.[539]
I don't think it was an intentional blooper, but it was funny to see Jango hit his head on the door of the Slave I when he entered it after Obi-Wan. A nice nod to the clumsy stormtrooper from *ANH*.[540]

---

[532]Chris2, "The Official *AOTC* Bloopers and Easter Egg Thread," *TheForce.Net,* op. cit. (16 May 2002).
[533]Raynar, ibid.
[534]The_Mountain_Man, ibid.
[535]Gingerjames, ibid.
[536]Darth-sennin, ibid.
[537]Death Stick Dealer, ibid.
[538]JMFMoore, ibid.
[539]ITDEFX101, ibid.
[540]XR73627794, ibid.

> I have to listen for Vader's breathing tomorrow. God . . . this is the best Thursday ever! Bye![541]

Amid the friendly jostling to post up new observations, an old EU canon debate was reopened with new evidence. The argument was prompted by ObiWanJane's offhand reference to a possible secondary text in-joke; a link to the *Jedi Apprentice* books.

> Obi-Wan's visit to Dex's Diner was sort of an Easter Egg for *Jedi Apprentice* readers. Except for the brief appearance of Aurra Sing in *TPM,* Dex is the only EU character included in the movies, I believe.[542]

Aurra Sing was a cameo character in *Phantom Menace* who subsequently gained starring roles in Expanded Universe comic books. Darth_Ignant pointed out that she should be defined according to the text she first appeared in, and he brought in another, more plausible example of an EU to film canon crossover:

> Aurra was in *TPM* before any EU stuff, so she isn't an EU character. An EU character is the blue Twi'lek Jedi female, who was modelled after someone called Aylaya Securra [*sic*].

Wild_Karrde chipped in, referring back as a side note to the proven case of the Outrider's appearance in *A New Hope*'s Special Edition.

> Aurra Sing is not an EU character. And, as far as I know, Dex isn't either. Aayla Secura is the blue-skinned Twi'lek Jedi in the final battle who is wearing a very non-Jedi outfit showing off her stomach. She is the only pure-EU character to appear in a film (not counting the Outrider).[543]

Finally, Genghis12, whose signature announces "Intelligently Fitting The Newer EU into Established *Star Wars* Continuity" alongside the quotation " 'Let's Roll': George W. Bush, 1.29.02," lays down an authoritative account of Aayla Secura's origins.

---

541 HBMC_Kloon, ibid.

542 ObiWanJane, ibid. (17 May 2002).

543 Wild_Karrde, ibid.

> That "blue Twi'lek Jedi female" is more than EU-inspired and isn't "modelled on" someone called Aayla Secura. That character *is* Aayla Secura—an EU character who was included in the movie. The character is credited as "Aayla Secura," not "blue Twi'lek female."[544]

The original comment about Dex is forgotten, and the Aurra Sing theory put aside, but the tertiary case about Aayla Secura is convincingly proven. This short discussion marks an important victory for EU enthusiasts—like Bib Fortuna and JediSabre from chapter 5—as a rare, unambiguous instance of Lucas appropriating an Expanded Universe character into the upper hierarchy of canon. There is no need for bluff or dredged-up quotes from ancient interviews here; the official site, *Starwars.com,* tells the story plainly.

> She was already an existing heroine, with a built-in audience of comic book readers who understood her origins before she ever made it onto the screen. After seeing artist Jon Foster's original cover art for issue #33 of the ongoing *Star Wars* series, writer/director George Lucas saw star potential. Aayla Secura, a blue-skinned Padawan, embodied Jedi strength and Twi'lek femininity in an eye-catching combination of beauty and power. It was the perfect ingredient for the action sequence recipe Lucas and Industrial Light and Magic were constructing, layer-by-layer.[545]

Given that the canon purists in chapter 5 were clinging to the line that "Lucas said he doesn't read the EU" and "Lucas is in no way changing his vision to accommodate the EU writers," the incorporation of a comic book character in *Attack of the Clones*—at Lucas's personal request—was a significant validation of the secondary texts, at the same moment that Boba Fett's EU origin was wiped off the canonical map.[546] During a leaner time for board discussion, these shifts in canon would probably have earned threads to themselves; but in the weeks following the new film's release, Aayla Secura was almost swamped by bloopers and Easter Eggs, and the only question being asked about Fett was whether Jango banged his head on the roof of Slave 1.

---

[544]Genghis12, ibid.

[545]"From EU to Episode II: Aayla Secura," http://www.starwars.com/episode-ii/feature/20020618

[546]Kevin J. Anderson had invented a past for Fett as Journeyman Protector Jaster Mereel. EU fans on *TF.N* have attempted to rationalize this story as a rumor about Fett, or as a possible disguise. See Anderson, *Tales of the Bounty Hunters,* op. cit.

Lacking an enemy within, *Clones* gushers had to look outside the *TF.N* community for someone to rail against. Threads like "What is The Most Stupid Complaint You Have Heard About *AOTC*" called for comments from non-fans, other websites, and the broader media, then gleefully swiped them down. "Someone at IMDB.com said that the Yoda/Dooku lightsaber battle looked too fast," railed Jedi_Xen. "This idiot got mad at GL, saying he should show us their skill with a lightsaber instead of dazzling us with speed. This guy probably rates the Kenobi duel on the Death Star as the greatest of all time. *Yawns*."[547]

With no dissent on the thread, the contributors cast the net wider, making movie reviewer Roger Ebert—who gave *AOTC* two stars—into a temporary bogeyman. "Ebert has become a joke as a critic," said Jedzelex, "more at home reviewing foreign movies that most people wouldn't go out to see. His review on *AOTC* is very dumb."[548] Matrags approved, adding "I wouldn't mind Ebert's job . . . watching movies all day and whichever company pays you the highest gets good review,"[549] while Sonic_Pumpkins scorned, "If *AOTC* is boring to him, I wonder what his daily life is like! Wow. What an enthralling flick that would be, A Day in the Exciting Life of Roger Ebert."[550]

The most interesting target, though, was the *Detroit News,* which had run a story on May 18 suggesting that "*Clones* Has Racial Stereotypes." Contextualizing the criticisms in terms of the furor around *The Phantom Menace*'s supposed ethnic caricatures—Watto as a Jewish salesman, Jar Jar as an alien Stepin Fetchit, and the Nemoidians' "Charlie Chan" accents[551]—the story drew its evidence for stereotyping primarily from a roundtable discussion that had been specially organized by the newspaper.

This time the controversial figure was Jango Fett, who allegedly represented the perceived threat of Latino immigration into the United States. The actor behind Fett, Temuera Morrison, is a New Zealander of Maori descent, but as the report blandly noted, "that didn't get in the way" of the newspaper panel.

---

[547]Jedi_Zen, "What Is The Most Stupid Complaint . . . ," *TheForceNet,* op. cit. (27 May 2002).

[548]Jedzelex, ibid.

[549]Matrags, ibid.

[550]Sonic_Pumpkins, ibid.

[551]See Brooker, "Readings of Racism," op. cit.

> "He looked totally Latino," says Martina Guzman, a Detroiter who is managing a State House election campaign.
>
> "And his kid," says Wayne State history professor Jose Cuello, referring to the young Boba Fett, "looked even more Latino."
>
> It reminds Cuello a little bit of "those Reagan ads in the 1980 campaign, that suggested if Nicaragua went communist, you'd have wild-eyed Mexicans with guns running across the California border."[552]

The actor's "Latino" appearance is the first plank of this interpretation; the second is that the planet he inhabits, Kamino, sounds like the Spanish word *camino,* meaning "I walk." That Jango is the source for the clone army, "swarthy look-alikes who march in lockstep by the tens of thousands . . . genetically modified for docility and obedience," is seen by Syracuse University professor Robert Thompson as either a result of Lucas's subconscious fears of Latinos or as a deliberate attempt to ignite Anglo prejudices. "And that's the scarier interpretation," concludes Thompson, who had not seen the film when he was interviewed.[553]

Further allegations reported by the *Detroit News* ironically tend to undermine the "Latino" argument and support the view that styles, accents, and languages in the *Star Wars* saga are open to many different real-life parallels, depending on the viewer's cultural position and interpretive framework.

> Three Arab-Americans on the *News*' panel seized on the fact that Jango's son calls him "Baba."
>
> "I frankly think the bounty hunter is Arab," says college counsellor Imad Nouri of Royal Oak. "He's basically a terrorist," explains Nouri, "and 'baba' is Arabic for 'father.' "[554]

These passionate but conflicting arguments, based on flimsy linguistic cues and a suppression of any troublesome counterevidence—Morrison is a Maori, but this interpretation depends on his "looking Latino," so his dark skin is made to signify accordingly—unfortunately read almost like parody.

---

[552]Michael H. Hodges, "Critics Say *Clones* Has Racial Sterotypes," *Detroit News* (18 May 2002), n.p.

[553]Ibid.

[554]Ibid.

The impression is that these theories were brainstormed within an afternoon's meeting, for the purposes of a story; the feelings behind them are no doubt genuine, but the textual evidence given here seems very thin.

Unsurprisingly, rumors of this attack on *Clones* were met on *TheForce.net* with a united front of hostility. "I think Detroit needed something to talk about since they are not doing much of anything else these days," remarked SithLord_77.[555] "*Detroit Free Press* should send an apology to Lucasfilm and its readers for this monstrosity," argued ShiftyJedi.[556] BigBossNass1138 dubbed the newspaper report "the dumbest criticism" of all the complaints he'd heard about the film and countered the racism claims with ammunition provided in the article itself.

> I mean, what are these people on? Get real. Jango and his clones is having some kind of go at Latinos? Well, besides that being a moronic concept to begin with, it's not helped at all by the fact that, well, Temuera Morrison isn't Latino at all . . . oops sorry to burst your bubble guys. Maybe you should check your facts and write some journalism instead of sensationalist articles that have no basis in fact whatsoever.[557]

With the basher-gusher skirmishes and stalemate of the past few years almost entirely swept aside in a wave of relief, the whole *TF.N* board was effectively turned into an *AOTC* Defense Force against threats from outside. But what about the stronghold of older fans who had been so disillusioned with *Phantom Menace* that they almost lost faith in Lucas's ability to guide the saga through *Episode II*? For the contributors to Darth Derringer's board, visited in chapter 4, *Clones* was their last and only hope. The film had a lot to prove to this group of alienated skeptics—they wanted to embrace the prequels, but their decades of investment in the saga seemed to have been thrown back in their faces.

The Fan Repaid

In June 2000, Darth Derringer's contribution to the thread "Top Ten Reasons Why *TPM* was a Huge Disappointment"—with its complaint that

---

[555]SithLord_77, "What Is The Most Stupid Complaint You Have Heard About *AOTC*?" *TheForce.net,* op. cit. (27 May 2002).
[556]ShiftyJedi, ibid.
[557]BigBossNass1138, ibid.

the film "had no heart and soul. It was a nice summer movie . . . but that's it"—was symptomatic of the general mood on the *Official TPM Bashers Board*. Almost two years later, Derringer gave his first response to *Attack of the Clones*. It was dishearteningly similar.

> I've seen the movie . . . and was disappointed. Lucas wasted another golden opportunity. Before everyone thinks, "big surprise—DD just likes bashing Lucas," I want to say that I really really wanted to like it. I had a secret fantasy that it would be the prequel's version of *ESB,* one of my all-time favorite movies. But it wasn't. Hell, it wasn't even in the same league. It was a fun summer action flick, nothing more, nothing less.[558]

Again, Derringer reminds us of the emotional investment that bashers had in *Episode II,* and of the fact that they genuinely wanted to enjoy it. A key difference this time for this long-term fan, though, is that he has chosen to cut his losses and protect himself against further disappointment. Darth Derringer has given up on the mythos, or at least the newer mythos of the prequel trilogy.

> This time around . . . I don't feel angry or betrayed. I guess I've lost my inner *Star Wars* child because I don't really care that much anymore. I still love the original series, but this prequel business has become nothing more than an interesting 2+ hour distraction from my work stuff.[559]

Clearly, there came a point for Derringer where Lucas finally crossed a line of acceptability—one mediocre episode was just about bearable, two was the last straw—and where the precious *Star Wars* of 1977–1983 had to be isolated and sealed off from these imperfect mutations. However, while *TheForce.net*'s dynamic shifted with the release of *Clones* from a series of conflicts to near-consensus—a culture of approval policed by the more militant gushers—the *Bashers Board,* which had been explicitly formed for people who felt the same way about *TPM* and wanted a space to vent, now failed to reach a comparable agreement over *Attack of the Clones*. In place of mutual consolation over a shared disappointment, the board was witness to a range of different opinions.

---

[558]Darth Derringer, "I Done Seen It," *Official TPM Bashers Board,* op. cit. (19 May 2002).
[559]Ibid.

Derringer met with affectionate jibes for his critical post—"Darth Derringer, only you would be so bold," joked fellow regular Quaff Down Gin, quoting Leia's line to Tarkin from *New Hope*[560]—and outright attacks from another poster, Shimmergloom.

> You had no intention of liking the movie. Especially since even though I like *TPM,* it's obvious to me that *AOTC* is light years better. But you have no intention of liking a *Star Wars* movie, so it doesn't matter. He's been posting anti-*Star Wars* stuff for 3 years every chance he gets and now he's claiming that he was hoping *AOTC* was going to be great all along but was disappointed. Do you honestly think we're supposed to believe that?[561]

The initial response to Shimmergloom's complaint was interesting—as a self-confessed fan of *The Phantom Menace,* he was ordered by Padméwan McGregor to "take it to *TF.N.* Like we need this crap here."[562] There was clearly a desire to keep the *Bashers Board* a separate territory where bashers could speak their minds without gusher rebukes; a territory explicitly defined against *TheForce.net*'s *Jedi Council,* which many of the contributors to Derringer's community scorned as overly censorious and blandly uncritical of the prequels. "My damn thread got locked at the *JC* for no reason," Quaff Down Gin grumbled, "don't need to post there anymore, methinks."[563] "Good, post here," responded Padméwan McGregor.

> The intelligence level at the [*Jedi Council*] boards is about 0. The mods have become extremely aggressive closing down "redundant" threads. Nice to know they learned so much from past experience (sarcasm).[564]

Quaff Down subsequently came home from work to find he was "banned from the *JCF*. . . . "

> I guess they didn't like my comment about the title of my locked thread "Gripes With *Attack of the Clones*" when I said "the title refers to the inevitable actions of the admins and their droid army." Go figure.[565]

---

[560]Quaff Down Gin, ibid.
[561]Shimmergloom, ibid.
[562]Padméwan McGregor, ibid.
[563]Quaff Down Gin, ibid. (18 May 2002).
[564]Padméwan McGregor, ibid.
[565]Quaff Down Gin, ibid.

Bashers Board regular Sith Acolyte offered immediate solidarity—"man, are they prickly. I'm gonna go get banned too. I don't think I want to bother with the place any longer."[566] These exchanges present an interesting confirmation, from a group of excluded outsiders, that the *TF.N* boards to some extent may have been forced into a fixed smile. Although we have to assume that the overwhelmingly positive response to *Clones* on the *TF.N* polls—and the generally upbeat mood around the film on the discussion boards—were representative of a genuine trend among contributors, it is also entirely possible that dissent was not just stamped upon by the community's gushers, but weeded out by the administrators.

Yet despite this resentment of *TheForce.net*'s culture of cheerfulness and the attempt on Padméwan's part at least to exile nonconformists like Shimmergloom to the *Jedi Council,* the *Bashers Board* did not, on the whole, follow Derringer's lead in grouping *Clones* with *TPM* and declaring the whole prequel trilogy redundant. Far more typical were responses like these, which positioned the new film somewhere between the horrors of *Episode I* and the beloved Original Trilogy, and expressed various degrees of tentative approval. All of these contributors shared a distaste for *The Phantom Menace,* but all of them were at least partially converted by its sequel.

> As most of you know, I strode into the theatre Thursday expecting to loathe *Episode II*. Fortunately, I did not. Unlike a *TPM* Gusher, I do not let my anticipated appreciation for a *Star Wars* flick dictate my actual opinion.[567]

> Overall, I'm not just relieved but quite happy . . . the overall product was stronger, much more coherent, and I walked out quite ready to Gush, with a liberal sprinkling of Bash. I'm seeing it tomorrow night and next week, so who knows where my opinions will be then?[568]

> You know, I really did try my best to be rational about this movie, to allow myself not to like certain parts, that sort of thing. But I couldn't . . . I loved it and I want to see it again.[569]

---

[566]Sith Acolyte, ibid.

[567]Frank Danger, ibid.

[568]Padméwan McGregor, ibid.

[569]Reka, ibid.

> I said I would need three viewings to give an adequate evaluation, so here goes . . . I feel nonplussed. Sorta neutral borderline negative. Dona geta me wrongo, I actually enjoyed the movie. Thankfully. Thank GOD! I had fun despite the movie's shortcomings . . . whereas I give *TPM* a rock solid D, I feel confident in giving *AOTC* a B-.[570]

> I totally agree with Quaff Down Gin [author of the previous post]. The Tatooine stuff really brought this home for me as a *Star Wars* movie. C-3PO and R2D2 bickering back and forth was the one of the things that *TPM* was missing.[571]

> Just came back from my second viewing. Still happy with the results. I tried to watch the background more during some of the busier scenes, and I determined that there's too much going on to capture it all. I can only think of one thing that I enjoyed in *TPM* that was missing in *AOTC*—where in the blazes is Ric Olié?[572]

> That . . . did not suck. I was settling in, waiting for the movie to start, feeling lackadaisical. I'd approached a sense of calmness about the whole proceedings. Yes, the dialogue was going to be irritating. Yes, there would be things that would not make sense. But the action should be cool, enough to get me through the viewing. And if it did suck, I would deal with it. Life would go on. I was almost welcoming the badness, preparing myself to feast on shite. Then Amidala's ship blew up. Not perfect, but not bad. Not bad at all.[573]

> That's funny, Sith Acolyte. You and I went through the exact same thing![574]

As the last post suggests, the boards could still yield a sense of shared experience and pleasure from the recognition of similar reactions, even though the feelings here were far more mixed than they had been with *Phantom Menace*. The *Bashers Board* judgement of *Clones* was based on repeated viewings within a short space of time, as was the case with the *TF.N* contributors. From these multiple screenings they came up, apparently

---

[570] Quaff Down Gin, ibid.
[571] Eric, ibid.
[572] Qui Gon Generic, ibid. (17 May 2002).
[573] Sith Acolyte, ibid.
[574] Eric, ibid. (18 May 2002).

independently, with some of the same observations that were discussed on the "Bloopers and Easter Eggs" thread.

> A few things I noticed on my third viewing: During Qui-Gon's vocal cameo, there is also a definite Vader "hoo-paah." It really does sound like Jango hits his head when he enters his ship.[575]

The accusations of racism were also picked up and mocked—"that Maori guy is offensive to Latinos. Sue Lucas now!"[576]—with specific reference to the various allegations in the *Detroit News* story. "Boba Fett in Arabic means 'Father Fett' . . . it's an obvious racist stab at terrorists! Gotta love Detroit."[577] However, in contrast to *TF.N*'s scornful closing of ranks against all such criticisms, the *Bashers Board* witnessed a thoughtful counterargument when a contributor labelled anyone who had found Jar Jar offensive as "sensitive in weird ways." JediEowyn responded, offering examples from the African American writer Langston Hughes to suggest that Jar Jar's dialect did have real-world racial parallels.

> Jar Jar's grammar sounds to me like it constructs pronouns and verbs in the same way one adjusts pronouns and verbs to recreate an old black Southern accent. The following lines from Langston Hughes' "Mother to Son" I think might help show how Jar Jar's speech seems to be constructed on a black accent: "But all the time I'se been a-climbin' on" reminds me of "Meesa sorry" and "Wees-a-goin' home!"[578]

The *Bashers Board* is, overall, made up of older contributors than *TF.N,* and is less rigidly moderated, which results in a community more open to debate and less prone to gang loyalties. There is more room here for ambivalence and evolving opinions, and little sense of a party line; the founder, Darth Derringer, was actually in the minority with his decision to abandon the prequel trilogy, and he made no effort to impose his views. However, bearing in mind that this was a gathering of *TPM*'s harshest critics, we can identify an overall feeling of relief and qualified approval; a feeling that the fans' investment in the saga was being at least partially

[575]DaedSiLuam, ibid. (22 May 2002).
[576]Zizou10, ibid. "The Race Card Bandwagon Thread," (10 June 2002).
[577]The Lounge Lizard, ibid.
[578]Jedi Eowyn, ibid. (11 June 2002).

Boba Fett in *Sins of the Jedi*

repaid. This was going to be a difficult group to win over, and they had had their spirits lifted enough for their hope to be renewed. "I enjoyed the movie despite its shortcomings," Quaff Down Gin concluded, "give it a solid B- . . . and hope that *Episode III* delivers like a motha."

Films, Slash and *Clones* Chicks

At the time of writing, fan filmmaking is only just beginning to respond to *Episode II*. *TheForce.Net*'s theater features a clutch of ongoing projects set in a post-*Clones,* pre–*New Hope* timeline, including Evolution Entertainment's seven-part serial *Sins of the Jedi*[579]—which features a Boba Fett who clearly wears a hybrid of the familiar Original Trilogy outfit and Jango's *Episode II* armor.

---

[579]See www.sinsofthejedi.com

Other *Clones*-era productions range from the endearingly inane to the hugely ambitious, often going to both extremes in the same film. Neo-Trinity Studios—made up of sixth, seventh, and eighth graders from a New York school and their teacher, Mr. Lucia—is currently working on *Fall of the Jedi,*[580] whose story begins at the end of the Clone Wars, while Håkan Andersson's *Kid Wars: Attack on the Father Clones*[581] is a play-fight between a Swedish dad and his children, boosted with stunning home-produced digital effects. Greg Sacrist and Rory Wallwork's *Dark Beginnings,*[582] apparently set in a post-*Menace,* pre-*Clones* galaxy where the Sith are active and the Republic subject to corruption, is essentially another saber-test expanded into a simple plot, much like Macomber and Thomas's *Duel.* As with many of the lower-budget fan productions, the CGI spacecraft are mind-blowing, while the characters look and sound like frat boys wandering in a desert.

Perhaps the most surprising offering is the award-winning *Rise of the Empire*[583] by Jay Silver, a speculative trailer for *Episode III* based entirely on Lego figures; despite the plastic performances, the film is so skillfully edited—in a neat pastiche of the *Episode II* trailers with their dramatic fades and fleeting glimpses—that it becomes gripping to watch. The *TF.N Theater* even places a spoiler warning on the link, in case Silver's predictions about Anakin's downfall and his pregnant wife's escape with Obi-Wan ruin anyone's enjoyment of the real *Episode III. Rise of the Empire* can be differentiated from speculative fan-fiction produced before *Clones* by its incorporation of specific details from that movie—Anakin's transformation into Vader is signalled by his lifting the claw-hand he gained after his duel with Count Dooku, and clenching it in a characteristic gesture from the Original Trilogy. "I have come to realize the truth . . . about power," he intones.

On the basis of this energetic response to *Episode II* in the fan film community, we would expect slash fiction to have produced a new wave of stories about the characters and relationships in *Attack of the Clones,* presumably taking inspiration from Hayden Christensen's brooding

---

[580]See http://www.geocities.com/thefallofthejedi/index.html

[581]See http://www.lysator.liu.se/~zap/kidwars/

[582]See http://www.secristfamily.com/brofilms/index.htm

[583]See http://users.eastlink.ca/~jaysilver/

Jay Silver's *Rise of the Empire*

Padawan and his strict but occasionally playful master, Obi-Wan. The new wave never came; and *Clones*' failure to spark anything like the body of same-sex erotic fiction that resulted from *Phantom Menace* seems symptomatic of its broader failure to stimulate or satisfy the largely female community of slash authors. My inquiries and research during the first month after the film's release cannot, of course, be used as the basis for sweeping conclusions about a whole community's response—still less for theories about gendered reception—but from the evidence I gathered, women writers were the one outstanding audience group who wanted more than *Clones* delivered.

They wanted to write *Clones* slash; they were planning to write *Clones* slash. They even wrote a significant body of *Clones* slash before the film came out, but the film didn't fill out the relationships in the way they had expected. Fee Folay offered an early report on this phenomenon, based on her visit to the Media West fan convention in Michigan in May 2002.

> One of the panels this year focused on the possibility of an Obi-Wan/Anakin relationship . . . there was also an Obi-Wan/Qui-Gon panel, and the Obi/Ani relationship was discussed there as well. The consensus? Most people do not see much basis for such a relationship; and in fact, they predict there will be very little Obi-Wan/Anakin slash (at least in comparison to the amount of Obi/Qui that is out there.)

> Some authors admitted to writing some Obi/Ani stories, but also said they had written them *before* the film was released. Even Yoda/Mace and Dexter Jettster/Obi-Wan were mentioned as having more potential than Anakin/Obi. (Don't ask! I didn't really want to have to consider those particular pairings too closely.)
>
> There was also a general sense of disappointment that there were no scenes between Anakin and Bail [Organa] as many had assumed the two had some sort of close relationship which led Obi-Wan to trust Bail with the infant Leia. There is already some Obi/Bail floating around, but the movie did not provide any support for it.[584]

Xehra Bethe, webmistress of the fantasy and science fiction fan site *Matherion,* confirmed that

> the *AOTC*-based fics are being very slow to trickle in. I haven't seen anything in the slash line yet, only Anakin/Amidala mush mixed with Obi-Wan love triangles (rolls eyes). There is, however, a ton of speculative fiction (including slash), which was written prior to *AOTC.* I know of one archive specialising in Obi-Wan/Bail Antilles slash.[585]

In keeping with Fee's implication that slash finds its couples in unusual places, Xehra also predicted "some serious Zam/Fett smut in the works."[586]

A glance at the *Master-Apprentice* archive[587] for *Attack of the Clones* slash supported these suggestions. The library held twelve Obi/Bail stories, submitted between November 17, 2001 and May 12, 2002. The film's May 16 release, with its absolute lack of any close interaction between Obi-Wan and Bail Organa, seemed to have immediately closed down the inclination to write any further stories in this subgenre, at least for the present. The Obi/Ani archive, by contrast, contained merely two stories—both written and submitted during 2000—suggesting that sexual explorations of this relationship had never taken off at *Master-Apprentice.* Stories within the Obi/Ani genre can be found elsewhere—the *SW-AL Slash Archive,*[588] for instance, holds Laura-Ann Troise's O/A fic "Shadows" and Lady Bard's "Right Path"—but again, both of these were archived

[584]Fee Folay, personal e-mail (1 June 2002).

[585]Xehra Bethe, personal e-mail (2 June 2002).

[586]Xehra Bethe, *Matherion,* http://www.angelfire.com/grrl/matherion/fantastic.htm

[587]*Master and Apprentice,* http://www.masterapprentice.org/html/archive.html

[588]*SW-AL Slash Archive,* http://www.squidge.org/swal/index.htm

well before *Episode II*'s release. "Shadows," focusing on Obi-Wan and his Padawan ten years after *Phantom Menace,* was written in April 1999.

The *Jedi Council*'s genfic boards provide examples of the strand described by Xehra as "mush." Meredith's "His and Hers Circumstances,"[589] categorized as "Ami/Ani/Vader," is a well-written mood piece that begins during the bedroom assassination scene of *Attack of the Clones,* but it was received on the forum as innocent, sweet romance. Fellow contributor Shezan enthused, "This was SO wonderful, and everything that was sorely needed in the movie! More of this please! When I read this I can understand how they fall in love at last!"[590] Perhaps surprisingly, Xehra's theory that Zam/Jango would be picked up as a new genre also finds some evidence here in "Killing me Softly," a mild hurt/comfort where Fett tends his fellow bounty hunter after a hit that goes wrong.[591]

Even the most obvious—and perhaps therefore the least interesting—pairing earns a story in the *Sith Chicks* archive. Moonscribe's "A Day At The Beach," set some time around the Naboo scenes of *Episode II,* has Padmé parading before Anakin in "the skimpiest little two piece bathing suit he had ever seen" and seducing him with the help of some suntan oil. "Tell me, Ani," she inevitably asks him. "Is that a lightsaber you're holding or are you just happy to see me?"[592] The fact is that, as Xehra and Fee suggest and this brief archival tour seems to confirm, a wide range of characters from *Attack of the Clones,* from the predictable to the bizarre, will be subject to slashing, and a thorough search will turn up stories about virtually every conceivable couple.

However, it is still possible to identify clear trends, and discussion on the *Master-Apprentice* slash mailing list during early June 2002 reinforced the notion that Obi/Ani was widely regarded as a nonstarter.

> I must say that I very much agree with the opinion that Obi and Ani's relationship is similar to that of an older and a younger sibling. I just do not see any slash potential at all, and, quite honestly, I find any Obi/Ani fics to be somewhat disturbing for that reason. Perhaps I am of the belief that Ani is very much heterosexual. He just doesn't seem

---

[589]Meredith, "His and Hers Circumstances," archived at *TheForce.net,* op. cit.
[590]Ibid.
[591]Zam, "Killing Me Softly," archived at *TheForce.net,* op. cit.
[592]Moonscribe, "A Day At The Beach," archived at *SithChicks,* op. cit.

> a logically slashable candidate, no matter how I think of him. However, I also seem to believe that Obi is as gay as all get out and there probably isn't a straight bone in that boy's body.[593]

> Strangely enough as hard as I tried (and believe me I did try very hard) I failed to see slash between Anakin and Obi-Wan. Now normally the only time that I don't see slash in a film is when I watched it with eyes closed. But I swear I was awaken. [sic] The person that I could see slashed: Obi-Wan/Mace (lack of Qui-Gon), Obi-Wan/Fett (he did give him some eyes in that scene.)[594]

> In regards to Obi and Ani's relationship, I really didn't see much affection and respect between them . . . the way Obi put Ani down: "You will learn your place." (shudders) Sounds like there was a LOT of friction between the two.[595]

> I had much the same feeling when I saw that scene. That is one of the reasons why I could never do Obi-Wan/Anakin slash. Too much resentment going on there. And not even in a good way.[596]

Siubhan, webmistress of the *Sith Academy,* also picked up on this sense within the slash community that *Attack of the Clones* was throwing up comparatively little erotic fiction, and that what there was went against expectations. "It's nothing like the massive Q/O explosion that happened almost immediately upon the release of *TPM* . . . "

> O/A, which seemed like the obvious pairing going in, was just not there. Hell, Padmé/Anakin wasn't really there either. The only remotely plausible pairing I've heard anyone come up with is Jango/Obi, and that's only because of the whole [*X-Files*] Mulder/Krycek "I hate you and yet I'm drawn to you" dynamic. There was tension in their scene together. Tension makes for interesting smut. But every other pairing I've seen espoused simply seems to me to be more of an intellectual exercise than something with real heat.[597]

---

[593]CrysBlues, post from *Master-Apprentice* slash list, quoted by Fee Folay, personal e-mail (7 June 2002).

[594]Strange Music, ibid.

[595]Glorianna, ibid.

[596]Indalia, ibid.

[597]Siubhan, personal e-mail (2 June 2002).

However, Siubhan's links her complaints about the lack of energy between Obi-Wan/Anakin to her own—and her friends'—deeper dissatisfaction with the film's handling of emotional relationships. As suggested by her comment that even Anakin and Padmé didn't come off as a couple, Siubhan was left cold by *Episode II* on a fundamental level and feels she isn't alone.

> *AOTC* really isn't as inspiring. I actually think it's a far inferior movie to *TPM* . . . most of my friends aren't impressed with it. Horrible as Jar Jar Binks was, the Padmé/Anakin love story was even worse. There was zero chemistry between them, there was nothing even remotely attractive about Anakin, every time they opened their mouths the dialogue was just awful (if only either of them had been introduced to the grammatical wonder that is the apostrophe . . .) I walked out the first time feeling actively annoyed, and the second time going "Well, okay, if you ignore the love story, it's not so bad, and I guess the story is kinda interesting." That's not what I go to movies for, especially *Star Wars* movies.
>
> Now, you may think that I just hang with a very critical group of people. But take this into account: I was at a sci-fi convention the weekend after this movie opened. The first day of the con we went as a group to see the film. The theatre was empty. And there was a sci-fi convention a block and a half away. That really says something. Another thing to consider. A good friend of mine who is a long-time, hard-core *Star Wars* fan has declared that she's not wasting her time and money on *Episode III*. That's how much she hated *Episode II*.[598] I know the movie has its fans, and I've spoken to some of them, and I honestly can't believe we watched the same movie.

There is a strong air of bullish defensiveness about Siubhan's criticism, as if she knows the climate has changed and that fandom as a whole tends to regard *Attack of the Clones* favorably; hence her pounding home of the argument and her rallying of support, both above and in the subsequent e-mails she sent me, forwarding reviews from her online acquaintances. "I was bored," states JediMom flatly,

> shifting-in-my-seat, checking-my-watch bored. I didn't care about any of the characters. I didn't believe in any of the relationships (especially the teacher/student relationship between Obi-Wan and Anakin and the

[598]Ibid.

> romantic relationship between Anakin and Amidala). The plot felt like the characters were being moved around on a chessboard. *Phantom Menace,* by contrast, though it had some awful dialogue and a rather thin plot, at least engaged my interest. I cared what happened to the characters.[599]
>
> This film offers NOTHING to the adult female viewer. Tween girls, perhaps, may be excited about Anakin, or identify with Amidala (or just covet her outfits) but those of us past puberty will only want to smack Anakin (and not in a good way), be supremely disgusted with Amidala, and find the "romance" plot—which is the part of the movie that we dames are supposed to like, anyway—an excruciating travesty that needs to be put out of its misery. Meanwhile, I am guessing that I am not the only woman in Lucas' audience who was incredibly bored by the toys vs. toys shoot-em-up that ends the movie.
>
> No doubt Lucas is under the impression that all his fans are male; but as the *Sith Academy* proves, he is wrong. However, if he keeps making movies the way he's been makin' them, he may eventually be right.[600]

The community around *Sith Academy,* on this evidence, gave *Clones* a rougher ride than the *Bashers Board* gang of disillusioned but hopeful diehards—the key difference being that the *Sith Academy,* like so many other slash-related sites, had found something to love in *The Phantom Menace*. By reading the "whiz-bang" adventure story of *Episode I* for its moments of potential homoerotic romance, by constructing histories and contexts for the Jedi couple and investing scraps of dialogue—even glances and occasional touches—with volumes of unspoken meaning, many slash writers had transformed *Phantom Menace* into something that was (to them, at least) sophisticated, subtle, and fascinating.

They had rehabilitated the film and made it something close to their hearts, playing up the elements that pleased them and tolerating the rest. Finding no hooks for this kind of reworking in *Episode II,* they had little reason to show it any mercy. Without a central slash relationship, which they had hoped and planned for, what remained seemed like little more than CGI action, imperfect acting, and flaws in character and plot. A rich mine of Obi/Bail nudges and gazes to play with would, I suspect, have

---

[599] JediMom, quoted in Siubhan, personal e-mail (5 June 2002).
[600] The Plaid Adder, ibid.

made Siubhan and her *Sith Academy* friends far more forgiving of the faults that, to some extent, exist within every *Star Wars* film; yet, lacking any moments of homoerotic potential to grab onto, reexamine, and pry open for new meanings, these female viewers found their attention skimming off the film's surface.

Watching *Attack of the Clones* Together

[Padmé's ship approaches Coruscant]

Will: I really like the sound of that ship. It's got that sort of World War II sound, a sort of chugging.

Adam: That's a Stuka bomber. A German warplane.

Paul: Or a Wellington.

Will: It's based on a stealth bomber.

Adam: S-1178. I know all this!

Will: So you're a planes expert.

Adam: No, I just play a lot of computer games. [laughter]

Mark: [seeing Captain Typho] That's Laurence Fishburne, isn't it?

Adam: No, Laurence Fishburne is a big black guy.

Mark: Yeah, the one with the patch.

Adam: No [laughter] flipping hell, Mark.

Mark: So who is it then? He looks like one of those New Zealand rugby players.

Adam: Laurence Fishburne was the guy from, um . . .

Will: *The Matrix*. He's about forty.

Mark: He looks good for his age here.

Will: Well, it isn't him.

Chatham, late June 2002: I was in Mark Williams' and Phil Espline's shared house with Tim Meader and two brothers, Paul and Adam Jenner. Paul, 28, worked for the Ford automobile dealership in Gravesend, Kent, and Adam, 20, was an ex-bouncer who now worked for his father's carpet firm. Duncan Wilson was suffering the effects of "a skinful at lunchtime" and was staying at home with his wife Emma. We were watching *Attack of the Clones* on a bootleg DVD.

Before the screening, Mark had demanded his right to reply to my comments in chapter 2, and I include his critique here because my return visit provided such a rare and, I think, valuable opportunity for a research subject to take the stand again and respond to the way he had been portrayed. Tim had explained to me as we drove to Mark's house that the publication of *Using the Force* had prompted a good deal of banter at the solicitors office where he worked with Mark and Phil. Tim had photocopied the relevant chapter and Mark had been the target of jibes about his lustfully macho comments on *Empire,* which were seen as protesting too much and as a possible symptom of secret homosexuality. Mark had recently "changed his image and started wearing beads," Tim added, and his decision to move in with Phil was a further gift to jokes about his "gayness."

Obviously, these lighthearted accusations construct homosexuality as something undesirable and suggest a degree of homophobia among this group of straight twenty-something men and their workmates. Adam in particular responded vehemently to reports of slash fiction that Tim had summarized from chapter 7, launching without being prompted into a rant that homoerotic *Star Wars* fiction "infuriates me. It brings down the character. You can't have two of the greatest characters ever to be written as gay. You can't have Jedis who are gay. That bothers me, it bothers me deeply."[601]

Mark's protest, however, seemed to be based not on a deep aversion to homosexuality so much as a desire to set the record straight; he complains that my comments portray him as either a closeted gay man or a rampantly prejudiced heterosexual, and plays to the crowd as he clears his name.

> Mark: [reading from *Using the Force*] "Having been invited into Mark's house, I can now blithely comment that perhaps he deliberately adopted a laddish performance to avoid being thought of as gay." [laughter] Either that means that I really just resent being thought of as gay and therefore go to the extremes, or, I am gay and I'm just covering it up! As they [his friends] like to believe. So, just for the record, I'm not gay . . . too bloody right I'm not! And any woman reading the book, if they're tasty I'm available.

Despite the fact that *Clones* had only been released in cinemas six weeks before this interview, Tim and Adam had seen the film twelve

---

[601]All quotations taken from tape-recorded transcript of interviews and commentary on *Attack of the Clones* (29 June 2002).

times on their illegal DVD, and were able to play the quotation game to almost the same level of skill that we saw in chapter 2. They dominated the conversation during the film, with the others holding back and allowing them to perform: Tim, retaining his old role as the Yoda expert, was encouraged to act out the character's new dialogue, particularly in the "Jedi younglings" scene where Obi-Wan has embarrassingly "lost a planet." Adam, in turn, claimed a special skill at Obi-Wan impressions, and continually delivered the line "R4, can you boost the power?" when Kenobi appeared on-screen, until this snatch of dialogue gained comic value through sheer repetition. Although Adam was absent from the chapter 2 gathering, he clearly has enough status in the group—enhanced by his superior knowledge of the film—to take this central role with Tim.

[*Anakin: I don't know why I keep dreaming about her now. I haven't seen her since I was little.*]

Adam: [as Obi-Wan] Dreams pass, in time.

[*Obi-Wan: Dreams pass in time.*]

[Laughter]

Paul: You've seen this far too many times.

Tim: [as Obi-Wan] He went *completely* the other way.

Will: I like the way he goes, [as Obi-Wan] "I felt it too."

Mark: They both feel it [the presence of the assassin bugs] at the same time, don't they?

Will: Let's have a look, who feels it first.

Adam: Anakin. [as Obi-Wan] I felt it too.

Tim: "I sensed it," I think.

[*Obi-Wan: I sense it too.*]

Paul: Lightsaber moment!

Mark: It's quite *Blade Runner,* all this, isn't it?

Will: That's Sebulba, isn't it?

Paul: It's a Dug.

[*Anakin and Obi-Wan pilot speeder through Coruscant traffic*]

Paul: You just know, when they bring the game out, this sodding bit's gonna be in it, and it's gonna be impossible, innit?

[*Obi-Wan and Anakin fly speeder through power couplings*]

Adam: [as Obi-Wan] That felt good.
[*Obi-Wan: That was good.*]
[Laughter]
Adam: That *was* good, or that *felt* good?
Will: That *was* good.
Mark: A lot of the language in this one, though, it's very twentieth century.
Adam: Here, Tim. [pointing out line]
[*Obi-Wan: He went* completely *the other way.*]
[Laughter]
Tim: [as Obi-Wan] He went *completely* the other way.

Note that there is still an ongoing learning process at work here, with members of the group helping one another out with dialogue cues and accuracy: Adam and Tim in particular are constantly improving their delivery and trying to ensure they have the correct wording. Paul's comment about the transition from film to computer game and Mark's comparison of the city's mise-en-scène to *Blade Runner* is in keeping with the intertextual remarks we saw in chapter 2, such as Tim's cross-reference to *Force Commander* and Duncan's drawing parallels to Harrison Ford movies. Paul takes it upon himself to announce any "lightsaber moments" during the film, having recently ordered a model weapon from a website.

Tim was of the opinion that Emma Wilson's absence would make no difference to the group, but in fact the dynamic was immediately different, and the atmosphere became more ribald and bawdy as the screening went on. Paul complained of the Coruscant nightclub that "it looks too much like . . . Soho or something," perhaps thinking of the London district's gay associations, but cheered up enough to comment that "there are some tasty birds here. Thonged-up." The lascivious observations about female clubbers in thong underwear gave over to mockery of Adam's girlfriends when Zam Wesell, the changeling bounty hunter, reverted to her reptilian form.

Paul: Looks like one of your birds.
Adam: That's one of the better ones. I have had a few mingers in my time. I'm a minger meself, really. [Laughs]

Although there is obviously a fair amount of sexism—as well as homophobia and even racial insensitivity—behind this group's commentary, note that Adam also makes jokes about his own appearance and gives himself the unflattering label of "minger," slang for an ugly woman. Later Paul makes a crack about his weight, watching the clones march through the Kaminoan factory: "I could have been Boba Fatt." The Kent working-class humor displayed by the Jenner brothers in particular may seem to reflect a slightly prejudiced worldview, but it also involves a significant amount of self-deprecation.

That said, the increase in boys-only banter during this screening, in comparison to the last, was dramatic. This may be partly because the film itself has more sexual imagery and situations than *Empire*—it does, after all, feature a story line of first love between two glamorous and hormonal young people, and Padmé's costumes are notoriously more revealing and provocative than anything seen before in the *Star Wars* saga. Designer Ian McCaig admitted, "It's a love story. There's a lot more of a sexy, seductive element. And so the costumes we were looking at didn't have to hide Natalie this time; they were revealing her."[602] Natalie Portman confirmed that "this time, I get to show a little more skin. There are some risqué outfits going on."[603]

I quoted above the *TF.N* contributor who wryly noted that "it appears that the ship itself is pretty cold because Padmé is certainly showing under her tight white bodysuit." This observation was widespread and not limited to male fans. Xehra Bethe's list of things to look for in *Clones* included "Padmé headlighting. You know what I mean. In the white battledress. Believe me, from the second row of the theatre, you're not paying attention to Obi-Wan's message."[604] Siubhan also remarked "I couldn't tell if it was cold on the spaceship or it was just the darts on her outfit, but either way, it was pretty regrettable for Natalie's dignity."[605] However, no online fan I came across paid quite the same unhealthy attention to Padmé's outfit as did Adam Jenner.

[*Padmé runs across field on Naboo*]

---

[602]Ian McCaig, quoted in Mark Cotta Vaz, *The Art of Star Wars: Attack of the Clones,* London: Ebury Press (2002), p. 58.

[603]Natalie Portman, interviewed by Mark Dinning, *Empire* no. 156 (June 2002).

[604]Xehra Bethe, *Matherion,* op. cit.

[605]Siubhan, personal e-mail (15 June 2002).

Adam: Now, you can see the shape of her pubic hair here, when she runs.
Mark: You what?
Adam: The shape of her pubic hair.
Will: That's part of her dress.
Adam: No, you can see the shape of it, if you're in a cinema . . .
Tim: You perve.

Later, the white bodysuit was the subject of similar debate.

Adam: You see her smuggling peanuts here.
Paul: It's the squares [on her outfit].
Adam: I'd have to touch them to find out. Feel how they're protruding.
Mark: I think it's just the corners. I think they're just covering them up. I said that when we came out, didn't we? I don't know if it's just the costume . . .
Paul: She does have these squares, doesn't she? On the pockets.
Mark: Yeah, I thought it was the corners . . .
Tim: In the arena, though, you see her stomach. And you think, ahhh . . . her stomach is nice.

It was partly Adam's presence, then, as well as Emma's absence, that changed the dynamic so significantly for this viewing. In addition to the comments quoted above, Adam remarked of Anakin's nightmare, "He's having a wank . . . cracking one off" and made repeated boasts about his own abilities at fighting, presumably based on his experience as a bouncer. When Anakin emerged from the Tusken Raiders' tent and cut two of them down with one stroke, Adam suggested, "He's like, 'you wanker' "—this time using the word to indicate Anakin's contempt for the Sand People, as if the Jedi was involved in a brawl outside a Chatham nightspot—and added, "I can actually do that." As an extension of this stereotypically masculine response, the whole group treated the climactic arena battle as if it were a sports game, freeze-framing the DVD and rewinding it to examine combat moves and pick out obscure players like Kit Fisto.

There were three interesting conclusions towards the end of the evening, if we gloss over the lads' examination of Mark's video collection for proof of "gayness," and reworking the titles so that *Back to the Future* became *Backs to the Wall* and *Monty Python* became *Monty's Python*. First, a discussion about discrepancies between the prequels and Original Trilogy led Mark to put on his video of *A New Hope,* and it was obvious that *Attack of the Clones* had placed the original *Star Wars* in a new perspective. The lightsaber duel between Vader and Obi-Wan was analyzed in terms of Anakin's fighting style from *Episode II* and the extent to which both combatants had lost their edge through age, lack of practice, or injury. Adam delivered his imitations of Kenobi's voice along with Alec Guinness's performance, effectively demonstrating the similarity between the 1977 Obi-Wan and Ewan McGregor's 2002 homage, and creating a sense of fluid continuity even as he drew out odd inconsistencies through his merging of *Episode II* and *Episode IV* dialogue. "I don't recall ever owning a droid . . . R4, can you boost the power?" The group discussed the existing *Star Wars* films as a five-part serial with one missing episode, a generous response that would probably have pleased George Lucas.

Second, however, the return to *A New Hope* immediately induced a rush of nostalgia and affection, and *Clones* suffered badly by comparison. "*A New Hope* knocks the prequels into a cocked hat," Paul announced. "Automatically, it's just so much better." The less advanced special effects were a small price to pay for what these fans saw as a much more involving emotional storyline. Adam joked, after admitting that he was drawn in and instantly moved by *Star Wars,* that he must be "in touch with my feminine side." This sudden shift in loyalties away from the prequels to the Holy Trilogy surprised everyone, given that the group had greatly enjoyed watching *Attack of the Clones;* it could well be due as much to the earlier film's associations of childhood and its importance as a long-term love object as it is to any difference in characterization, acting, or plot.

Finally, at the start of the evening everyone in the group had given a favorable response to *Attack of the Clones,* apart from Paul. His criticism was that the film didn't contain enough action and therefore wasn't "truly *Star Wars*." How he could want more action from a film that opens with a spacecraft explosion and climaxes with a score of Jedi against a platoon of battle droids, the arrival of a clone army, and a four-way lightsaber duel remained a mystery, but at the end of the screening he too was won over. The experience of watching in a group had transformed the movie for him "because you can talk and take the piss out of the bits you don't like. They should let you talk in cinemas, have a room just for the six of you." The banter and running commentary, particularly the lampooning of slow or unsuccessful scenes, had helped Paul to work through a negotiated reading that played down less pleasing aspects and enhanced the moments he enjoyed. When the evening was over, it was also clear that the rapid bonding I noted in chapter 2 had taken place again, but this time with one of the group's new members. As Tim drove us to our respective homes, Adam turned to me in the back of the car and confided, "I've only just met you, but I feel like I've known you for years."

The Best of Times

In 1997 I wrote a list in the back of a notebook in an attempt to establish what events, characters and locations had to be worked into the prequel trilogy. It included some guesses that are satisfying to look back upon now—"Jabba: almost definitely as CGI in-joke," "Coruscant," "Boba Fett? How old is he," "Skywalker trained by Obi-Wan," "Clone Wars: General Kenobi, Bail Organa"—and others that seem wide of the mark, such as "Chewbacca," "Lady Skywalker," and "Obi-Wan trained by Yoda." Five years later and two prequels in, the task of predicting the remaining episode is far easier.

Episode III is sandwiched between known events, and its options are significantly limited unless Lucas dodges continuity—as he did with Obi-Wan's never owning a droid and being trained by Yoda—or actually reworks the Original Trilogy, as some fans expect he may, in an Ultimate Edition that resolves all narrative bloopers and inserts prequel characters into scenes from *Episodes IV–VI*. If the original movies are digitally reshuffled one final time, Jar Jar could be placed in a new scene on Alderaan during *A New Hope*; but barring this kind of cheat, it is a fairly safe bet that he, like other major characters such as Dooku, Mace, and Padmé, will die in *Episode III*. The question then is not when or whether it will happen, but how.

Following the revelations of *Attack of the Clones,* the *Episode III* boards at *TF.N* were loaded with debates along these lines. "How Do You Think

Mace Will Die?" asked The_Doode.[606] "Horrible boating accident," guessed Justified,[607] while more sensible answers argued that the killer had to be Boba Fett "since it's the only way I can see Lucas making Boba into a more dangerous bounty hunter than his dad,"[608] or "Anakin/Vader's first Force Choke, I'd reckon."[609] These speculative posts are based on notions of character development—Mace would provide an opportunity for viewers to witness the evolving ability and callousness of the Dark Lord or the bounty hunter—while another, more complex suggestion took its cues from a line of *Empire Strikes Back* dialogue, Boba's subsequent behavior in *Return of the Jedi,* and the evidence from the *Clones* arena scene where the young Boba watches Mace kill his father.

> I imagine that Mace will be aiding the getaway of Obi-Wan and Amidala. In like manner that Mace fends off the many droids in the arena, he will be attacked round about by many Clone (Storm) Troopers. Mace will take down these and then from the smoke will come Darth Vader to confront Mace. They exchange a few words, then the battle will begin. What will cut the battle short will be a laser cannon blast catching Mace from behind off guard. Vader looks in the direction of the blast and sees none other but Boba Fett. Vader is angry, but he sees and understands. [all *sic*]
>
> So in *ESB,* when Vader confronts Boba and says "no disintegrations" he will have been referring to when Boba robbed him of taking down Mace those years ago. Anyway, Boba almost made the same mistake his father made in *ROTJ* when he got too close to Luke . . . he got smart again and opted to try to take him down from long-range as Luke was preoccupied on the other skiff. I think this is how he would take out Mace.[610]

Other explanations of similar depth are offered for the anticipated deaths of Padmé and Jar Jar, with the latter given greater odds of survival: "in the *Ultimate Edition* depicting Alderaan just before its destruction he can appear in hologram form in a conversation with Bail Organa";[611]

---

[606]The_Doode, "How Do You Think Mace Will Die?" *TheForce.Net,* op. cit. (14 May 2002).
[607]Justified, ibid.
[608]Uncle Owen, ibid.
[609]Darth-Mauls-Torso, ibid.
[610]Darth Sin, ibid. (28 May 2002).
[611]Darcphoenyx, "And What Will Be The Fate of Jar Jar Binks," *TheForce.Net,* op. cit. (20 May 2002).

"actually, I place Jar Jar in the Rebel Alliance. I wouldn't put it past GL to insert him in the *SW:UE*."[612] Additional threads propose the theory that Vader gains his armor from his various kills during *Episode III*—"Parts of Plo Koon's mask, maybe . . . ,"[613] "Dooku's cape, Mace's gloves and boots"[614]—and ask whether the apparent continuity errors between Owen Lars, Anakin, and Threepio will be resolved.

> 1. Why doesn't he recognize C-3PO in *ANH* if he lived with him for five years when Anakin came back?
>
> 2. In *ANH,* Kenobi said that Owen thought Anakin should stay on Tatooine and not have gotten involved. Will Owen have time to explain this? IMO he hardly even knows Anakin, and by the time he does, Anakin is a major player in the universe.
>
> Or could Obi-Wan just chalk this up as "another point of view" thing? I hope Lucas lets us in on some of these things in *Episode III*.[615]

As the last post implies, *Episode III* is seen as Lucas's last chance to straighten out the contradictions between what we were told in the Original Trilogy and what we saw in the prequels. Although hopes are high on these boards following the perceived return to form of *Clones,* there is still anxiety that Lucas could, as Forja-Bingbey puts it on the "Uncle Owen" thread, "mess this whole saga up."[616] Another poster, Damn_I_Love_Yoda, protests in broken English, "hoe can he mes it up? It's his story, not ours, whateer he sais go,"[617] to which Marcusith replies, "true, it's his story not ours, but he can STILL ruin it!"[618]

The detection process is already underway, even at this early stage before any snatched location photos, leaked storyboards, or torn call-sheets have reached the community; there are sufficient clues in the existing primary texts now to sketch out a rough idea of the plot and establish characters' ultimate fates. "Anakin never gets to see Luke . . . Vader

---

612Ternian, ibid.
613RamblinJ, "The Official Vader's Armor Thread," *TheForce.Net,* op. cit. (5 May 2002).
614Anakindbud, ibid. (6 May 2002).
615Kabal, "Will The Owen Confusion Be Explained?" *TheForce.Net,* op. cit. (18 May 2002).
616Forja-Bingbey, ibid. (20 May 2002).
617Damn_I_Love_Yoda, ibid.
618Marcusith, ibid.

must hunt down the remaining Jedi . . . Obi-Wan and Anakin have a duel . . . Anakin gets hurt enough to put on the suit . . . Count Dooku is killed."[619] Yet despite the fact that only one gap now remains in the saga, there is still enough uncertainty to debate the how and why. These fan theories and projections are enjoyable, of course—or none of the contributors would bother with their often lengthy posts—and they are also, as seen above, edged with anxiety that the overall coherence of the *Star Wars* mythos, and to an extent its wider reputation, now rests on the final episode.

So far it is hard to catch a sense of melancholy or regret, but it will surely emerge as the release date of *Episode III* approaches; this is, as all these fans must know, the last time any of this pleasurable debate will be possible. The confirmation that *Episode I* would finally be made was the revival of a dead hope for many *Star Wars* aficionados, and it prompted a new wave of enthusiastic guesswork and background research, as is clear from my own circa-1997 notes above. Unless Lucas reconsiders his decision that a final trilogy is out of the question, the *Star Wars* saga will be complete after 2005; and while fandom will not be finished, it will change gears as it did in 1983. This kind of speculation, certainly, will be finished: and so, while the contributors to the *Jedi Council* eagerly anticipate a morning in mid-May 2005, the knowledge that this will be the last time they take in the opening crawl of a new *Star Wars* film must make the waiting bittersweet.

The last I heard, *Star Wars: Episode III* is going to be called *Rise of the Empire*. But don't trust me on that.

---

[619]Pancrase, "List Events that MUST HAPPEN in *Episode III*," *TheForce.Net*, op. cit. (3 May 2002).

Bibliography

Secondary Texts

Audience studies

Bacon-Smith, Camille. *Enterprising Women,* Philadelphia: University of Pennsylvania Press (1992).

Bacon-Smith, Camille. *Science Fiction Culture,* Philadelphia: University of Pennsylvania Press (2000).

Bobo, Jacqueline. "The Color Purple: Black Women as Cultural Readers," in Deirdre Pribham (Ed.), *Female Spectators,* London: Verso (1992).

Brooker, Will. "New Hope: The Postmodern Project of *Star Wars*," in Peter Brooker and Will Brooker (Eds.), *Postmodern After-Images,* London: Arnold (1997).

Brooker, Will. "Internet Fandom and the Continuing Narratives of *Star Wars*, *Blade Runner,* and *Alien,*" in Annette Kuhn (Ed.), *Alien Zone II,* London: Verso (1999).

Brooker, Will. *Batman Unmasked,* London: Continuum (2000).

Brooker, Will. "Readings of Racism: Interpretation, Stereotyping and *The Phantom Menace,*" London: Continuum vol. 15 no. 1 (April 2001).

Brooker, Will. "Living on *Dawson's Creek*: Teen Viewers, Cultural Convergence and Television Overflow," *International Journal of Cultural Studies*, Vol. 4, No. 4 (December 2001).

Fiske, John. *Television Culture,* London: Routledge (1987).

Gillespie, Marie. *Television, Ethnicity and Cultural Change,* London: Routledge (1995).

Jenkins, Henry. "Star Trek Rerun, Reread, Rewritten," in Constance Penley et al. (Eds.), *Close Encounters: Film, Feminism and Science Fiction,* Minneapolis: University of Minnesota Press (1991).

Jenkins, Henry. *Textual Poachers,* London: Routledge (1992).

Lavery, David (Ed.). *Full of Secrets: Critical Approaches to Twin Peaks,* Detroit, MI: Wayne State University Press (1994).

Liebes, Tamar, and Katz, Elihu. *The Export of Meaning: Cross-Cultural Readings of Dallas,* Oxford: Oxford University Press (1990).

Morley, David. *The "Nationwide" Audience,* London: BFI (1980).

Penley, Constance. *Nasa/Trek,* London: Verso (1997).

Tulloch, John, and Jenkins, Henry. *Science Fiction Audiences,* London: Routledge (1995).

Wood, Robin. *Hollywood from Vietnam to Reagan,* New York: Columbia University Press (1986).

Key Primary Texts

Reference

Arnold, Alan. *Once Upon A Galaxy: A Journal of the Making of The Empire Strikes Back,* London: Sphere (1980).

Baxter, John. *George Lucas,* London: HarperCollins (1999).

Bresman, Jonathan. *The Art of Star Wars Episode One: The Phantom Menace,* London: Ebury Press (1999).

Henderson, Mary. *Star Wars: The Magic of Myth,* London: Bantam Books (1997).

Jenkins, Garry. *Empire Building: The Remarkable Real Life Story of Star Wars*, London: Simon and Schuster (1997).

Johnston, Joe, et al., *Return of the Jedi Sketchbook,* New York: Ballantine Books (1983).

Sansweet, Stephen J. *Star Wars: From Concept to Screen to Collectible,* San Francisco, CA: Chronicle Books (1992).

Sansweet, Stephen J. *Star Wars Encyclopaedia,* London: Virgin (1998).

Titelman, Carol. *The Art of Star Wars: A New Hope,* London: Titan Books (1997).

West Reynolds, David. *Star Wars: Incredible Cross Sections,* London: Dorling Kindersley (1998).

West Reynolds, David. *Star Wars: The Visual Dictionary,* London: Dorling Kindersley (1998).

West Reynolds, David. *Star Wars: Episode One, The Visual Dictionary,* London: Dorling Kindersley (1999).

Novels and comics

Anderson, Kevin J. *Jedi Academy Trilogy,* London: Bantam (1994).

Anderson, Kevin J., and Moesta, Rebecca. *Young Jedi Knights* series, London: Berkley Books (1995–1996).

Anderson, Kevin J. (Ed.), *Tales from the Mos Eisley Cantina,* London: Bantam Books (1995).
Anderson, Kevin J. (Ed.), *Tales of the Bounty Hunters,* London: Bantam Books (1996).
Anderson, Kevin J. (Ed.), *Tales from Jabba's Palace,* London: Bantam Books (1996).
Brooks, Terry. *Star Wars Episode I: The Phantom Menace,* London: LucasBooks/Random House (1999).
Daley, Brian. *Han Solo at Star's End,* New York: Del Rey (1979).
Hambly, Barbara. *Children of the Jedi,* London: Bantam Books (1995).
Kube-McDowell, Michael P. *Tyrant's Test,* London: Bantam Books (1997).
Lucas, George. (Alan Dean Foster), *Star Wars: From The Adventures of Luke Skywalker,* London: Sphere Books (1976).
Lucas, George. *Star Wars: A New Hope,* London: Faber and Faber (1997).
Lucas, George. *Star Wars: Episode I, The Illustrated Screenplay,* London: Ebury Press (1999).
Perry, Steve. *Shadows of the Empire,* London: Bantam Books (1996).
Smith, L. Neil. *Lando Calrissian and the Mindharp of Sharu,* New York: Del Rey (1983).
Smith, L. Neil. *Lando Calrissian and the Star Cave of ThonBoka,* New York: Del Rey (1983).
Thomas, Roy, and Chaykin, Howard. *Star Wars*, reprinted in the *Star Wars Annual* no.1, London: Brown Watson (1978).
Richardson, Nancy. *Junior Jedi Knights* series, London: Berkley Books (1995).
Various, *Star Wars: The Official Souvenir Annual 1998,* Cheshire, England: World International (1997).
Veitch, Tom, and Anderson, Kevin J. *Dark Lords of the Sith,* Dark Horse Comics (1994–1995).
Watson, Jude. *Star Wars: Jedi Apprentice: The Uncertain Path,* London: Scholastic Ltd. (2000).
Zahn, Timothy, *Heir to the Empire,* London: Bantam Books (1991).
Zahn, Timothy. *Dark Force Rising,* London: Bantam Books (1992).
Zahn, Timothy. *The Last Command,* London: Bantam Books (1993).

Radio drama

Daley, Brian. *Star Wars Radio Drama,* reissued London: Hodder (1993).

Fan fiction

Analise, "A Matter of Control," archived at Analise's Nest.
Ellen Blair, "Falcon's Flight," archived at The Fanzine Archives.

Toni Carlini, "Can't Run," archived at Fanfix.
Kirby Crow, "Stepping To Jonah," archived at members.tripod.com/~Slash-Girls/jonah1.html
DarthCleo, "Darth Maul Gets Internet Access," archived at The Sith Academy.
Dianora, "Need," archived at Fanfix.
Duncan, "Against the Sith," archived at The Fanzine Archives.
The Emu, "The Offering," archived at The Emu's Feathers.
Esmeralda, "Lost," archived at the Jedi Hurtaholics' Archive.
Esmeralda, "Recovery," archived at the Jedi Hurtaholics' Archive.
Amy Fortuna, "Across the Great Divide," archived at Master and Apprentice.
Frostfyre, "Elementary, my dear Obi-Wan," posted at TheForce.net
Angela Jade, "Lost Innocence," archived at Fanfix.
Kaelia and Teza, "Darth Maul vs the Spice Girls," archived at The Sith Academy.
Kelly Kanayama, "Return of the . . . Jade?," archived at Fanfix.
Karrde289, "Harem Pants and Explosions," archived at Fanfix.
Kass, "Listen To The Force, Padawan," archived at the Phantom Menace Lair.
Kass and Kate, *Hearts of Darkness,* archived at the Phantom Menace Lair.
Gina Leeds, "Also a Woman," archived at Fanfix.
Marie, "Escape to Yavin," archived at Fanfix.
Maygra, "Faithless," archived at Maygra's Musings.
Monique Robertson, "A Matter of Trust," archived at Fanfix.
Lilith Sedai, "L'Histoire D'Obi," archived at the Obi-Wan Torture Oasis.
Shadow, "The End of the Beginning," archived at Fanfix.
Shadow, "Darth Maul vs eBay," archived at The Sith Academy.
Siubhan, "Life Lessons at the Sith Academy," archived at The Sith Academy.
SiriGallia, "Good Day, Mr Kenobi," posted on TheForce.net
D. L. Slaten, "Archaeology in Hyperspace," archived at Fanfix.
Margo Witkowska, "DuneJedi," archived at Fanfix.

Filmography

Star Wars: A New Hope, directed by George Lucas (1977).
The Star Wars Holiday Special, (TV), directed by David Acomba and Steve Binder (1978).
Star Wars: The Empire Strikes Back, directed by Irvin Kershner (1980).
Star Wars: Return of the Jedi, directed by Richard Marquand (1983).
Star Wars: A New Hope: Special Edition, directed by George Lucas (1997).
Star Wars: The Empire Strikes Back: Special Edition, directed by Irvin Kershner (1997).

Star Wars: Return of the Jedi: Special Edition, directed by Richard Marquand (1997).
Star Wars Episode I: The Phantom Menace, directed by George Lucas (1999).

Fan filmography

Attack Droids, directed by Scott Layman, archived at TheForce.net
Bounty Trail, directed by Justin Dix, archived at TheForce.net
Duel, directed by Dave Macomber and Mark Thomas, archived at TheForce.net
Duality, directed by Dave Macomber and Mark Thomas, archived at TheForce.net
Episode II (fan trailer), directed by Anonymous, archived at TheForce.net
George Lucas in Love, directed by Joe Nussbaum, available at Amazon.com
Jabba on the Dais, directed by Petch Lucas and Matthew Beal, archived at TheForce.net
Matrix Jedi, directed by Darel Finley and Jim Skipper, archived at TheForce.net
Phantom Edit, directed by Anonymous, available as rare bootleg.
Prelude to Hope, directed by Nathan Butler, archived at TheForce.net
Return of the Dude, directed by Richard Cando, archived at TheForce.net
Star Dudes, directed by Richard Cando, archived at TheForce.net
Star Wars Gangster Rap, directed by Jason Banning and Chris Crawford, archived at Atomfilms.
Star Wars Legacy, directed by Kevin Blades, archived at *Star Wars* Legacy.
Stargeeks, directed by Marc A. Samson, archived at Atomfilms.
Sev Wars, directed by John Cook, archived at Atomfilms.
The Bad Dudes Strike Back, directed by Richard Cando, archived at TheForce.net
Troops, directed by Kevin Rubio, archived at TheForce.net
The Dark Redemption, directed by Peter Mether, archived at TheForce.net
Two-ness, directed by Steven Ballew and Roy Thomas, archived at TheForce.net
Way of the Force, directed by Josh Taylor, P.J. Tamayo and D.C. Sariti, archived at TheForce.net
Wookiee, directed by Petch Lucas and Matthew Beal, archived at TheForce.net

Key Internet Sources

Message boards

http://www.boards.theforce.net
http://www.ezboards.com/officialtpmbashersboard

News sites

http://www.theforce.net
http://www.starwars.com
http://www.nabooonline.com
http://www.echostation.com

Technical commentaries

http://www.theforce.net/swtc/

Star Wars Special Edition sites

Paul Ens' Special Edition Annotations, http://www.theforce.net/swse/
Treadwell's Star Wars Special Edition FAQs, http://www.jax-inter.net/users/datalore/starwars/sepage.htm

Star Wars scripts

http://www.starwarz.com/starkiller/frame.htm

Speculation

The Virtual Edition, http://www.theforce.net/virtualedition

Slash and genfic

Analise's Nest, http://the-nesting-place.com/analise.html
Jedi Hurtaholics Archive, http://www.ktnb.net/jedi/
Master and Apprentice, http://www.sockiipress.org/ma/warn.html
Master and Apprentice survey, http://www.slashcity.com/sockii/ma/results.html
Maygra's Musings, http://7parabian.com/Maygra/Musings/swtpm/
Obi-Wan Torture Oasis, http://members.tripod.com/~SlashGirls/toto/
Sex Tips For Slash Writers, http://www.squidge.org/~minotaur/classic/eroc.html
Sith Chicks, http://www.starwarschicks.com/sithchicks/tosith.html
Slash-Informational, http://www.fanficweb.net/directory/slash/slash.htm
Slash Tutorial, http://adult.dencity.com/Krychick/slash_tutorial/tutorialindex.html
Star Wars Fanfix, http://www.fanfix.com/

The Emu's Feathers, http://www.zip.com.au/~emu/offer.html

The Phantom Menace Lair, http://www.geocities.com/soho/workshop/3293/lair/q_o.html

The Fanzine Archives, http://members.aol.com/fzarchive/home/html

The Sith Academy, http://www.siubhan.com/sithacademy

Fan films

http://www.theforce.net/theater

http://www.atomfilms.com

http://www.starwarz.com/swlegacy

Junior fan sites

http://www.starwarskids.com

Rebel Friends, http://www.theforce.net/kids/

Online articles

AC. "In Defense of Slash," http://www.chisp.net/~zoerayne/defense.html (no date).

Brown, Janelle. "Fan fiction on the Line," Wired.com, http://www.wired.com/news/topstories/0,1287,5934,00.html (August 11, 1997).

Durack, Elizabeth. "Fan.Starwars.con," http://www.qui-gonline.org/features/fanstarwarscon.htm (no date).

Granick, Jennifer. "Scotty, Beam Down the Lawyers!" Wired.com, http://www.wired.com/news/topstories/0,1287,7564,00.html (October 9, 1997).

Hazlett, Sue. "Filling in the Gaps: Fans and Fan Fiction on the Internet," reprinted at *X-Files University,* http://www.geocities.com/Hollywood/Lot/8254/xfuis.html (no date).

Jenkins, Henry. "The Poachers and the Stormtroopers," reprinted at http://web.mit.edu/21fms/www/faculty/henry3/pub/stormtroopers.htm (1998).

Karko, James. "In Defense of Starwars.com," Echo Station, http://www.echostation.com/editorials/defendsw.htm (March 24, 2000).

Nact, Su. "Two Men Are Better Than One: Why Women Like Slash," reprinted at *X-Files University* (April 9, 1999).

Plotz, David. "Luke Skywalker is Gay?," Slate.com, http://slate.msn.com/Features/fanfic/fanfic.asp (April 14, 2000).

Phillips, David R. "It's Not Wise To Upset A Wookiee," Echo Station, http://www.echostation.com./features/lfl_wookiee.htm (September 1, 1999).

Film technical sites

Desormeaux, Eric, et al. "Sound Effects," http://theforce.net/theater/postproduction/soundfx/

Finley, Darel. "Rotoscoping Lightsabers," http://www.theforce.net/theater/software/premiere/rotoscoping/rotoscoping_finley.shtml

Roman, Darryl. "Lighting in CGI Scenes," http://www.theforce.net/theater/software/3dstudiomax/romanlighting_tutorial/index.shtml

Trenor, Brian. "Star Wars Fan Films for Dummies," http://www.theforce.net/theater/preproduction/brian_tutorial/index.sht ml

Index